The Economics of Small Business

of

Small Business

An Introductory Survey

The Economics of Small Business

An Introductory Survey

Roger A McCain

Drexel University, USA

World Scientific

NEW JERSEY · LONDON · SINGAPORE · BEIJING · SHANGHAI · HONG KONG · TAIPEI · CHENNAI · TOKYO

Published by

World Scientific Publishing Co. Pte. Ltd.

5 Toh Tuck Link, Singapore 596224

USA office: 27 Warren Street, Suite 401-402, Hackensack, NJ 07601

UK office: 57 Shelton Street, Covent Garden, London WC2H 9HE

Library of Congress Cataloging-in-Publication Data

Names: McCain, Roger A., author.
Title: The economics of small business : an introductory survey /
    Roger A McCain (Drexel University, USA).
Description: 1 Edition. | New Jersey : World Scientific, [2018] |
    Includes bibliographical references and index.
Identifiers: LCCN 2017045441 | ISBN 9789813231245
Subjects: LCSH: Small business--Management. | Personnel management. |
    Family-owned business enterprises--Succession.
Classification: LCC HD62.7 .M3873 2018 | DDC 338.6/42--dc23
LC record available at https://lccn.loc.gov/2017045441

British Library Cataloguing-in-Publication Data

A catalogue record for this book is available from the British Library.

For any available supplementary material, please visit
http://www.worldscientific.com/worldscibooks/10.1142/10743#t=suppl

Desk Editor: Shreya Gopi

Typeset by Stallion Press
Email: enquiries@stallionpress.com

Contents

v

About the Author

Dr. Roger A. McCain, a native of Louisiana, had his education at Louisiana State University and has been a university faculty member, specializing in economics and game theory, since 1967. He is Professor in the School of Economics, Drexel University, Philadelphia, PA, where he has been since 1988. McCain is the author of eight books, including textbooks in Game Theory and Microeconomic Theory, and research monographs on cognitive economics, computational models of economic growth, and applied game theory. He has also written more than 100 scholarly papers and addresses and is guilty of two published short stories.

Chapter 1

Introduction

The purpose of this book is to introduce the economic research on enterprises of small and medium scale. This has been a topic of active economic research for about a generation. In earlier economics, there was little or no special study of small business, probably because economists thought of small business as the norm. Agricultural enterprises, which are typically small, were the special study of agricultural economics. Otherwise, it seemed that it was "big businesses" that needed specialized study — monopoly and oligopoly. Much was learned about these enterprises in the specialized studies of industrial organization and public utilities. These studies showed how the abstract idea of "the firm" in economic theory could give way to a more detailed, empirical understanding of business organizations. In the late 1980s, some economists began to study small business in a similar way. The journal *Small Business Economics* began to be published in 1988. In the quarter century that has followed, a great deal has been learned, some of it built on work that had already been done before 1988 and proved particularly valuable for the study of small- and medium-scale businesses, and much of it novel. The purpose of this book is to convey the results of this research in a form accessible to undergraduate students in economics and others with some preparation in economics. The focus will be on non-agricultural small and medium enterprises (SMEs).

Why study small businesses? First, there are a lot of them. There are many more small businesses than big businesses. In the United

States, about 99.75 percent of businesses are "small." Over the years, in the United States, small businesses have employed about half of the work force and produced about one-third of GDP. There is reason to believe that small businesses often face different conditions than larger businesses. Small businesses are more likely to be located in rural areas. Small businesses tend to be in different industries than large businesses: industries in which increasing returns to scale are less important. Finally, but most importantly, government policies often give small businesses special consideration.

1. Small and Medium Enterprises as a Topic for Economics

In the first issue of *Small Business Economics*, Brock and Evans wrote (1989, p. 7) "About 13 million of the 17 million corporations, partnerships, and sole proprietorships that filed (United States) federal tax returns in 1986 had no employees other than their owner. All but approximately 10,000 of the 4 million businesses with employees had fewer than 500 employees." We will see that the numbers of firms have continued to grow in the interim. They continue (p. 7)

> Small-business economics seeks to better understand why firms come in different sizes, how and why firm behavior varies with size, what determines the formation, growth, and dissolution of small firms, the role of small firms in the introduction of new products and the evolution of industries, and the dynamic relationships among small firms and macroeconomic variables such as output and employment.

A first step is to get a better idea of just what we might mean by "small business." How is the business scale best measured? Should we focus on sales, capital value, employment, or use different measures for different purposes? Where can we find the boundary between small-, medium-, and large-enterprise scales? Certainly, the range given by Brock and Evans includes enterprises that will operate very differently. A self-employed businessman without any employees is a very different kind of operation than a firm with 20 employees, and the firm with a few hundred employees is a different kind of operation yet again.

The most common measure of the size of the enterprise is the number of employees. This has the advantage that it is relatively easily comparable. If one company sells tractors and the other sells cheesecakes, it will be easier to compare the number of employees of the tractor company and the number of employees of the cheesecake company than it is to compare the output of tractors to the output of cheesecakes! On that basis, we will treat the number of employees as the principle measure of the size of the firm. From time to time, for specific purposes, we will also measure the size of the firm by revenue or capital value.

2. How Small is Small?

The U.S. Small Business Administration serves businesses with 500 or fewer employees, for most purposes. At the other extreme, about three-quarter of businesses have no paid employees. They employ the proprietor (maybe part-time) and, in some cases, family labor. In the United States and some other countries, firms with fewer than 50 employees are excluded from certain regulations as "small businesses." For other regulations, there are different thresholds below which the enterprises are excused as "small businesses." Thus, what is a "small business" depends on the purpose for which we ask the questions. We should probably say "small and medium enterprises" (SMEs) for enterprises with 500 or fewer employees.

Caruso (2012) writes "In 2012, large enterprises employed 59.9 million people (51.6 percent of all employees), very small enterprises employed 20.4 million people (17.6 percent), small enterprises employed 19.4 million people (16.7 percent), and medium enterprises employed 16.3 million people (14.0 percent)." For these statistics, very small enterprises have fewer than 20 employees, but do have employees other than the owner, small enterprises have 20–99 employees, medium enterprises 100–499 and large enterprises 500 or more. This book will use those categories whenever possible. This is summarized in Table 1. But, as we will see, other studies use other

Table 1. Categories of SMEs.

Microenterprise	Self-employed part time
Non-employer	No paid employees
Very small employers (VSE)	19 or fewer paid employees
Small employers (SE)	20–99 employees
Medium-size enterprise (MSE)	100–499 employees

Table 2. Businesses of Different Sizes in the United States in 2014.

Enterprise employment size	Number of firms	Proportion of firms	Employment	Proportion of employment
1–4	3,598,185	0.62	5,940,248	0.051596141
5–9	998,953	0.17	6,570,776	0.057072816
10–19	608,502	0.10	8,176,519	0.071020069
20–99	513,179	0.09	20,121,588	0.174773223
100–499	87,563	0.0150	17,085,461	0.14840186
500+	19,076	0.0033	63,175,352	0.548732032

break points. Table 2, based on data from the U.S. Bureau of the Census, presents some data for the United States in 2014. (Data for 2016 is not yet available as I write.)

In studying small business, it is important to distinguish between the firm and the establishment. Some firms have multiple locations — establishments — so the establishment may be small even if the firm itself is medium or large. Headd (2000, p. 13) writes, "First, with regard to small businesses, establishment data... can result in incomplete figures, because many small establishments are parts of large businesses." Franchises generate a slightly different problem. Most employees that we see in a franchised operation such as a McDonald's® restaurant are not employees of McDonald's, a large business, but of the franchisee, which will often be a small business.

3. Non-Employer Businesses

Many of our statistics refer only to employer firms, since they are classed by number of employees. However, about three-quarters of all business firms in the United States have no employees. The same is true of Britain (BMG Research, 2013): "The 2012 Business Population Estimates calculated that there were 4,794,105 businesses in the UK private sector.... However, 74 percent of these businesses had no employees...." (p. 13). These are self-employed individuals and some family firms that deploy only the labor of family partners in the enterprise. I think of a firm I have done business with in which the work (paving) is done by a father and son and the mother is the telephone receptionist, scheduler and bookkeeper. At the other extreme, some businesses employ a proprietor only part-time. After my sister's retirement, she sold some craftwork but did not work at that full-time.

Here are some data on non-employer firms (some of the following bullet points are adapted from Nazar, 2015):

- There were 23.8 million non-employer firms in 2014.
- Approximately 75 percent of all U.S. businesses are non-employer businesses.
- Of the nearly 24 million non-employer businesses in the United States, over twenty million, that is 86 percent, are individual proprietorships as of 2014.
- Over 1.7 million are partnerships, comprising about 7 percent.
- Almost 1.5 million are corporations, comprising 6 percent. (This includes both C corporations and S corporations, distinctions of tax treatment.)
- To be classified as a "non-employer" business you must have annual business receipts of $1,000 or more and be subject to federal income taxes. (For less than that, you are not considered to have a business.)
- Total revenue of non-employers was over one trillion dollars in 2014.
- Around 80 percent of non-employer businesses for 2014 (over 18 million businesses) reported less than $50,000 in receipts

Table 3 below gives some detail on the distribution of sizes of non-employer businesses in 2014, where size, in this case, is annual revenue.

Table 3. Size Distribution of Non-Employer Businesses.

Size class: Revenue per year	Number of establishments	Proportion of establishments (%)
All establishments	23,836,937	100
<$5,000	5,776,674	24.23
$5,000–$9,999	3,858,277	16.19
$10,000–$24,999	5,915,940	24.82
$25,000–$49,999	3,269,756	13.72
$50,000–$99,999	2,348,629	9.85
$100,000–$249,999	1,812,554	7.60
$250,000–$499,999	570,491	2.39
$500,000–$999,999	248,636	1.04
$1,000,000–$2,499,999	33,624	0.14
$2,500,000–4,999,999	1,991	0.0084
>$5,000,000	365	0.0015

Source: Author's computations from Bureau of the Census, American FactFinder, https://factfinder.census.gov/faces/tableservices/jsf/pages/productview.xhtml?pid=NES_2014_00A3&prodType=table, accessed on 3/29/2017.

Who are the proprietors of non-employer businesses? Fairlee and Robb (2007, p. 226) write "A few patterns are beginning to emerge in the young and expanding literature on self-employment. The empirical studies in this literature generally find that self-employment is positively associated with being male, white, older, married, and an immigrant, and with having more education and higher asset levels. Another important determinant that has been identified in the literature is having a self-employed parent." Relying on their statistical analysis, they argue that it is the experience of working in the parent's business that provides the key advantage, even though only a very small proportion of the businesses are inherited.

4.   Who Are The Proprietors of Small Businesses?

The "demographic" characteristics of small business employers have been studied for some time. The word "demographic" means how they fit in the overall population, that is, for example, are they older?

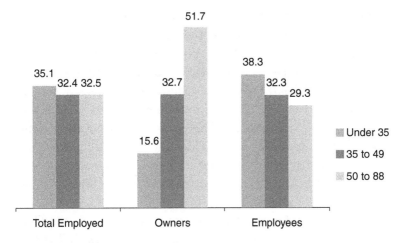

Figure 1. Ages of Employers and Employees.
Source: Headd (2013).

Are they likely to be more or less educated? Headd writes (2013, p. 2) "In 2013, the age makeup of business owners was much older than that of employees. While the proportion of those of prime age in the workforce did not differ between business owners and employees, business owners were much less likely to be younger (under age 35) than employees, 15.6 percent versus 38.3 percent, respectively." This is illustrated in Figure 1. These data are for all business owners, but they are mostly the owners of small businesses — as we learned earlier in this chapter, small businesses are the huge majority of all businesses — so the data for small business owners could not be very different. The contrast, however, is with the *employees* of all businesses, and an important proportion of all *employees* are employed by big businesses.

Further, Headd (2013, pp. 2–3) writes "Business owners were more likely to have a bachelor's degree or higher education level than employees, 39.2 percent versus 29.2 percent, respectively. In addition, owners were less likely than employees to have a high school degree or less." Business owners are less likely to be nonwhite, Hispanic or women (Headd, pp. 1–2). "Minority and Hispanic business owners made up less than 15 percent of all U.S. business owners in 2013.

Asian business owners represented 4.3 percent of all owners versus 4.8 percent of all private sector employees. Blacks represented 7 percent of all owners compared to 12.1 percent of all employees. Hispanics represented 10.6 percent of all business owners versus 16.7 percent of all employees in 2013. Women's share of business ownership in 2013 was 35.4 percent of business owners compared to 47.3 percent of private sector employees.... This ownership proportion is in line with an Office of Advocacy study which found that 29 percent of U.S. firms were owned by women." Business owners are also more likely to be married, to own a home and to be veterans. This is shown in summary form in Table 4.

These data are for the United States, but studies for Canada, Britain and Australia, and an international survey by the Organization for Economic Cooperation and Development, suggest that similar patterns will be found in other industrialized countries.

5.   The Employees of Small and Medium Employers

Small, medium and large enterprises differ in a number of ways, and there are corresponding differences in the characteristics of their employees. For this section, we will be concerned with enterprises that have from 1 to 500 employees — very-small-, small- and medium-scale employers. If the firm has more than one establishment, employees at all establishments are included. Headd (2000) summarized data from the Bureau of the Census on some of the characteristics of small business employees in the United States, as of 1999. For example, he found that small-business employees were somewhat more likely to be part-time employees than the employees of other businesses, and more likely to have lower educational attainments — and more likely to have postgraduate degrees. He writes (pp. 14–16) "Small firms' share of part-time workers (22.0 percent) was almost 25 percent greater than large firms' share (17.8 percent). In addition, the part-time share of very small firms (those with fewer than 25 employees), at 28.4 percent, was more than 50 percent greater than the share for very large firms (those with more than 1,000 employees), namely, 18.3 percent.... overall, whites and Hispanics were somewhat more

Table 4. Demographic Characteristics of Business Owners and Employees, 2013 (%).

		Total employed	Owners	Employees
Age	Under 35	35.1	15.6	38.3
	35 to 49	32.4	32.7	32.3
	50 to 88	32.5	51.7	29.3
Gender	Male	54.4	64.6	52.7
	Female	45.6	35.4	47.3
Race	Non-Minority	80.4	85.9	79.5
	Minority	19.6	14.1	20.5
Ethnicity	Hispanic	15.9	10.6	16.7
	Non-Hispanic	84.1	89.4	83.3
Veteran Status	Veteran	6.0	9.0	5.5
	Non-Veteran	94.0	91.0	94.5
Marital Status	Married	53.8	66.3	51.7
	Non-Married	46.2	33.7	48.3
Education	High School or Less	33.6	28.0	34.6
	Some College	35.7	32.8	36.2
	Bachelor's or Higher	30.6	39.2	29.2
Citizen	Yes	91.1	91.6	91.0
	No	8.9	8.4	9.0
Homeowner	Yes	67.1	77.5	65.4
	No	32.9	22.5	34.6
Location	Metro	80.8	79.1	81.1
	Non-Metro	14.9	16.7	14.6
	Not Identified	4.3	4.2	4.3

Source: Headd (2013).

likely to work in smaller firms, while women, Asians, and blacks were somewhat less likely.... Small firms employ more workers under age 25 and workers aged 65 or older.... Employees under age 25 were 21.4 percent of very small firms (firms with fewer than 25 employees) and 20.1 percent of very large firms (firms with 1,000 or more employees).... Very small firms also had more than twice the share of employees 65 or older than very large firms had (4.8 percent versus 2.0 percent).... Small firms had higher percentages of employees who had less than a high school education and employees whose highest degree was a high school diploma, ... While small and large firms had similar shares of employees with doctoral or professional degrees, the greatest shares of employees with those degrees showed up in the very small firms (possibly because of individual doctors' and lawyers' offices)."

We see that the employees of smaller businesses are often drawn from the extremes of the distributions of age and education. These data are given in more detail in Tables 5–7. These data, of course, date from about the year 1999, and more recent data would be interesting, but no similar summary study seems to have been done with recent data.

6.   Some Contrasts

Thus far, we have focused mostly on information on the United States. There are two reasons for this, apart from the author's nationality: on the one hand, small businesses in the United States are well documented and much studied, and on the other hand (as we will see in later chapters), the patterns observed in the United States tend to parallel those in other large relatively industrialized countries. For example, "99% of businesses in Canada have fewer

Table 5. Some Characteristics of Small Business Employees (%).

Size of firm	Women	Asian	Black	White	Hispanic
All firms	46.5	4.7	11.3	84.0	10.9
Under 10	46.8	5.3	7.9	86.8	12.8
10–24	44.1	4.2	8.7	87.1	12.4
25–99	43.7	4.3	10.7	85.0	12.2
100–499	46.2	4.2	11.8	84.0	11.5
500–999	48.8	5.0	13.8	81.2	9.6
1,000 or more	48.0	5.0	13.2	81.8	8.9
Fewer than 500	45.3	4.5	9.8	85.7	12.2
500 or more	48.1	5.0	13.3	81.7	9.0

Source: Headd (2000, p. 14).

Table 6. Age Distribution of Employees by Size of Firm (%).

Size of firm	Under 25 years	25 to 34 years	35 to 44 years	45 to 54 years	55 to 64 years	65 years or older
All firms	19.3	24.1	25.9	18.5	9.1	3.0
Under 10	19.7	21.3	24.8	17.8	10.8	5.6
10–24	24.1	24.8	23.3	15.7	8.5	3.7
25–99	19.3	25.3	25.9	17.8	9.0	2.6
100–499	15.0	25.7	28.6	19.1	9.2	2.5
500–999	16.1	26.7	25.7	19.4	9.9	2.1
1,000 or more	20.1	23.7	26.2	19.6	8.5	2.0
Fewer than 500	19.2	24.2	25.8	17.7	9.5	3.6
500 or more	19.5	24.1	26.1	19.6	8.7	2.0

Source: Headd (2000, p. 15).

Table 7. Education of Employees (%).

Size of firm	Less than a high school diploma	High school graduate	Some college	Bachelor's degree	Master's degree	Doctoral or professional degree
All firms	16.1	32.9	28.5	16.4	4.0	2.1
Under 10	20.3	33.3	27.0	13.8	2.7	3.0
10–24	20.4	32.8	28.4	13.0	3.0	2.4
25–99	18.0	34.1	27.2	15.6	3.4	1.7
100–499	15.6	34.5	27.7	16.1	4.4	1.8
500–999	12.4	32.3	29.0	19.2	5.0	2.2
1,000 or more	12.8	31.8	30.1	18.6	4.9	1.8
Fewer than 500	18.5	33.7	27.5	14.7	3.4	2.2
500 or more	12.7	31.8	30.0	18.7	4.9	1.9

Note: Based on the NCEMP, A_HGA and CLWX = 1CPS variables. The category of "some college" includes those who attended, but did not graduate from, college, which in turn includes those who received associate's degree.

Source: Headd (2000, p. 15).

than 500 employees and they employ 64% of workers in the private sector." Moreover, some Canadian policies in support of small business parallel those in the United States (Chandler, 2012). However, it is appropriate before moving on to consider a few contrasts.

In the European Union, "in Greece, for example, SMEs account for almost the total employment (91 per cent) in the non-primary sector, while in Portugal and Ireland the shares are also very high (82 per cent and 78 per cent respectively)" (Liargovas, 1998). For smaller countries, and particularly less industrialized countries, small businesses are likely to be even more important. "The role of small business is more critical in small states where size, technology, capital and other resource constraints limit establishment of large business. In such states, small businesses have leading role in providing goods and services for the society" (Reddy, 2007, p. 304). In Fiji, an island nation with a population of less than 1 million, for example, SMEs employ about 64 percent of the employed population. In Kosovo, a small and embattled post-Soviet European nation of less than 2 million, 56.3 percent of enterprises are individual enterprises with no employees other than the proprietor and they employ 13.7 percent of the economically active population, while enterprises with fewer than 50 employees comprise 43 percent of enterprises and employ just over half of economically active people (Oberholzner, 2014). Referring back to Table 2, though, we see that Kosovo's economy is less concentrated on small business than that of the United States, where businesses with less than 50 employees comprise 98 percent of employer enterprises but employ only a little over one-third of employees. Probably this difference reflects Kosovo's history as a Soviet-type economy and subsequently as a part of Yugoslavia.

India, for a further contrast, is a large country, with a population of over 1 billion, larger than any other country except China. Its small business sector is rather well documented, although less studied than that of the United States; India has a long history of policy in favor of small businesses. It is, however, a developing country, with a substantial part of its population engaged in a low-productivity traditional sector of production. Coad and Tamvada

(2012, pp. 383–384) write "...in developing countries the roles of small firms differ from those in developed ones. One major reason why micro and small firms exist in developing countries is that they offer individuals a livelihood and a source of independent revenue. In many cases, new small businesses are founded as a last resort rather than as a first choice." This is quite uncommon in more developed countries such as the United States. Further, "India has, historically, been especially supportive of its small enterprises. For example, the Indian government has granted exclusive production rights of certain goods and services to Small Scale Industry (SSI) businesses and even though the Indian economy has undergone considerable deregulation in recent years, the production of many goods continues to be reserved for small businesses" (p. 384). For this purpose, small businesses are those that at startup have capital of less than 10 million Indian rupees, about US$200,000. Again quoting Coad and Tamvada (p. 384), "It is estimated that, in 2001, SSI businesses in India accounted for around 95% of the industrial units in the country, contributed 40% of the manufacturing sector output and close to one-third of India's export. By 2009, the share of SSI's contribution to manufacturing output increased to 45%, and the share of exports rose to 40%."

7. An Agenda for the Study of the Economics of Small Business

The later chapters of this book will introduce and discuss some topics and results from the research of economists over the last 25 years. Following are some issues about small businesses that we will explore.

7.1. *Do Economies of Scale Handicap Small Businesses?*

Do bigger businesses have a technological advantage over smaller businesses? To say that another way, are there *economies of scale* for most businesses? If so, how do small businesses survive? We say that there are economies of the scale of the firm if larger firms are able to produce more cheaply than smaller ones. If that is so, then it would seem that smaller businesses would be at a disadvantage and might not survive. In economics, generalizations about the economy that are simple, observable and persistent are sometimes called "stylized facts." They are something between simple observed facts and theories, since the generalization makes a "stylized fact" a very simple sort of theory. On the other hand, "stylized facts" say nothing about causes and effects, and in that sense they are something less than theories. Here are two "stylized facts" about economies of scale and small and large business: first, economies of scale differ from one industrial sector to another. Economies of scale are much more important in some industries than others. Second, in many industries, large and small companies coexist, and this coexistence is quite persistent. How can we account for this?

For a small business challenged by economies of scale, are there strategies that can enable the business to cope and survive and even prosper? Could this be done by making business-to-business (B2B) contracts with larger businesses that would take advantage of the scale economies? In particular, franchising is a B2B arrangement in which a large business typically develops products and does national or regional advertising, branding and quality assurance, where economies of scale seem more important, while affiliated small businesses provide local service. Thus, franchising will be considered in a later chapter.

7.2. *Are Growth and Failure Related to Firm Size?*

How does firm size affect the tendency of the firm to grow? We have a theory that says that the growth rate of a firm is *unrelated* to the size of the firm. This theory was proposed in 1931 and is called "Gibrat's law" after the French engineer Robert Gibrat who put it forward. But is Gibrat's law really a law? We have learned a great deal since 1931. Do we need to modify Gibrat's law in light of what we have learned? We also know as "stylized facts" that smaller firms are more likely to fail than larger firms, on average. Does this require us to modify Gibrat's law, and more generally, how does it fit into our understanding of the dynamics of small business and firm growth? Does the age of the firm modify the answers to these questions?

7.3. *What is the Role of Family Ownership and Management?*

Not all "family firms" are small businesses. The Ford Motor Company and the Fox entertainment complex are family businesses that are not small. Conversely, not all small businesses are "family firms." However, many small businesses are "family firms," and the relation of small business to family ownership and management will be studied. The category of "family firms" has somewhat blurry boundaries. A business may be predominantly owned by the members of a family but managed by a hired manager or managers. On the other hand, it is very common for a family-owned company also to be managed by a family member. Further, some small businesses may rely partly or completely on the work of family members. In such a case, the company may be organized more or less formally as a family partnership, in which the family member employees may be compensated partly or completely with a partnership share rather than a wage or salary. If the family members are not paid a wage or salary, then the firm may appear in the statistics as a non-employer firm.

What are the implications of family participation in the ownership, management and work force of the firm? There are at least two possibilities:

- Family management and work are an asset, as family members have strong incentives to put in extra effort.
- Family managers are amateurs, and a shift to professional managers would increase productivity and the profitability of the firm for the family.

The latter idea is probably more applicable to medium-size enterprises (MSEs), as professional management would not be feasible in the smallest categories.

Family management poses another issue. The retirement of a family member who has founded the firm or has been a long-time successful member of it will present the enterprise with a challenge. Sometimes the retiree will have a child or other relative who will take over without difficulty. But what if there is no younger relative who wants to take over? What if there is a conflict within the family between two or more relatives who want to take over? This is called *the succession problem*. It will be the topic of a later chapter.

A relatively rare category of firms are *cooperative enterprises*. A cooperative enterprise is an enterprise owned and operated by a membership organization (an association) with membership open to some category of stakeholders, such as customers, employees, or farmers specializing in a particular crop in a particular district (such as potato growers in certain counties of Idaho and neighboring Oregon). The management of a cooperative enterprise is based on the democratic principle of one member, one vote. Not all cooperatives are small businesses, but many are, and face many of the same challenges and issues that family businesses face. This book will sometimes, but rarely, digress on cooperative enterprise.

7.4.   Are Small Firms Especially Job Creators? Innovators?

We often hear that small businesses are especially likely to innovate and grow by employing more workers. This is expressed by saying that small businesses are "job creators." On the other hand, there is evidence that employment in small business is more volatile than employment in larger businesses, which means that more of the employees of small businesses, proportionately, lose their jobs in an average period. There is also evidence that small businesses pay less for similar work, and that the employees of small businesses are more likely to be part-time. We shall have to try to disentangle these matters.

Small business is also often associated with innovation, which is seen as leading to rapid growth. Borrowing ideas from the great economist Joseph Schumpeter (1883–1950), the creation of innovative new firms is described as "entrepreneurship." Yet Schumpeter suggested that in modern society, big businesses would be more likely to innovate: this was sometimes called "the Schumpeterian hypothesis." It must be stressed that small business and entrepreneurship are two different topics, and this is not a book on entrepreneurship. However, the *relationship* of small business and entrepreneurship will be discussed. Are small firms more likely to innovate and to grow? Does this vary from small to medium and large firms? These issues will be addressed.

Start-up companies usually are small at first, although there are some exceptions. Are start-ups more likely than other firms to innovate? Are start-ups net job creators? Do former employees of successful small businesses have more success in start-ups? What is the role of formal education and learning by doing or experience in the success of small-firm start-ups?

7.5.   *Do Small Firms Lack Access to Capital Markets?*

One of the "stylized facts" about small business is that "efficient markets" hypothesis does not seem to apply to small businesses. One symptom of this is that, while the profits of small businesses vary widely — on the whole, even more widely than the profits of larger businesses — the average profit in the small business sector seems to be larger than the average rate of profit for larger businesses. How can this be, in a world of well-informed, profit-seeking investors? Conversely, it is often suggested that many small businesses are unable to get access to capital for profitable expansion or recovery from temporary shocks. Are these two anomalies related, perhaps as cause and effect or as effects of the same third cause? This brings us back also to the common pattern of family businesses — companies predominantly owned by a single family. In many cases, the ownership of the company will also constitute most of the wealth of the family. Financial theory tells us that diversification of assets will give rise to a better trade-off between risk and the rate of return. Why, then, is family ownership common, and how is this related to the other two capital market questions? These issues will be addressed in future chapters.

7.6.   *What are Appropriate Government Policies for Small and Medium Business?*

There are a number of government policies to encourage small businesses, including both agricultural and non-agricultural enterprises. For non-agricultural enterprises in the United States, many of these policies are coordinated by the Small Business Administration. What are these policies, and how are they justified on economic grounds, if at all?

7.7.   *What Public Policies Address the Role of Women and People of Color in Small Business, and How May They be Understood?*

Historically, women and some minority groups, including people of color, have been subject to legal and social conditions that limited their role in business. Two hundred years ago, for example, most women were not legally persons, which means that they were not able to own property or enter into contracts voluntarily; the great majority of people of color in the United States were neither legal persons nor even the proprietors of their own bodies, but slaves. Over decades, these inabilities have been largely removed and the inequalities that resulted from them have been partly eliminated, though there is still more to be done. Thus, the U.S. Government, including the Small Business Administration, and some other governments have instituted policies designed to further encourage the participation of people of color and women in small business, particularly as proprietors. In a later chapter, these policies and their context will be discussed.

8.   Summary and Prospect

The economics of small business is a relatively new field of research in economics, but a great deal is known. Firms of smaller size are at the same time more numerous, so that their large numbers offset their small size: the small business sector, however we define it, is important. Also, there are some predictable differences in the operation and economics of small versus big business. Employment, growth, revenues and profits tend to be more volatile for small businesses than for bigger businesses. Small businesses are more likely to be challenged by an inability to realize economies of scale and by inadequate access to capital. Despite all these factors, they remain a large and important sector of the American economy and that of other countries as well.

In Chapter 2, we discuss the population of small businesses, with some stress on the diversity and the problem of describing such a diverse population in statistical terms. Chapters 3 and 4 address economic theory in relation to small business. We first review the theories of perfect and monopolistic competition and their applications to small business, and discuss economies of scale in more detail. Chapter 5 reviews the theory of entrepreneurship and explores the relation of small business to entrepreneurship.

With this preparation, Chapters 5–10 introduce some topics of relatively recent research on the economics of small business, focusing typically on one or two studies which are summarized with background on the theory applied. Topics include the relationship of small business to job creation, the role of experience in business startups, the role of family participation and the succession problem, access to capital markets and franchising. A following chapter addresses a controversy in the theory of small business, another explores the importance of non-monetary rewards in small business and Chapters 13 and 14 address the public policy toward small business, first with respect to women and people of color, and then more generally.

Discussion Questions

1. The Small Business Administration considers businesses with fewer than 500 employees as "small businesses." Within that limit, however, we can distinguish several subtypes at different size ranges. Enumerate some different size ranges that fall within this group and discuss their importance in terms of the number of firms in each category and their economic activities.
2. Criticize the following statement: "The average American employee is employed in a large firm; therefore, we can ignore small business."

3. How can we account for the fact that small businesses have a larger proportion of employees with graduate degrees than larger businesses?

References

BMG Research. (2013), *Small Business Survey 2012: SME Employers* (London: Department for Business, Innovation and Skills).

Brock, W. A. and D. S. Evans. (1989), "Small business economics," *Small Business Economics* v. 1, pp. 7–20.

Caruso, A. (2012), *Statistics of U.S. Businesses Employment and Payroll Summary: 2012* (United States Bureau of the Census).

Chandler, V. (2012), "The Economic Impact of the Canada Small Business Financing Program," *Small Business Economics* v. 39, no. 1, pp. 253–264.

Coad, A. and Tamvada, J. P. (2012), "Firm Growth and Barriers to Growth among Small Firms in India," *Small Business Economics*, v. 39, no. 2, pp. 383–400.

Fairlie, R. W. and A. Robb. (January 2007), "Families, Human Capital, and Small Business: "Evidence from the Characteristics of Business Owners Survey," *Industrial and Labor Relations Review*, v. 60, no. 2, pp. 225–245.

Headd, B. (2000), "The Characteristics of Small-Business Employees," *Monthly Labor Review* v. April, pp. 13–18.

Headd, B. (2013). *Issue Brief Number 6: Demographic Characteristics of Business Owners and Employees: 2013* (Washington, DC: U.S. Small Business Administration Office of Advocacy).

Liargovas, P. (1998), "'The White Paper on Growth, Competitiveness and Employment' and Greek Small and Medium Sized Enterprises," *Small Business Economics* v. 11, no. 3, pp. 201–214.

Nazar, J. (2015), *16 Surprising Statistics About Small Businesses*, Forbes Magazine, accessed online at http://www.forbes.com/sites/jasonnazar/2013/09/09/16-surprising-statistics-about-small-businesses/2/ (accessed on 19/12/2015).

Oberholzner, T. (2014), *Report in SMEs in Kosovo* (Austrian Institute for SME Research, Section 3.1).

Reddy, M. (2007), "Small Business in Small Economies: Constraints and Opportunities for Growth," *Social and Economic Studies* v. 56, no. 1/2, *The Caribbean and Pacific in a New World Order* v. March/June, pp. 304–321.

Chapter 2

Small and Medium Businesses: A Diverse Population

As we have seen, there are far more small businesses in the American economy than big businesses, although small businesses account for a less-than-proportional mass of production and employment; this is no less true in most countries. Indeed, the small business sector is itself very diverse. Small and medium enterprises as we have defined them include non-employer proprietorships and partnerships and employers of 1–500 employees. Certainly, an employer of four or five will operate quite differently than an employer of 45–50, which again will operate differently than an employer of 400 or 450. At the same time, the boundaries between the different size categories are blurry and arbitrary. An employer of 95 may be categorized as a small employer and an employer of 105 as a medium-size enterprise, but they are likely to be more similar in their operation. This is a problem not only for classification but also for statistics: how may we summarize the statistics of such a diverse population of business firms?

1. Some Useful Theory: Probability and Distribution Functions

This section will refresh the reader's knowledge of probability and distribution functions. These will be applied again and again in the economics of small business. Those who know probability and statistics well can skip Section 1.1 but will probably profit by skimming Section 1.2.

1.1. *Probability*

McCain (2014, pp. 157–159) writes

> Uncertainty plays a role in many human experiences. In gambling, uncertainty may be created deliberately by throwing dice or shuffling cards. Let's consider the example of throwing a single die. (The word "dice" is the plural of "die," which means a cube with numbers from one to six on its six faces. So we say: one die, two or more dice, a pair of dice.) When we throw the die, will it show a number greater than three? Yes, no, or maybe? Since the answer is uncertain, it is maybe. But can we do better than that?
>
> In an absolute sense, we can do no better. The statement about an event is either true, false or uncertain, and in this case it is uncertain. But in a relative sense, some uncertain statements are less likely than other uncertain statements. When we throw the die, for example, the statement that the number will be greater than five is less likely than the statement that the number will be greater than three. The reason is that there are three different ways we can get a number greater than three — it can be four, five or six — whereas there is only one way that we can get a number greater than five. We can often make these comparisons of likelihood, and we put more confidence in the likelier prediction.
>
> Probability is a way of measuring relative likelihood in numerical terms. A probability is a number between zero and one, inclusively. If we know that an event is certain to occur, the probability of that event is one and if we know for certain that the event will not occur, the probability of that event is zero. Among uncertain events, the more likely the event is, the larger the probability number that is assigned to it. Thus we might say that when we throw a die, the probability of a number greater than five is one sixth, while the probability of a number greater than three is one half. Thus, the more likely event has the larger probability.
>
> In some cases, we can do better still. We can tie the probability of an event to the frequency with which we observe that event in a whole series of similar experiments. Suppose, for example, that we throw a die 100 times. We can be reasonably certain that we

will observe a number greater than five in approximately one sixth of all the throws. Similarly, we will observe a number greater than three in approximately one half of all the throws. Not only that, but if we throw the die a thousand times, the proportions will be the same, and the approximation will be even better. The proportions remain the same, and the approximations get better, as the number of throws increases. The "limiting frequency" of an event is the number approximated in this way as the number of trials increases without limit. Thus, we identify the *probability* of an event with the *limiting frequency* whenever a limiting frequency makes sense.

In some other important cases, a limiting frequency may not make much sense. Think of the outcome of a research project to find a new technology for automobile engines. Until the research is done, we do not know whether it will be successful or not. As researchers say, that's what makes it research. But once the research is done and the results are in, that same research project will neither need to be done again, nor could it be done again. So a limiting frequency makes no sense in this case. Nevertheless, it seems to me that success in a research project to produce automobile engines using fuel cell technology would be *more probable* than success in a research project to produce automobile engines using nuclear fusion. It would be likelier, so we assign a larger probability number to it. Of course, there is a subjective element in my judgment that success with fuel cell technology is more likely than success with nuclear fusion technology. So there is a subjective element in the probability attached to it. Nevertheless, we will assume that probabilities for unique events like a research project have the same properties as probabilities identified with relative frequencies, despite the subjective element. This is a common assumption in many applications of probability.

We can also use the relative frequency approach to *estimate* probabilities, when the relative frequencies are observable. Meteorology gives some good examples of this. What are the chances of a white Christmas next year? Although it is too far in the future to know what cold or warm fronts may be passing through, we can look at the frequency of white Christmases over the past decades and use that information to estimate the probability of a white Christmas next year. The records show that about 20% of Christmases in the Philadelphia area have been white Christmases. So we can say with good confidence that the probability of a white Christmas is about 20%.

1.2. *Skewed Distributions*

Another probability concept that will be used in this book is the concept of a *probability distribution*. Suppose we were to ask the question: If a firm was chosen at random among all the business firms in the United States, what is the probability that the firm would have N or fewer employees, where N can take any value from $1, 2, \ldots$ and onward to 100, 250, etc., and any value in between. To say that the firm is chosen at random is to say that every firm in the country has the same probability of being chosen. This selection of a firm at random is an experiment we can carry out again and again, as many times as we wish, so we can use the relative frequency approach to probability in this case. This means the *probability* of selecting a firm with N or fewer employees will be identical with the *proportion* of all firms that have N or fewer. We could calculate an approximate answer to that question using data from Table 2 in Chapter 1.

One of the most familiar ideas from statistics is the "bell curve," that is, the normal distribution. Figure 1 shows an example, which is an approximation to the distribution of heights, in inches, of adult women in the United States. It is a good example of a normal

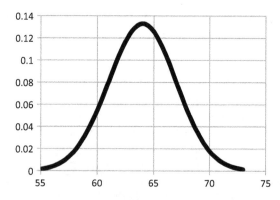

Figure 1. Normal Distribution of Height of Adult Women.

Source: Author's computation from data in Centers for Disease Control (2016), *Anthropometric Reference Data for Children and Adults: United States, 2011–2014*, p. 14.

distribution. What the bell curve tells us is that (1) the average (or *mean*) height of women corresponds to the top of the curve, and is 64 inches, that is, 5 feet, 4 inches, or in metric terms, about 163 cm. (2) The proportion of women whose height is approximately 5 feet is proportional to the height of the curve, that is, women with height close to 5 feet (152 cm) are less than half as common as women with height close to 5 feet 4 inches. In other terms, the normal distribution is an instance of a *frequency distribution* — it tells us approximately how frequently we will encounter women about 5 feet tall, in this example. (3) Women whose height is 4 inches over the mean, 5 feet 8 inches (173 cm), are exactly as common as women who are 4 inches below the mean, 5 feet tall. In general, the normal distribution is *symmetrical*. (4) This in turn means that the median is exactly the same as the mean. The *median* is a value large enough that 50%-1 of the observations are less than the median and 50%-1 are greater. In this example, approximately half of all women are 5 feet 4 inches or taller, and approximately half are 5 feet 4 inches or shorter. Because of the symmetry of the normal distribution, the median of the normal distribution is identical to its mean.

The normal distribution, like any frequency distribution, can also be interpreted in terms of probabilities. Suppose we choose a woman at random in such a way that the probability of being chosen is the same for every woman in the population. We measure her height. Since the *proportion* of women who are about 5 feet tall is proportional to the value of the normal distribution, this also gives us the *probability* that the person chosen will be approximately 5 feet tall. More generally, the normal distribution is connected to the *central limit theorem*, which tells us that the average value of a random sample (in this example) will itself be distributed normally with the same mean value. The larger the sample, the more closely its mean will approximate the mean of the original distribution. Turning this around, we can estimate the mean of the original population by taking a sample and calculating its mean, and if the sample is large, we can be sure that the estimate is very accurate. Further, it is not the relative size of the sample that determines the accuracy of the estimate, but its absolute size — which means that we can use this approach to estimate the mean of a very large population at reasonable cost.

All of this so far will be familiar (and pretty old hat) to readers who have studied statistics. For our purposes, unfortunately, it is a negative example. For the economics of small business, the distribution functions we will be most concerned with will not be normal distributions. In particular, they will not be symmetrical. Instead, they will be *skewed*. In particular, they will be skewed to the right, in the sense that there will be a longer "tail" of observations to the right of the mean than to the left. Figure 2 shows an example of a distribution that is skewed to the right, a *lognormal distribution*. A lognormal distribution means that the logarithm of the variable on the horizontal axis is normally distributed. The mean of this distribution is 12.2, which is greater than the median, 7.4. There is a heuristic rule[1] that tells us that, if the distribution is skewed to

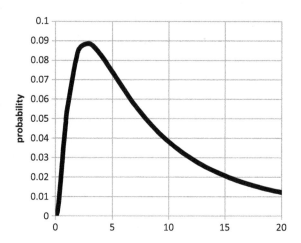

Figure 2. The Lognormal Distribution Function.

Source: Author's computation from a numerical example.

---

[1] A rule is said to be *heuristic* if it may not be true in absolutely every case, but is true in most cases of interest, so that it can be used with confidence that it will only very rarely lead to errors. The rule will be applicable for all examples of skewed distributions used in this book.

the right, its mean is greater than its median, and this will be true for our examples. A distribution function can also be skewed to the left, but the distributions important for this book will be skewed to the right.

In fact, skewed distributions have a long history in economics. One of the best-known skewed distributions is the Pareto distribution, named after the economist and sociologist Vilfredo Pareto (1848–1923). Studying the distribution of incomes in various countries, Pareto discovered that those distributions were similar and could all be described by the same sort of skewed distribution functions. (Further study shows that the Pareto distribution fits bigger incomes better than the lower incomes.) Figure 3 gives an example of a Pareto distribution.

To illustrate how skewed distributions are applied in the economics of small business, let us suppose that the distribution function shown in Figure 3 describes businesses in an imaginary country, which we shall imaginatively call "Imaginaria." The number of employees is shown on the horizontal axis and the frequency on the vertical axis. The distribution shows the number of employees in businesses, so that half of all businesses have just one employee, one-quarter have two employees, one-sixth have three employees, one-eighth have four employees and so on. Clearly the median number of employees is one — one half minus one of all companies have just

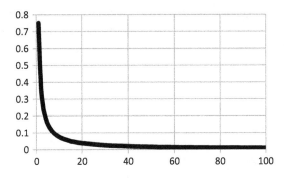

Figure 3. A Pareto Distribution.

Source: Author's computation from a numerical example.

one employee, and one-half minus one have more. However, the mean number of employees is 50.

As we have seen, there is more than one way that a skewed distribution can be represented mathematically. We have seen two: the lognormal and the Pareto distribution. We will see some others in later chapters.

If we have a normal distribution, we can think of the mean as being representative of the whole population. We know that nobody is average, but most observations are close, and those that are less may roughly offset those that are more. In a skewed distribution such as this, we need to be very cautious in identifying the mean as typical. In the Imaginaria example, just one percent of all firms have exactly 50 employees, while 90 percent have fewer. Should we therefore treat the median, with one employee, as the representative case? That could also be confusing, since in some ways, the bigger firms may be more important. We had best be cautious about treating *any* size as representative; instead, we must always allow for the wide and skewed distribution of the sizes of firms.

In fact, even the Pareto distribution is too simple for our purposes, and the example given is far less skewed than firm sizes are in the real world. We will see this as we use these concepts to discuss some of the simpler things that are known about small business.

2.   Some "Stylized Facts" About Small Business

Here are some "stylized facts" about small and large businesses that have been known and consistently observed for decades. In the first issue of *Small Business Economics*, Brock and Evans (1989, p. 2) wrote

> Financial economists know that the efficient markets model breaks down for small firms, labor economists know that smaller firms pay lower wages for apparently comparable workers, and industrial organization economists know that small firms are more likely to fail and have faster and more variable growth than large firms.

Another "stylized fact" is that there are very many more small than large businesses. We can see this in Table 2 in Chapter 1: in every case, the larger size category has fewer firms. This has been observed for many years, as long as we have had data to answer the question. It can be illustrated in a graphic form, in a diagram with the number of employees on the horizontal axis and the relative proportion of all firms that have approximately[2] that number of firms on the vertical axis. This is shown (for 2014) in Figure 4, but Figure 4 also shows how extreme the change in the number of firms is with the increase in size. For much of the range, it is barely visible as distinct from the axes. To make the curve more visible, we might instead measure the *logarithm* of the number of employees on the horizontal axis. Since the logarithm of zero is not defined, we instead measure the logarithm of the number of employees *plus one*. This is called a "zero-inflated" distribution, since zero is inflated to one, and it is often a useful

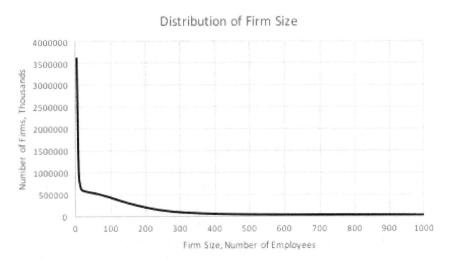

Figure 4. Distribution of Firm Sizes in the United States in 2014.
Source: The author's calculations from U.S. Census Data.

---

[2]In order to make this idea precise, it would be necessary to use some calculus, which is the mathematics of approximations. Rather than digress on calculus, we will make the language a bit imprecise. If you want to know more and want a very precise explanation, a course in mathematical or business statistics would fill in the blanks. For those of you who have taken mathematical or business statistics, please bear with the rest of us.

Figure 5. Distribution of Firm Sizes in the United States in 2014, Logarithmic Scale.

Source: The author's calculations from U.S. Census Data.

modification in small business statistics. This is shown in Figure 5. Similar diagrams for other years, both earlier and more recent, will have similar appearance, although the exact details will of course be different.

For some purposes, it is more useful to measure firm size by sales receipts. It will come as no surprise that sales receipts and employment scale are correlated. Figure 6 illustrates this. Perhaps a little more surprising is the fact that larger firms pay higher wages. This is illustrated in Figure 7. It will come as no surprise at this stage, however, that the distribution of firm sizes by sales receipts is skewed! This is shown in Figure 8. These figures all use U.S. Census Data for 2012.

A study by Hurst and Pugsley (2011, p. 78) provides an overview of the role of small businesses in 2007. This is shown in Figure 9. On the horizontal axis, we have the size of businesses and on the vertical axis we have the proportion of the various economic measures that are attributed to firms of the corresponding size or smaller, in 2007. Hurst and Pugsley show an alternative way of displaying a skewed distribution, the *cumulative* distribution function. For

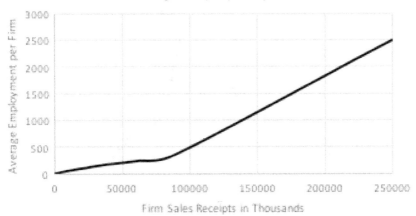

Figure 6. Firm Sales Revenue and Employment.
Source: The author's calculations from U.S. Census Data.

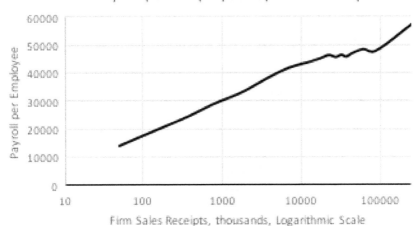

Figure 7. Distribution of Firm Receipts by Size, Logarithmic Scale.
Source: The author's calculations from U.S. Census Data.

Number of Firms by Sales Revenue

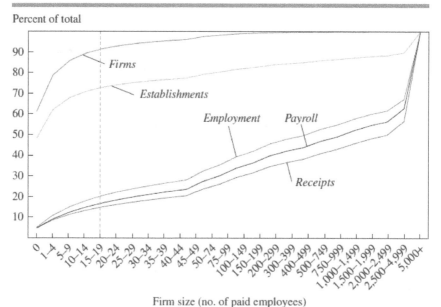

Figure 8. Distribution of Firm Receipts by Size, Logarithmic Scale.
Source: The author's calculations from U.S. Census Data.

Cumulative Shares of Firms, Employment, Receipts, and Payroll,
by Firm Size Category, 2007

Figure 9. Firm Size and Various Economic Measures.
Source: Hurst and Pugsley (2011, p. 78).

example, in Figure 9 the black line shows the proportion of all payrolls paid by firms with no more employees that the ranking shown at the corresponding point on the horizontal axis, including all firms with fewer employees. Thus, continuing the example, we see that industries with fewer than 20 employees paid about 15 percent of all payrolls, though they accounted for about 90 percent of all businesses. In this display, the skewness of the distribution is less obvious, but is seen in the curvature and height of the graph, and lends itself to comparison as we see here. We see that the curve for the proportion of all firms with fewer employees than the value shown on the horizontal axis is above the curve for receipts, and oppositely curved, indicating that the distribution of firm sizes is much more skewed to the right than the distribution of firm receipts, for example.

3. Summary

The categories of small and medium enterprises include a very wide range of sizes and kinds. For statistical purposes, we can describe a population by a distribution function, that is, a curve that expresses the relative frequency with which we observe various size categories. We find that the distribution functions for the employment sizes of enterprises, and for several other dimensions of enterprises, are highly skewed. This skewness is in itself an important fact about the economics and statistics of small businesses. Whatever we mean by "small," there will always be more enterprises in the "small" category than in the "larger" category, despite the fact that there will always be an element about the categories that is arbitrary.

Discussion Questions

1. The "bell curve," with variation symmetrically distributed around its mean, does not seem to be applicable to small businesses. What alternative is there? What does this tell us about the usefulness of averages in the study of small business?
2. Define a lognormal distribution. Does it seem likely that business employment is lognormally distributed? Why or why not?
3. Contrast a Pareto distribution with a normal distribution.

References

Brock, W. A. and Evans, D. S. (1989), "Small Business Economics," *Small Business Economics*, v. 1.

Hurst, E. and Pugsley, B. (2011), "What Do Small Businesses Do?" *Brookings Papers on Economic Activity*, Fall, pp. 73–142.

McCain, R. A. (2014), *Game Theory: A Nontechnical Introduction to the Analysis of Strategy*, 3rd Edition (World Scientific).

Chapter 3

Microeconomics and Small Business

The purpose of this chapter is to review some ideas of microeconomics in the context of the economics of small business, for readers who have limited preparation in microeconomic theory. Readers who are confident of their knowledge of microeconomics might skip Sections 1 and 2 of this chapter without losing the thread. Among the most important concepts for this purpose are perfect competition, monopolistic competition and economies (and diseconomies) of the scale of the firm.

1. The Theory of "Perfect" Competition

Recall for a moment what many economists call "Perfect Competition." This is an idealized structure of an industry in which price competition is dominant — in fact the only form of competition possible. A "perfectly competitive" market structure is defined by four characteristics:

- Many small buyers and sellers
- A homogenous product
- Perfect knowledge
- Free entry

The requirement of "many small sellers" suggests that small business leads to perfect competition. In fact, the case is a bit more complex. Nevertheless, it will be worthwhile to recall some of the theory of perfect and also of monopolistic competition.

First, consider the condition that there are many small sellers. The idea is that the sellers are small *relative to the size of the market,* so that no one of them can "fix the price." If there are "many small sellers," it makes it much harder for any seller or any group of sellers to "rig the price." Each seller reasons as follows: "If I try to charge a price above the market price, my customers will know that they can get a better price from my competitors. My own share of the market is so small that all of my customers will be able to buy what they want from the competition — and I won't have any customers left!" Thus, the seller treats the price as being given and determined by "the forces of the market" independently of her own output.

"Homogenous products" means all suppliers sell products that are perfect substitutes. If the product (or service) of one seller differed significantly from that of another seller, then each seller would probably be able to retain at least some of the customers, even at a very high price. These would be the customers who just prefer this seller's product (or service) to that of someone else. Thus, the price would be somewhat under the firm's control. The assumption of homogenous products serves to rule that out.

But this assumption should not be taken too literally. No two potatoes are exactly alike. We are not assuming that the goods are alike: only that the goods produced by one supplier are good substitutes for those offered by another seller. Thus, the potatoes don't need to be just alike — provided that, on the average, Farmer Jones' potatoes are just as good as Farmer Green's. This is especially important with respect to services. It would be hard to prove that two haircuts are just alike! But so long as the haircuts supplied by one barber are substitutable for the haircuts supplied by another — and their conversation is about equally amusing — then perhaps the "homogenous products" assumption is fulfilled.

Perfect information is a little less clear than the other assumptions — we can hardly assume that people know everything there is to know! In practice, what is important is that each buyer and seller knows all about her or his opportunities to make deals, that is, knows the terms on which other market participants will buy and sell. Remember what we said in the paragraph on "many small sellers": a seller would assume that her or his customers would know whether the competition was selling more cheaply. If the customers didn't know that they had alternatives, then even a very small seller might get away with pushing the price up, without losing many customers. Thus, the "perfect information" assumption complements the other assumptions. The assumptions that there are many small buyers and many small sellers mean that buyers have many alternatives of potential sellers to choose among. The assumption of perfect information says that they know what those alternatives are.

Remember Adam Smith's concept of the "natural price": when the price of beer is high, so that brewing is especially profitable, people will enter the brewing trade and their competition with the established breweries will force the price of beer down toward the "natural" price. As Smith was aware, in the long run the entry of new competition — or the exit of unprofitable firms from the industry, to go into other trades — is one of the most important aspects of competition and is thus one of the four characteristics of the perfectly competitive structure.

Free entry means that new companies can set up in business to compete with established companies whenever the new competitors feel that the profits are high enough to justify the investment. This is, first and foremost, a legal condition. That is, in a "perfectly competitive" market there are no government restrictions on the entry of new competition. This legal status is often expressed by the French phrase "laissez faire," meaning "let them make (whatever they want to make for sale)." But it could also be a practical condition. For example, if no one could set up in business without enormous capital investments, that might prove an effective limit on the entry of new competition — especially if, for some reason, the capital cannot be raised by borrowing or issuing shares.

Other, more or less noncompetitive market structures are also defined in terms of these characteristics. The other three market structure models can be defined in terms of the ways in which they deviate from the characteristics of "perfect" competition.

In a "monopoly," there is just one seller of a good or service for which there is no close substitute.

In an "oligopoly," there are two or more but only a few sellers.

In "monopolistic competition," the products are not homogenous but are "differentiated."

At first thought, it might seem that these forms could only exist with "big business" — that they will not correspond to small business. However, since small businesses may exist in small local markets, any of the three, even monopoly, might in principle include some small businesses. However, of these three, monopolistic competition may be the most relevant for small business. The reason is that local markets are likely to overlap. Thus, we might say that for many small businesses, the product or service is *differentiated by location*. On the whole, the model of monopolistic competition with product or service differentiation by location seems the best general model for the economics of small business. In what follows, we will recall some of the basic ideas from the models of perfect and monopolistic competition in order to contrast them.

1.1. *Cost*

For either sort of firm, cost is an important determinant of supply, so let us first review the analysis of cost in elementary economic theory. There are two dichotomies: fixed cost (FC) and variable cost (VC) (on the one hand) and money and implicit or opportunity cost (on the other.) By looking at the firm from the point of view of costs, we gain a much more direct understanding of supply.

In the short run, we have two major categories of costs:

- Fixed costs and
- Variable costs

Variable costs, VCs, are costs that can be varied flexibly as conditions change. In the John Bates Clark model of the firm that is pretty standard in elementary economics, labor costs are the VCs. FCs are the costs of the investment goods used by the firm, with the idea that these reflect a long-term commitment that can be recovered only by wearing them out in the production of goods and services for sale.

The idea here is that labor is a much more flexible resource than capital investment. People can change from one task to another flexibly (whether within the same firm or in a new job at another firm), while machinery tends to be designed for a very specific use. If it isn't used for that purpose, it can't produce anything at all. Thus, capital investment is much more of a commitment than hiring is. In the 1800s, when John Bates Clark was writing, this was pretty clearly true. Over the past century, (1) education and experience have become more important for labor, and have made labor more specialized, and (2) increasing automatic control has made some machinery more flexible. So the differences between capital and labor are less than they once were, but all the same, it seems labor is still relatively more flexible than capital. It is this (relative) difference in flexibility that is expressed by the simplified distinction of long and short run.

What is the connection between the distinction we have just made — fixed costs, FCs, versus variable costs, VCs — and opportunity cost, a key concept for economic theory? In general, economists define the "opportunity cost" of any good or service as the value of all the other goods or services that we must give up in order to produce it. The opportunity cost of any decision consists of everything we must give up in order to carry out that decision. In economics, all costs are included — whether or not they correspond to money payments. If we have opportunity costs with no corresponding money payments, they are called "implicit costs." The implicit costs (as well as the money costs) are included in the cost analysis we have just given. The distinction can be illustrated by a conversation I had with a taxicab driver many years ago. I asked if he were driving his own cab or working for a cab company. He said he was working for a cab company, and added that he formerly had been a small businessman driving his own cab. He had been able to cover his own costs, he said, but found that he could actually take home more money working for another company. However, the taxicab driver was thinking only of the money costs that he had to lay out to keep his taxicab going — gasoline, maintenance and so on. He was overlooking the opportunity cost of his own labor. If he drove his own cab, he had to give up the opportunity to work for another company a for a salary or wage, and that — the greater amount he made working for another company — was his opportunity cost for his labor when he drove his own cab. Since he did not have to pay it out in money, it was an implicit cost. He had not studied economics, so he could not have defined "opportunity cost;" but when he gave up his business and went to work for another company, he responded to opportunity costs, just as economic theory says he would.

There is some correlation between implicit costs and fixed or variable costs, but this correlation will be different in such different kinds of firms as

- A factory owned by an absentee investor
  This is the easiest case to understand. All of the labor costs to the absentee investor are money costs, including the manager's salary. If the investor has borrowed some of the money he invested in the factory, then there are some money costs of the capital invested — interest on the loan. However, we must consider the opportunity cost of invested capital as well. The investor's own money that she has used to buy the factory is money that she could have invested in some other business. The return she could have gotten on another investment is the opportunity cost of her own funds invested in the business. This is an implicit cost, and in this case the implicit cost is part of the cost of capital and probably a FC.
- A "mom-and-pop" store
  A "mom-and-pop" store (family proprietorship or partnership) is a store in which family members are self-employed and supply most of the labor. Typically, "mom" and "pop" don't pay themselves a salary — they just take money from the till when they need it, since it is their property anyway. As a result, there are no money costs for their labor. But their labor has an opportunity cost — the salary or wages they could make working similar hours in some other business — and so, in this case, the implicit costs include a large component of variable labor costs.
- A large modern corporation
  The corporation has relatively few implicit costs, but generally will have some. All labor costs will be expressed in money terms (though benefits and bonuses have to be included), since the

shareholders don't supply labor to the corporation as "mom and pop" do in a family proprietorship. The corporation will pay interest to bondholders and dividends to shareholders. Moreover, the typical corporation will retain some profits and invest them within the business, a "plowback" investment. Conversely, shareholders may take a large part of their payout in appreciation of the stock value — and plowback investment is one reason for the appreciation. Thus, we would say that the corporation has a net equity value, that is, that the corporation "owns" a certain amount of capital that it invests in its own business (very much like the absentee owner in the first example). This capital has an opportunity cost, and this opportunity cost is an implicit cost. The stockholders, who own the corporation, ultimately receive (as dividends or appreciation) both the opportunity cost of the equity capital and any profit left over after it is taken out.

Figure 1 is a picture of the FCs, VCs and the total of both kinds of costs (TC) from a spreadsheet numerical example. Output produced

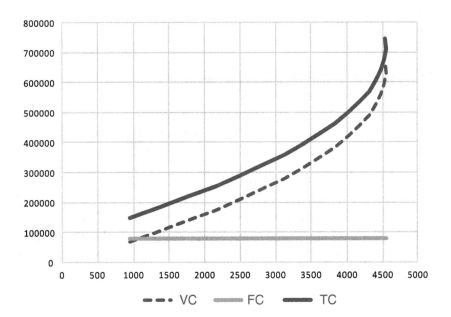

Figure 1. Fixed, Variable, and Total Cost.

Source: The author's numerical example.

is measured toward the right on the horizontal axis. The cost numbers are on the vertical axis. Notice that the variable and total cost curves are parallel, since the distance between them is a constant number — the FC.

Costs may be more meaningful if they are expressed on a per-unit basis, as averages per unit of output. In this way, we again distinguish

Average fixed cost (AFC)

This is the quotient of FC divided by output. In the numerical example we are using, when output is 4,020 FC is 80,000, so AFC is 80,000/4,020 = 19.9.

Average variable cost (AVC)

This is the quotient of VC divided by output. In the example, at an output of 4,020 the VC is 357,000, giving AVC of 357,000/4,020 = 82.71.

Average total cost or simply average cost (ATC or AC)

This is the quotient of total cost divided by output. In the example, with 4,020 of output total cost is 413,500, so AC is 430,000/4,020 = 106.96 = 87.06 + 19.90.

Figure 2 shows the average cost (AC), AVC and AFC in a diagram. This is a good representative of the way that economists believe firm costs vary in the short run.

In economic theory, we often focus particularly on the marginal variation. In this case, of course, it is marginal cost. Marginal cost is defined as

$$\mathrm{MC} = \frac{\Delta C}{\Delta Q}$$

As usual, Q stands for (quantity of) output and C for cost, so ΔQ stands for the change in output, while ΔC stands for the change in cost. We assume that ΔQ is "small." As usual, marginal cost can be interpreted as the additional cost of producing just one more ("marginal") unit of output, and the marginal cost is an approximation to the derivative of cost with respect to output. If the reader has studied calculus and understands the concept of a

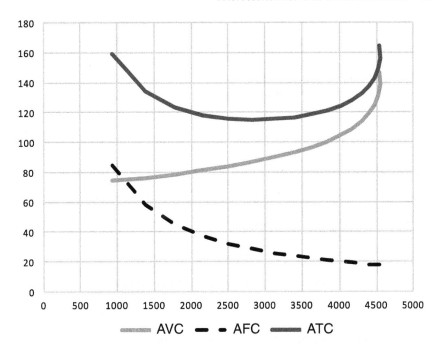

Figure 2. Average Cost Curves.

Source: The author's numerical example.

derivative, he/she will not go wrong interpreting the marginal cost as a derivative. Those who have not studied calculus can pass over that: they will not go wrong by thinking of marginal cost as the cost of producing just one more unit. (In either case, all opportunity costs must be included in the computation).

Let's have a numerical example of the marginal cost definition to help make it clear. In the spreadsheet example we have been using, total cost is 280,000 for an output of 3,120, and it is 33,000 for an output of 3,625. So we have

$$\Delta C = 360,000 - 318,000 = 42,000$$

$$\Delta Q = 3625 - 3120 = 505$$

$$\frac{\Delta C}{\Delta Q} = \frac{42,000}{505} = 83.16$$

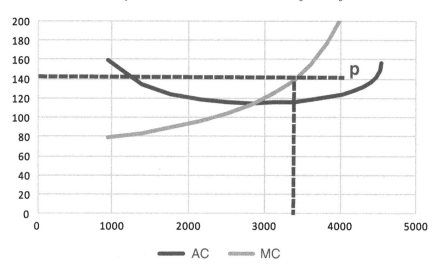

Figure 3. Average and Marginal Costs.
Source: The author's numerical example.

for a marginal cost of \$99.01 for the next unit produced. As usual, this is an approximation, and the smaller the change in output we use, the better the approximation is.

Figure 3 is a picture of marginal cost for our spreadsheet example firm, together with average cost as output varies.

As before, the output produced is measured by the distance to the right on the horizontal axis. The average and marginal cost are on the vertical axis. Average cost is shown by the lighter grey curve, and marginal cost in darker grey. Notice how the marginal cost rises to cross average cost at the lowest point of the average cost curve.

1.2.   *Demand and Equilibrium*

One of the most familiar ideas from the theory of perfect competition is that, from the point of view of the seller, the price is given. We say that the demand curve for a perfectly competitive firm is infinitely elastic. In fact, the demand curve for a perfectly competitive firm is a "horizontal line corresponding to the going price."

And that makes sense, because the price in a perfectly competitive market is determined by supply and demand — not by the seller or the buyer. Conversely, so far as the seller or the buyer is concerned, the price must be a given, since it is determined by supply and demand. The seller has no control over the price, and to say that the seller has no control over the price is to say that the price is given — a constant, a horizontal line — from the point of view of the seller. Economists sometimes express this by saying that the price is "parametric," meaning that while it may change from time to time, it does not change in response to the firm's output decision.

This assumption that price is parametric simplifies the maximization of profit. The rule for maximization of profit for a perfectly competitive firm is: increase output until

$$p = \mathrm{MC}$$

Notice, in Figure 3, the maximum profit will correspond to the point where the price line crosses the marginal cost curve, an output of 3,300. If the price rises or falls, the quantity sold will rise or fall along the marginal cost curve. That is to say, the supply curve of a perfectly competitive firm is the firm's marginal cost curve.

Thus, marginal cost = price is the same as quantity supplied = quantity demanded for the individual firm. When marginal cost = price for each firm in the industry, we have quantity supplied = quantity demanded in the industry as a whole. See Figure 4.

In Figure 4, the lower case q, s and d refer, respectively, to output, supply and demand from the point of view of the individual firm, and the capital S, D and Q are for the industry as a whole. Price (per unit

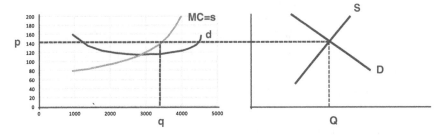

Figure 4. The Firm and Industry in Equilibrium.

Source: The author's example.

sold) is the same from all points of view. In an industry of this sort, the small business takes the price it can get, and adjusts accordingly. When I was a boy living on a farm that produced feeder cattle, the price we got for each animal was determined by an auction — a price that we could not set nor, so far as we knew, influence by bringing fewer animals to the market. But not all small businesses operate that way.

2.   Small Business and "Monopolistic" Competition

We have said that monopolistic competition differs from perfect competition in that products (or services) are differentiated. To say that products are differentiated is to say that the products may be (more or less) good substitutes, but they are not perfect substitutes. For an example of a monopolistically competitive "industry," we may think of the hairdressing industry. There are many hairdressers in the country, and most hairdressing firms are quite small. There is free entry, and it is at least possible that people know enough about their hairdressing options so that the "perfect knowledge" condition is fulfilled. But the products of different hairdressers are not perfect substitutes. At the very least, their services are differentiated by location. A hairdresser in Center City Philadelphia is not a perfect substitute for a hairdresser in the suburbs — although they may be good substitutes from the point of view of a customer who lives in the suburbs but works in Center City. Hairdressers' services may be differentiated in other ways as well. Their styles may be different; the decor of the salon may be different, and that may make a difference for some customers; and even the quality of the conversation may make a difference. A very good friend of mine changed hairdressers because her old hairdresser was an outspoken Republican. My friend said that she just couldn't take it any more without answering back — and it's not a good idea to get into a controversy with one's haircutter!

In the previous paragraph, the word "industry" was put in quotes, when it referred to a group of firms with product differentiation. That's because the boundaries of the industry become much more vague when we talk about product differentiation. A hairdresser in Center City Philadelphia and another in a Philadelphia suburb may be pretty close substitutes — but the Philadelphia hairdresser's service will be a very poor substitute for the services of a hairdresser in Seattle! Are they in the same industry? Or should we think of hairdressing industries as localized, so that Philadelphia hairdressing is a different industry than Seattle hairdressing? Also, barbers may cut women's hair, and hairdressers may cut men's hair. Are hairdressers and barbers part of the same industry, or different industries? There really is no final answer to this question, and some economists have avoided any reference to industries in dealing with monopolistic competition. Instead they talk about "product groups." A product group is a group of firms selling products that are "good," but not necessarily "perfect" substitutes. And, of course, a product group is not unique, since it depends on how "good" we require the substitutes to be, so there will be broader and narrower product groups. Coke and Pepsi are both members of the product group "cola drinks," while Coke, Dr. Pepper, Sprite and Squirt are members of the broader product group "carbonated soft drinks." (Coke, Pepsi, Dr. Pepper, Sprite and Squirt are all registered trade-marks.)

This illustrates another point. Product differentiation is characteristic of monopolistic competition, but not limited to monopolistic competition. Oligopolies, too, may have product differentiation. Cola drinks would probably be thought of as a differentiated oligopoly, an oligopoly product group, rather than a monopolistically competitive group.

And what about "free entry?" For monopolistic competition, that means free entry into the "product group." Again, let's think of hairdressers as the example. If a hairdresser is especially successful with a Seattle-punk style at a certain location in Center City Philadelphia, there is nothing to prevent other hairdressers from setting up at a nearby location, and cutting in a similar style. In that sense, there is "free entry" into the product group. In general, when one monopolistically competitive firm is quite profitable, we may expect that other firms will set up in business producing similar products, and established firms may change the characteristics of the products they produce, to make those products more similar to the successful one. In that sense, there is free entry into the monopolistically competitive product group.

In the short run, then, the monopolistically competitive firm faces limited competition. There are other firms that sell products that are good, but not perfect, substitutes for the firm's own product. In the words of British economists Robinson and Eatwell (1973, p. 173) every firm has a monopoly of its own product. When the product is differentiated, that means the firm has some monopoly power — maybe not much, if the competing products are close substitutes, but some monopoly power, and that means we must use the monopoly analysis.

Let us digress to recall what the monopoly analysis tells us. The demand curve for the monopoly is the demand curve for the industry — since the monopoly controls the output of the entire industry — and the industry demand curve is downward sloping. So, the monopoly's demand curve is downward sloping. That means the monopoly can push the price up by limiting output. If the monopoly cuts back on its output, it can move up the industry demand curve to a higher price. We need one more concept: marginal revenue.

We define the marginal revenue, MR, as the increase in TR = price times quantity sold for a small increase in quantity sold. That is, in parallel to marginal cost, MR $= \Delta TR/\Delta Q$ where ΔQ is small. Notice that price and quantity sold will vary in opposite directions, so that in general MR will be less than the price. This is shown for a spreadsheet example in Figure 5. While, we recall, a perfectly competitive firm will maximize profit by increasing output until $p = $ MC, a monopoly will instead maximize its profits by increasing output until MR $= $ MC. This rule also applies to a monopolistically competitive firm. This analysis is illustrated by Figure 6.

We see that, as usual in monopoly analysis, the marginal revenue is less than the price. The firm will set its output so as to make marginal cost equal to marginal revenue, and charge the corresponding price on the demand curve, so that in Figure 6, the

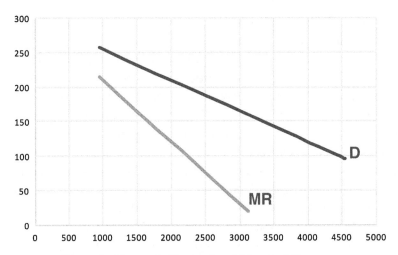

Figure 5. Monopoly Demand and Marginal Revenue.
Source: The author's numerical example.

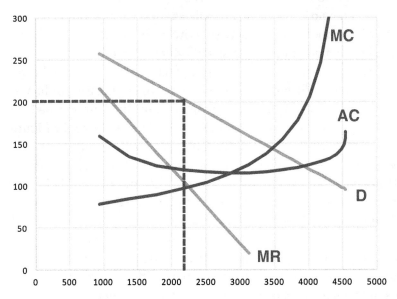

Figure 6. Monopoly Cost, Demand and Marginal Revenue.
Source: The author's numerical example.

monopoly sells 1,905 units of output (per week, perhaps) for a price of $132.85 per unit.

We should notice an assumption underlying all of this. The assumption is the "law of one price," that is, that the monopoly or monopolistically competitive firm sells everything for the same price — no price discrimination. That may actually be more realistic for a monopolistically competitive firm than for a pure monopoly. If the monopolistically competitive firm discriminates on price, the sellers of good substitutes may respond with offers that will take some of their customers away. A pure monopolist does not face that limit.

But the example in Figure 6 is just a short-run situation. We see that the price is greater than the average cost (which is $108.14 per unit, in this case) giving a profit of over $45,000 per week. We remember too that this is "economic" profit — net of all implicit as well as explicit costs — so this profitable performance will attract new competition in the long run. What that means is that new firms will set up, and existing firms will change their products, so that there will be more, and closer, substitutes in the long run. That will shift the demand for this firm's products downward, and perhaps cause the cost curves to shift upward as well, squeezing the profit margins. This will go on as long as the firm and its product type remain profitable. A new "long-run equilibrium" is reached when (economic) profits have been eliminated. This is shown in Figure 7.

What all of this means is that a small business may nevertheless have some "pricing power," some power to increase the price by cutting back on the supply of the product or service. This pricing power is likely to exist only if the product or service of the business is differentiated, either by location or on some other dimension. Most farmers will not have that power (although farms that become tourist attractions are an exception), but many personal services and some kinds of craft production or art will have differentiated products and thus determine their own price subject to a demand curve for their own product. In theory, that is an advantage in the short run (since it can result in profits) but only a temporary advantage for the short run, since new competition will always limit profits in the long run. But the theory assumes that the seller has some knowledge that

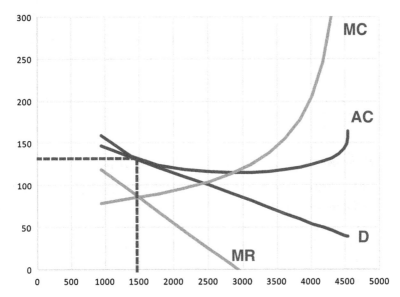

Figure 7. Long-run Equilibrium in Monopolistic Competition.
Source: The author's numerical example.

may, in practice, be difficult and costly to obtain. What, in fact, is the marginal revenue? And what is the marginal cost? For a small business that sells a differentiated product or service, pricing power is no less a dilemma than an advantage: just how high should I set my price, allowing both for the decrease in marginal revenue as I sell more output and for the threat of new competition in the long run? In a successful small business, this will be determined by experience, but a bad guess for a start-up company could mean that the company will never have a chance to gain experience. Mark-up pricing rules are widely used in practice, and for good reason. The right mark-up rule can correspond to the MR = MC rule, at least on the average, and with very limited information the small business may not be able to do better than that.

3.   Economies of Scale

We say that there are "economies of scale," or that "returns to scale are increasing," if an increase in the scale of the firm can result in lower average cost. Remember, average cost is the total cost divided by the output of the firm. Conversely, if an increase in firm scale will result in higher average cost, we say that there are diseconomies of scale," or that "returns to scale are decreasing." This is a little vague. We need to be a bit more precise as to what we mean by "the scale of the firm," but we will leave that for later.

3.1. *Economies and the Scale of the Output*

Economies or diseconomies of scale, or returns to scale, can be under-stood in terms of the long-run cost curves of the firm. We usually define "the long run" as "a period long enough so that all inputs are variable." This includes, in particular, capital, plant, equipment and other investments that represent long-term commitments. Thus, here is another way to think of "the long-run": it is the perspective of investment planning.

So we might approach it this way: Suppose you were planning to build a new plant — perhaps to start-up a new company — and you know about how much output you will be producing. Then you want to build your plant so as to produce that amount at the lowest possible average cost. To make it a little simpler, we will suppose that you have to pick just one of three plant sizes: small, medium and large. The three possible plant sizes are represented by the "short-run" average cost curves AC1, AC2 and AC3 in Figure 8.

The plant size that is best for you depends on how much you expect to produce. If you expect to produce 1,000 units, the small plant size gives the lowest cost. If you expect to produce 3,000 units, the medium plant size gives the lowest cost. If you expect to produce 4,000 units, the large plant size gives you the lowest cost. The average cost you face before making a commitment to one plant size or the other is the lowest of the three, for whatever quantity you expect to produce, and is known as the long-run average cost (LRAC) curve. Therefore, the LRAC — the lowest average cost for each output range — is described by the "lower envelope curve," shown by the thick, shaded curve that follows the lowest of the three short-run curves in each range.

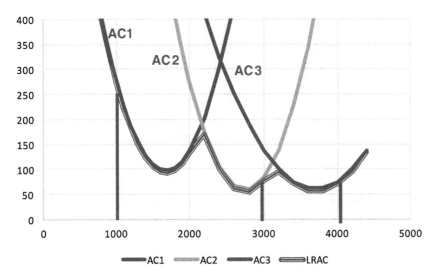

Figure 8. Three Possible Scales of Plant and their Average Cost Curves.
Source: The author's example.

We see that in this example, a larger plant size *together with* sufficiently larger production and sales can result in lower average cost, so in this case, economies of scale are predominant — "returns to scale increase" — at least, in the range shown. Conversely, in this example, when we speak of an "increase in scale" we mean an increase in output and sales.

More realistically, an investment planner will have to choose between many different plant sizes or firm scales of operation, and so the LRAC curve will be smooth, something like Figure 9. As shown, each point on the LRAC corresponds to a point on the SRAC for the plant size or scale of operation that gives the lowest average cost for that scale of operation. In the example shown in Figure 9, we see that increasing returns are predominant at $Q = 20$, but for sufficiently larger outputs, more than 30, diseconomies of scale become predominant, "returns to scale diminish." In general, the "returns to scale" will change as the quantity produced changes. In other words, returns to scale are a *local property* of the LRAC curve. That is, the returns to scale are defined in the neighborhood of a specific output, and may be different at different points along

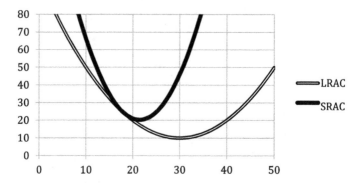

Figure 9. A Short-run and a Corresponding LRAC Curve.
Source: The author's example.

the curve, although similar returns to scale also may predominate over a range of outputs.

We often assume that the LRAC curves have the shape shown in Figure 9, roughly a U-shape, with first "increasing" and then "decreasing returns to scale." This is convenient, because it means that there is a definite, well-defined optimal scale as shown at 30. However, neither assumption of "increasing" or "decreasing returns to scale" can be justified without some further explanation, and the explanations for "increasing" or "decreasing returns to scale" are different, not equally plausible, and in neither case is the explanation obvious. Why indeed should average cost decrease as the scale of production increases? Or, indeed, why should it increase? We will take the first of these questions first in order.

It seems that economists before John Stuart Mill never thought to ask the question whether average cost might be lower when output is greater. However, Adam Smith had postulated that an increase in the division of labor would bring about an increase in labor productivity. Mill (1909) returned to that idea and wrote, "The larger the enterprise, the farther the division of labour may be carried. This is one of the principal causes of large manufactories. As a general rule, the expenses of a business do not increase by any means proportionally to the quantity of business." And if the expenses do not increase in proportion to the quantity of business, we have decreasing average cost — economies of scale. This idea was also adopted by some 20th century economists, such as Nicholas Kaldor.

In the 20th century, economists were more likely to explain economies of scale by "indivisibilities" inherent in the technology. For example, the machines needed for the most efficient production might be machines capable of producing a very large quantity of output, by comparison with market demand. Since the machine is indivisible, a small company would have the choice of paying its cost, but only using it part-time, or purchasing a smaller, less-efficient machine. Either would mean production at higher average cost.

Economies of scale, then, reflect something about the technology: whether because it requires very extensive division of labor, or because it requires large and costly machines, or both, the best technology cannot be put to effective use without a large organization to deploy it.

However, this leaves a bit of a blank if we are to explain diseconomies of scale at quantities greater than the hypothetical optimum scale. Suppose my company has bought one of those big machines and is running it full time producing the optimum output. Suppose, then, that we want to double our output. We can do that by buying another big machine and hiring a second team of employees, dividing their labor in the same way, to produce the increased output. Thus, we double our output while exactly doubling our cost — at exactly the same average cost as before. In general, it is sometimes argued that, once we reach the optimal scale, we can simply replicate that optimal scale of production to multiply output at a constant average cost. If that argument is right, then economies of scale make sense, up to a point, but diseconomies of scale never do, and a firm's LRAC curve would look like Figure 10.

However, Alfred Marshall argued that replication would not work, since the replicated units of production will require a larger organization, and the cost of management of the larger organization will increase more than in proportion to the capacity of the firm to produce goods and services, so that overall average costs would rise beyond some limit. At the very least, the organization would

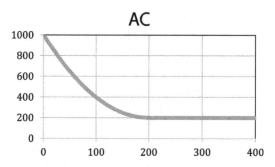

Figure 10. An LRAC Curve with Replication.

Source: The author's example.

need another level of supervisors to coordinate the duplicated units of production. In a world of perfectly rational economic men, it is hard to understand "cost of management." However, in a real world of bounded rationality, in which a manager has a limited span of control, Marshall's assumption has a certain plausibility. However, diseconomies of scale have remained controversial in a way that economies of scale have not.

In any case, diseconomies of scale are not very important for our purposes, since a *small* business is not likely to experience diseconomies of scale, but may experience economies of scale. We can state a few propositions that seem so probable, on the face of the evidence, that they should be considered true until proven otherwise:

(1) Different industries are differently affected by economies of scale.
(2) There are industries in which economies of scale are important so that the minimal efficient scale of operation is quite large by any reasonable standard.
(3) There are other industries in which economies of scale are not important.
(4) There are still other industries in which there are some economies of scale, but nevertheless a firm can operate approximately efficiently at what any reasonable standard would regard as a small scale.

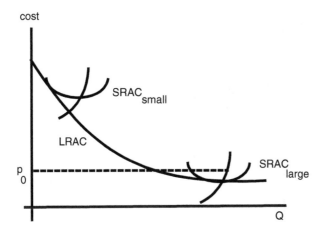

Figure 11. Small and Large Firms and the Economies of Scale.
Source: The author's example.

Clearly, it is industries in the latter two groups that will be important for our study, since a small business is unlikely to survive or even to be started up in the sort of industry described in number (2). But there is one kind of exception.

To illustrate the problem of a small firm in an industry characterized by economies of scale, consider Figure 11. In Figure 11 economies of scale are shown by the LRAC. We also see short-run costs for a small firm, $SRAC_{small}$, and for a large firm in the same industry, shown by $SRAC_{large}$. In these circumstances, the small firm is not likely to survive, since a price like p_0 could be very profitable to the large firm but not to the small firm. The one exception would be the case if this were a new industry, with no established large firm such as shown by $SRAC_{large}$. Then we have a situation more like Figure 12.

Industry demand is shown by the dashed line. In a situation like Figure 12, the small firm without larger-scale competition can charge a price like p_1 and, by reinvesting its profits, grow rapidly, taking advantage of economies of scale, cutting its price as costs decrease and might in the process become a very large firm indeed. This story could be told about Microsoft®, Apple Corp.® and Google®, and perhaps the Ford Motor Company® in 1905–1915 and Comcast®

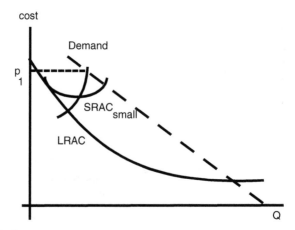

Figure 12. A Small Firm in an Industry Characterized by Economies of Scale but without an Established Large Firm.

Source: The author's example.

in 1972–1985. There is an ideological talking point that "small companies are job creators" which is based on the mistaken idea that this pattern is typical. It is not typical — just the opposite. Companies that are highly successful and expand rapidly do, as a rule, create a lot of jobs, but companies that are highly successful are for that very reason not typical. The most successful businesses, whether they begin small like Apple and Ford or are companies that have built innovative success on large scale, such as Dupont® and General Electric® in the 20th century, are exceptional just to the extent that they are highly successful. You don't achieve exceptional success without being exceptional.

Thus, we will not understand small business by limiting our attention to businesses that create many jobs because they are highly successful. (Nor could we understand big business by studying only the outstanding successes.) Well, can we not learn how to be highly successful by studying the very successful companies? Probably not — as just pointed out, you don't become exceptionally successful without being exceptional, and you don't become exceptional by imitating what has already been done and is established.

In contrast, consider the firm that applied a sealing coat to my driveway in '13. It comprises three partners: Henry, his son who assists him, and his wife who serves as telephone receptionist, scheduler, office manager and bookkeeper. It is, in the American (southern) jargon, a mom, pop and bubba enterprise. It has been operating for several years and, if all goes well, will continue to "create jobs" for Henry and his wife and son, provide resources for retirement for Henry and his wife and get the son started on his own independent enterprise. If so, it will be an extremely successful small business!

This is not to say that Henry's successful mom, pop and bubba enterprise is a "typical" small business, either. For one thing, it is another instance of extremely successful small business, and extreme success is not typical. But more importantly, there really is no "typical small business." What distinguishes small and medium enterprises (SMEs) is their diversity, and the attempt to find a "typical" one is likely to be confusing.

To return to the theme of this section — economies of scale — it would seem that Henry's industry is an example of case (3) or (4) above. Figure 13 shows an example that might correspond

An Example of Case 4

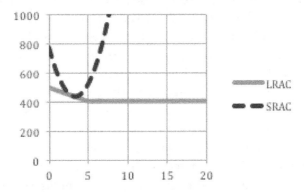

Figure 13. An Example of Case 4.

Source: The author's example.

(in a very rough way) to Henry's situation if it is an example of case (4).

In this case, the scale of the firm is measured by the number of people working in it, whether they are employees or family members. We see in this example that the three-person enterprise is not quite of an efficient scale. It could produce a little more cheaply if there were five or more employees. Why then would it remain smaller? One possible reason is that Henry and his partners like it that way and are willing to settle for a slightly smaller income to avoid the stresses and strains of employing a few wage-earners to operate at a larger scale. Of course, these are conjectures — I have no actual data on returns to scale in Henry's firm, and these reflections should be taken only as examples and possibilities.

3.2. *Economies and Scale More Generally*

It is time to return to the question of how best to measure the scale of a firm and what is likely to be meant by "any reasonable standard." The diagrams and definitions given so far (except for Figure 13) refer to a relationship between average cost and the quantity of output. However, we need a measure of enterprise scale that can be compared between firms in different industries, and the quantities of output for different industries will usually be measured in different units. Indeed, there may be no natural units of output for some industries — the scale may seem much greater if we measure output in ounces rather than carloads! Further, output is limited by sales as well as by productive *capacity*, and the economies of scale refer to productive capacity, not to sales *per se*. In turn, productive capacity is determined by the quantities of inputs available, with a given technology. Thus, in order to compare the scales of firms in different industries, we may choose to use the scale of the inputs, rather than the scale of output.

But which inputs? Mill's explanation of economies of scale in terms of division of labor suggests that we focus on the number of employees — the more there are, the more complex the division of labor that can be adopted. By contrast, if we think of indivisible machines, we might want to focus on the capital investment in the business as the indicator of business scale. However, on the whole, bigger indivisible machines will need bigger teams of employees to work with them, and in some cases indivisibilities may be directly expressed in terms of labor, as, for example, if each business in a particular industry needs at least one person with some specific skills, an accountant for example, even if it cannot keep him busy all the time (and part-time or temporary employment is not feasible.) For these reasons, the number of employees is the most common measure of business scale. For this book, we recall, "small business" means, more completely, SMEs, and a small business will be considered a business with fewer than 100 employees, while the upper limit for medium enterprises will be 500 employees.

We can translate economies of scale from the scale of output to the scale of the inputs, but that would require a bit more advanced theory. It was said above that economies of scale are an aspect of the technology of the industry. In more advanced economics, we express the technology of a firm or industry as its production function. Economies of scale can be defined in terms of the production function, but that requires a bit of mathematics, so it is reserved to Appendix A. Readers who have taken intermediate microeconomic theory should find Appendix A understandable, but others may skip it.

3.3. *Some Evidence*

We have some evidence that bears indirectly on the role of economies of scale for small business. Hurst and Pugsley (2011, p. 74) write "By 'small businesses' we primarily mean firms with between 1 and 19 employees; firms in this size range employ roughly 20 percent of the private sector workforce. We show that over two-thirds of all small businesses by our primary definition are confined to just 40 narrow industries, most of which provide a relatively standardized good or service to an existing customer base." They examined the relative importance of small businesses in the four-digit the North American Industry Classification System (NAICS) categories, quite a narrow set of categories. Some examples (in which small businesses are important) are residential building construction (2,361), offices of physicians (6,211), legal services (5,411) and building equipment contractors (2,382). Hurst and Pugsley ranked the two-digit industries from those with the highest proportion of businesses with 1–19 employees to those with smaller proportions and measured the proportion of all business receipts, employment, payroll, firms and establishments. Figure 14 shows how these industries are related to the proportion of all small businesses. On the horizontal scale, we see the ranking of the industrial sectors, and on the vertical scale we see the proportion of all small businesses that are accounted for by industries at or above that ranking (where "ranked above" means a smaller number). Thus we see that, as Hurst and Pugsley write, "The first 20 industries accounted for just about half of all firms

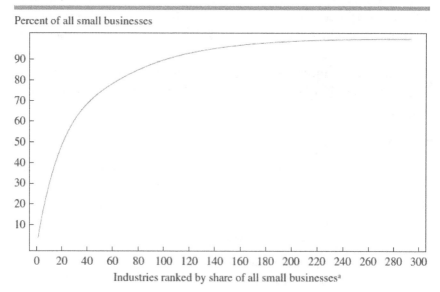

Cumulative Share of All Small Businesses across Ranked Four-Digit Industries, 2007

Percent of all small businesses

Industries ranked by share of all small businesses[a]

a. The 294 four-digit NAICS industries are ranked by their share of all businesses with fewer than 20 employees, starting with the industry with the largest share.

Figure 14. Industries and the Proportion of all Small Businesses.
Source: Hurst and Pugsley (2011, p. 79).

with fewer than 20 employees in that year, and the top 40 for about two-thirds."

Hurst and Pugsley (2011) then compare the performance of industries with greater and lesser proportions of all small businesses, as they define small business. They observe (pp. 77–78) "First, most small businesses are concentrated in a few detailed industry classifications. Second, within these few detailed industries, the distribution of employment across all firm sizes differs from the overall distribution for all other industries. Most of the industries in which small businesses reside are also industries in which a disproportionate amount of economic activity takes place in small firms." Nevertheless, (pp. 83–84) "even within the industries where most small businesses are located, many firms are still quite large." Their evidence suggests that (p. 75) "some industries (such as insurance agencies) may have a natural scale of production at the establishment level that is quite low" while others are characterized by economies of scale up to a substantial employment size, although much larger firm sizes usually seem to be possible. All of this seems consistent with the remarks (1)–(4) about economies of scale in Section 1.1.

3.4. *The Importance of Economies of Scale*

However we express economies of scale — in terms of quantity of production and average cost curves, of employment scale, or mathematically in terms of a production function — economies of scale will play a key role in many small businesses. There probably are some industries in which economies of scale, beyond the individual self-employed proprietor, are not important. Hairdressing comes to mind as an instance. However, many small businesses will find themselves in in a situation like that shown in Figure 13, in which they could produce more cheaply if they could operate at a somewhat larger scale. This might be six employees rather than three, or 600 rather than 100. In this situation, small scale is a handicap. Why do businesses remain smaller than the "minimum efficient scale?" There are several reasons.

(1) Limited demand. Many small businesses operate in local markets in which demand is too small to sustain a firm of the "minimum efficient scale."

(2) Search frictions. In order to grow, to attract and select a larger, appropriate work-force, it would be necessary for the company to commit its resources to the search for those employees. This is in effect an investment, and the investment might not be a profitable one, despite the gain in efficiency of day-to-day operations.

(3) Finance. Small business growth may often be restrained by an inability to obtain financing for an expansion.

(4) Preference. As we suggested with the example connected with Figure 13, the proprietor or partners may like it that way. A small enterprise that employs family members or a few long-term employees may provide a more attractive lifestyle than one that brings in new employees, strangers, and that faces uncertainty as to whether demand will be adequate and that bears the burden of borrowed money with the risk that the business will be lost through bankruptcy. This is an example of a *nonpecuniary motive* for a business decision. The term "nonpecuniary" comes from the Latin, pecunia, meaning money. (In the earliest Latin, the term was pecu, meaning cattle, and therefore wealth!) Thus nonpecuniary motives are subjective satisfactions that are an alternative to money. In the example of Henry's paving enterprise, the subjective satisfaction is the independence of his family both from employers and from the responsibility and trouble of employees. As we will see in later chapters, nonpecuniary motives play an important role in small business.

Economies of scale are also recognized as a barrier to new entry, that is, to start-ups. If there are economies of scale, the new enterprise may face a period of losses before it "gets up to scale," that is, finds a market and a business plan for a minimum efficient scale. (This has been often observed in world wide web start-ups where advertising is the major source of revenues and it does not make sense to advertisers until the web service has an audience of some size, i.e., can operate at a large scale.) This can be true for start-ups that remain small or medium enterprises. Even if the efficient team size is 10 or 20, there are likely to be (on the one hand) search costs of assembling a new team and (on the other hand) some time lag before customers can be found for the product of an efficient scale of operation. Losses are likely in the meantime, and those losses are themselves an investment that may or may not be profitable. These barriers to entry may protect established, but smaller than efficient size, enterprises from new competition at an efficient scale, allowing them to remain small if that is what the proprietor prefers.

4. A Brief Chapter Conclusion

In conclusion, competition, including monopolistic competition, and economies of scale are considerations we must keep in mind throughout our study of small business. One or another may not be applicable in every case, but because our focus is *small* business, we cannot assume them away. All in all, basic economics can provide us with some ideas useful in understanding small business, not so much by answering the important questions, but rather, by helping us to pose those questions clearly. That's a valuable first step.

Discussion Questions

1. Criticize the following statement: "Since small businesses face competitive markets, we can apply the theory of perfect competition to any field of small business."
2. How does "free entry" influence a small business field such as hairdressing?
3. Define economies of scale and explain your definition.
4. How would economies of scale influence a family business, in most cases?
5. Why do most small businesses remain small?

Appendix A. Production Functions and Economies of Scale

The production function would be written $Q = f(R_1, R_2, \ldots, R_n)$, where Q is output, R_i is the quantity of input i used and the function f defines the maximum output that can be produced with the corresponding quantities of inputs. We often group the inputs into two or three components, such as labor and capital or land, labor and capital, but each of these categories is diverse and we will not adopt that assumption here. (Output may also be diverse but, for simplicity, we will follow the conventions and ignore that diversity here.) Suppose that each of the inputs is increased by the same factor (percent increase) λ. Then Q is increased by a factor μ. If, for every $R_1, R_2, \ldots, R_n$ and every λ, we have $\mu = \lambda$, that is, output increased (or decreased) in the same proportion as the inputs, then we have constant returns to scale. If $\mu \neq \lambda$, then returns to scale are not constant, but the situation is a little more complex. In that case, the relation of μ to λ could depend on the size of λ, depending, for example, on whether λ is big enough to move from a region of increasing returns to scale to a region of decreasing returns to scale. Accordingly, we will have to use a mathematical limit process. Consider $lim_{\lambda \to 0} \frac{\mu}{\lambda}$. If the limit of the quotient $\frac{\mu}{\lambda}$ is greater than 1, given that the starting point is $R_1, R_2, \ldots, R_n$, then we have increasing returns to scale at $R_1, R_2, \ldots, R_n$. If the limit of the quotient $\frac{\mu}{\lambda}$ is less than one, then we have decreasing returns to scale at $R_1, R_2, \ldots, R_n$. It also might be that the limit of the quotient $\frac{\mu}{\lambda}$ is exactly one, at $R_1, R_2, \ldots, R_n$. Then we have constant returns to scale at $R_1, R_2, \ldots, R_n$. The answer to the question "increasing, decreasing, or constant returns to scale" depends on the starting point, which is what we mean when we say that returns to scale is a local property.

There is no disagreement between this approach and the previous one that defined returns to scale in terms of the LRAC function. Here is the reason. Suppose the unit cost of input i is V_i. Then the cost of production with inputs $R_1, R_2, \ldots, R_n$ is $\sum_{i=1}^{n} V_i R_i$. Then the cost of production with inputs $\lambda R_1, \lambda R_2, \ldots, \lambda R_n$ is $\sum_{i=1}^{n} V_i \lambda R_i = \lambda \sum_{i=1}^{n} V_i R_i$. If, then, output increases by factor μ, average cost is

$\frac{\sum_{i=1}^{n} V_i \lambda R_i}{\mu Q} = \frac{\lambda}{\mu} \frac{\sum_{i=1}^{n} V_i R_i}{Q} = \frac{\lambda}{\mu} AC_Q$. With increasing returns to scale, $\frac{\lambda}{\mu} < 1$, so average cost decreases by comparison with what it was when Q was produced with $R_1, R_2, \ldots, R_n$.

References

Hurst, E. and Pugsley, B. (2011), "What Do Small Businesses Do?" *Brookings Papers on Economic Activit*, v. Fall.

Mill, J. S. (1909), *Principles of Political Economy with Some of Their Applications to Social Philosophy*, 7th Edition; Book I, Chapter IX, http://www.econlib.org/library/Mill/mlP.html# (accessed on 1/10/2016).

Robinson, J. and Eatwell, J. (1973), *An Introduction to Modern Economics* (McGraw-Hill).

Chapter 4

Entrepreneurship and Small Business

Entrepreneurship is one of the most popular topics in the business press and popular economics of the 21st century and is often casually identified with small business. But there is less to this than meets the eye. Entrepreneurship and small business certainly are interrelated, and this chapter will discuss some of the interrelations. More importantly, there are a number of different definitions of entrepreneurship. The most popular definition — one associated with the ideas of Joseph Schumpeter — is the one that is least useful for the study of small business, however important it is for other purposes. For the American Internal Revenue Service, an entrepreneur is simply the person who receives the net proceeds of a business. This is a key point! The one thing all definitions agree on is that the entrepreneur is the recipient of the profits, if there are any. This chapter will review some of the definitions of the word "entrepreneur," including Schumpeter's, and will then consider some of the evidence on the relation of Schumpeter's conception in particular to small business in the American economy.

1. Defining the Term

We can trace the concept of the entrepreneur at least to J. S. Mill, and according to some accounts, to J. B. Say and the Physiocrats. Coming from the classical tradition of economic thought, Mill envisioned a society with three classes: landowners, who receive rent, employees, who receive wages, and capitalists. By Mill's time, however, financial markets had matured enough so that some capitalists simply supplied their capital in return for interest, taking none of the responsibility to run the business and little of the risk. By contrast, other businessmen paid interest and received profits. Thus, there was a clear distinction in practice between the capitalists who would finance a business and the active owner who manages the business. Mill described the active managing owner as the "undertaker." Therefore, the income of Mill's undertaker is a mixture of profit, payment for the labor services of management and interest and risk premium on his or her ownership of some part of the capital of the business. This conception of entrepreneurship is still the primary one in national income accounting. "Entrepreneur" is French for "undertaker." Since the word "undertaker" often has a narrower meaning in English, English-speakers have adopted the French word. The same word in German is "unternehmer."

1.1. *The Elder Austrian School*

The Elder Austrian School of thought in economics comprises Carl Menger (whose son, Karl Menger, was a noted mathematician), Friedrich von Wieser, and Eugen von Bohm-Bawerk. The "unternehmer" in the work of the elder Austrian School is something of a cousin of Mill's undertaker. Menger's comments on entrepreurial activity are characteristic of the Elder Austrian School. Menger understands entrepreneurial activity in the light of his "roundabout" theory of production, in which goods of the first order, that satisfy human wants, are produced by means of goods of the second and higher order, some of which are themselves products of labor and goods of still higher order. The higher order goods do not directly satisfy human wants. Broadly speaking, they are capital goods and raw or semi-finished materials. Menger writes (Menger, 1871, pp. 160–161) "Entrepreneurial activity includes (a) obtaining *information* about the economic situation, (b) economic *calculation* — all of the various computations that must be made if a production process is to be efficient ... (c) the *act of will* by which goods of a higher order ... are assigned to a particular production process, and finally (d) *supervision....* With progressive division of labor and an increase in the size of enterprises, ... entrepreneurial activity is just as necessary a factor of production of goods as technical labor services. It therefore has the character of a good of higher order, and value, too, since like goods of a higher order it is also generally an economic good." By saying that entrepreneurial services are an economic good Menger is saying that they are scarce. (Menger, 1871, p. 94). Nevertheless, (Menger, 1871, p. 172) "*Entrepreneurial activity* must definitely be counted as a category of labor services. It is an economic good as a rule, and as such has *value* to economizing men. Labor services in this category have two peculiarities: (a) they are by nature not commodities (not intended for exchange) and for this reason have no prices; (b) they have command of the services of capital as a necessary prerequisite since otherwise they cannot be performed. This second factor limits the amount of entrepreneurial activity in general that is available to a people."

It seems that this definition can be readily applied to small businesses. Menger notes that "In large firms, not only the entrepreneur himself, but often several helpers, are fully occupied with these (entrepreneurial) activities." (1871, p. 160) Menger's entrepreneur will often be a small businessperson, and a small businessperson can hardly avoid being an entrepreneur in Menger's sense. Nevertheless, there are some difficulties with Menger's conception of entrepreneurship. On the one hand, although entrepreneurship is a (qualified, difficult and responsible) form of labor service, and an "economic good," it cannot be offered for sale. Why not? Perhaps the key to it is characteristic (c): "the *act of will* by which goods of a higher order ... are assigned to a particular production process," that is, the decision to initiate and continue the business. The person who commits herself to that "act of will" is presumably the one who does the hiring, not one who is hired.

1.2. *Leibenstein, Alchian and Demsetz*

In the second half of the 20th century, two important discussions of entrepreneurship took place that have much in common with that of Menger, and extended this understanding. Schumpeter's ideas were already known, but not at that time given the priority that they probably would be today; thus, Schumpeter will be discussed later.

Leibenstein begins, from the observation that "the labor contract is almost always incomplete," (Leibenstein, 1969, p. 603). Recognition of the incompleteness of many contracts, and especially labor contracts, is an important step forward in economic theory in the second half of the 20th century, often associated especially with Williamson's Nobel Laureate (2009) work. If information and lawyers are costly, it is unlikely that businesspeople will invest the cognitive and other resources necessary to arrive at and administer complete contracts, which, in fact, would be inordinately complex. But this implies that some resources needed for production will not be available by contract: "The central assumptions on which our theory is based follow that: (1) Not all inputs are purchaseable in terms of the units in which they are used in production." (Leibenstein, 1969, p. 602). Therefore "those who directly or indirectly cooperate to carry out the entrepreneurial role must (1) promote change over resistances implicit in the inert areas,[1] (2) *fill gaps* in the input market, and (3) be responsible for *input completion....* Hence our notion of the entrepreneur as basically a self-propelled input gap-filler and input-completer." (Leibenstein, 1969, p. 612, italics in the original.) The latter two of these functions (which are not clearly distinct) are new in Leibenstein's work, and provide a clear reason why entrepreneurial services cannot be purchased in the market so that the entrepreneur must be the recipient of the residual claim. *By definition* the inputs supplied by the entrepreneur are just those inputs that cannot be procured from the market, due to the incompleteness of contracts (and the boundedness of rationality).

If we take this conception literally at face value, it would seem to be applicable only to very small firms. It does seem to be quite descriptive of the small businessman who pitches in to do whatever

---

[1]Leibenstein also argues that the cost of information and calculation will lead to inertia when the decision is already fairly near the optimum. These limits define the "inert area;" Leibenstein is saying that one of the functions of an entrepreneur is to take action to reduce this region of inertia.

job is needed on a particular day. In a larger organization, no one person would be likely to be able to supply, from his own effort, resources necessary to complete the input set. However, employees can take initiative to supply resources beyond their contractual obligation, and can be recognized and rewarded *ex post* for doing so, and if the chief manager receives the residual revenue of the firm and is attentive, she will find ways to do so. Indeed this is just what Leibenstein has in mind. It is necessary that "some people within the firm attempt to promote change by utilizing or manipulating the inducements present in the existing incentive reward system...." (Leibenstein, 1969, p. 612)

In Alchian (1950), Armen Alchian had argued that there is no need for an entrepreneur in an evolutionary concept of economic progress — that random variations in firm activities, with selection according to profitability, would be sufficient. With Demsetz (1972), however, he provided yet another concept of the entrepreneur. They do not use the word "entrepreneur" as a rule but they instead refer to "the specialist *who receives the residual rewards*," and in all of the theories considered here that is the entrepreneur (Alchian and Demsetz 1972, p. 782, italics in the original.).

Like Leibenstein, Alchian and Demsetz observe that labor inputs are not determined by contract and indeed "Almost every contract is open-ended in that many contingencies are uncovered." (Alchian and Demsetz, 1972, p. 778). This being so, for team production motivation of effort becomes a central issue; due to the noncooperative tendency for team members to shirk, low effective productivity is the result. Thus, supervision or "monitoring" is necessary to maintain effort in the team. "But who will monitor the monitor? ... give him title to the net earnings of the team, net of payments to other inputs. ... the monitor will have an added incentive not to shirk as a monitor. Specialization in monitoring plus residual claimant status will reduce shirking...." (p. 782).

Thus, for Alchian and Demsetz, it is of key importance that the recipient of the residual claim (the entrepreneur) is the ultimate monitor (supervisor) of all other supervisors. We recall that supervision is one of the entrepreneurial services listed by Menger. Alchian and

Demsetz have provided a partial answer to the question why this service cannot be purchased in the marketplace: at least part of supervisory service, the ultimate level of supervision, can come only from the residual claimant.

Since the service of monitoring the monitors is a service that cannot be procured on the market, through contracts, it is one of the inputs that a Leibensteinian entrepreneur will have to complete — and arguably by far the most important one. Thus the concepts of Alchian and Demsetz seem to complement and reinforce that of Leibenstein and also of Menger.

All in all, the definitions we have from Menger, Leibenstein, and Alchian and Demsetz seem to stress different aspects of the same concept, and it is one that can be applied to the proprietor of any small business, though it also has applications to big businesses as Alchian and Demsetz stress. In later chapters of this book, when the word "entrepreneur" is used without modification, it will refer to the entrepreneur as understood in the ideas of Menger and Leibenstein, and by implication in Alchian and Demsetz. However, Schumpeter uses it in a different way, and Section 3 will explore his ideas.

1.3. *Schumpeter*

No economist is more associated with concepts and theory of entrepreneurship than Joseph Alois Schumpeter. Schumpeter had studied with Wieser and Bohm-Bawerk of the Elder Austrian School and was very influenced by them, and by Menger, especially in Schumpeter's own earliest work. Recall that the entrepreneur is the recipient of profits. When Schumpeter began writing (between 1900 and 1910), the purpose of a theory of entrepreneurship was to explain how the existence of profits could be reconciled with market equilibrium. Schumpeter (1934) had adopted a concept of equilibrium partly from the Physiocratic school of thought — he used the term "the circular flow" that had originated from them — along with the ideas of Leon Walras. Thus, it seemed to Schumpeter that there could be no profits — correctly understood — in an equilibrium. Profits could only occur as a result of "breaking the circular flow," that is, of actions that deliberately create disequilibrium. Thus, the entrepreneur must be someone who breaks the circular flow.

It is understood that, for Schumpeter, the "entrepreneur" is an innovator, that is, one who incorporates a "new combination" in economic activity. (Schumpeter, 1934, pp. 66, 75) The innovation, that is, is a new combination of higher-order goods, as Menger uses the terms. Schumpeter writes, "One necessary distinction is that between enterprise and management: evidently it is one thing to set up a concern embodying a new idea and another thing to head the administration of a going concern, however much the two may shade off into each other.... Again, it is essential to note that the entrepreneurial function, though facilitated by the ownership of means, is not identical with that of the capitalist.... In the third place, it is particularly important to distinguish the entrepreneur from the 'inventor.'"

Schumpeter's system of thought is set out in his first book, *The Theory of Economic Development*, and while his later work uses language less influenced by Austrian Economics, these ideas are elaborated rather than changed in his later writing. *The Theory of Economic Development* was published in German in 1911, and Schumpeter tells us that it was largely complete a few years earlier. Neoclassical Economics, then, was in its infancy. The 20th century neoclassical controversy over the efficiency of market processes remained in the future. And while Schumpeter can fairly be accused of a certain amount of hero-worship with respect to the innovative entrepreneur, he is far less starry-eyed than most of his 21st century followers. In (Schumpter, 1934, p. 66) he lists five possible forms that innovation may take:

(1) "The introduction of a new good, ..."
(2) "The introduction of a new method of production, ..."
(3) "The opening of a new market, ..."
(4) "The conquest of a new source of supply, ..."
(5) "The carrying out of a new organization of any industry, like the creation of a monopoly position. ..."

In context, (3) and (4) are suggestive of colonialism, and few orthodox economists would think of "the creation of a new monopoly position" as a good thing, although some of the most successful entrepreneurs from Rockefeller to Gates have innovated in just that way.

Innovations are a product of human creativity, whether we find them in new economic combinations or in new art or science. As Schumpeter (1947) says, entrepreneurship is "the creative response": in a sense the innovations that drive the capitalist economy are not merely discovered by entrepreneurs but are created by them. The creative response creates not only the innovation, but the standard by which it is judged adequate (p. 151). "Thirdly, creative response ... has obviously something ... to do ... with individual decisions, actions, and patterns of behavior.... It should be observed at once that the 'new thing' need not be spectacular or of historic importance. It need not be Bessemer steel or the explosion motor. It can be the Deerfoot sausage. To see the phenomenon even in the humblest levels of the business world is quite essential though it may be difficult to find the humble entrepreneurs historically." (Deerfoot was a very popular and expensive brand of sausages in the US in the 19th and early 20th century, known for high quality and healthy production — a problem with other sausages at the time. Not so humble — this was a pretty major step forward in branding and marketing consumer goods!)

Schumpeter concedes that entrepreneurship is found in "all who actually fulfill the function, ... even if ... employees...." (Schumpeter, 1934, p. 230) and that, with the development of capitalism, innovation might become routinized, so that entrepreneurship would no longer be needed to produce innovations. "Technological progress is increasingly becoming the business of teams of trained specialists who turn out what is required and make it work in predictable ways." (Schumpeter, 1950, p. 132). This sentence written in the 1940s could be a description of the emergence of cellular telephones in the 1970s and 1980s, one of the most fundamental innovations of the second half of the century and one in which an established regulated monopoly and government were the key players.

Schumpeter's theory of innovation is crucial for any understanding of capitalist economic development, but his concept of the entrepreneur is inconsistent with the others we have seen. For Schumpeter, it is history-making creativity that distinguishes the entrepreneur. Schumpeter has linked together two things that seem to be distinct: what Menger calls "the *act of will* by which goods of a higher order ... are assigned to a particular production process" and creativity. More than that, he sees creativity only when it "breaks the circular flow." A person who starts a new business that finds its niche, or who solves troubling problems in order to keep an established business from failing, is not from Schumpeter's viewpoint "creative." Is that quite fair to the business-people who do these things? One could make a case that most businesses demand a certain amount of creativity, just to solve the problems that will always challenge them from time-to-time.[2]

From this point on book, when I mean to refer to Schumpeter's concept of entrepreneurship I will use the term "creative entrepreneurship," while the term "entrepreneurship" without modifier will refer to the common ideas of Menger, Leibensten, and Alchian and Demsetz.

2. Small Businesses and Entrepreneurs

This book is about small businesses. To what extent are small businesspeople entrepreneurs? If we mean the concept as understood by Menger, Leibenstein, and Alchian and Demsetz, the answer seems to be that every small businessperson has to be an entrepreneur much of the time, and perhaps many other things as well. However, if we ask, to what extent are small businesspeople creative entrepreneurs, as Schumpeter understands the terms, it is much less clear. This has been the topic of an important recent study by Hurst and Pugsley (2011). They argue that small businesses are typically quite different from Schumpeter's creative entrepreneurs.

---

[2]This seems to be the view of Nobel Laureate Edmund Phelps (2006), though in other ways he has much in common with Schumpeter. See his *Mass Flourishing* (2013), Princeton University Press.

Their study focused on very small employers, that is, firms with 1–19 employees. They write (Hurst and Pugsley, 2011, p. 77) "In 2007 roughly 6 million firms had paid employees; the 90 percent of these firms that had fewer than 20 employees accounted for about 20 percent of aggregate paid employment and about 15 percent of sales receipts and payroll." They drew on a questionnaire study that asked businessmen and potential businessmen about their plans and objectives. They used (Hurst and Pugsley, 2011, p. 93) "data from the Panel Study of Entrepreneurial Dynamics II.... The PSED started with a nationally representative sample of 31,845 individuals. An initial screening survey in the fall of 2005 identified 1,214 "nascent entrepreneurs." To be considered a nascent entrepreneur, individuals had to meet the following four criteria. First, the individual had to currently consider himself or herself as involved in the firm creation process. Second, he or she had to have engaged in some business start-up activity in the past 12 months. Third, the individual had to expect to own all or part of the new firm being created. Finally, the initiative, at the time of the initial screening survey, could not have progressed to the point that it could have been considered an operating business. The goal was to sample individuals who were in the process of establishing a new business. "... They were asked detailed questions about their motivations for starting the business, the activities they were currently undertaking as part of the start-up process, the competitive environment in which the business would operate, and their expectations about the desired future size and activities of the business. Follow-up interviews occurred annually for 4 years, ..."

They write (Hurst and Pugsley, 2011, p 94) "... only 5 percent of the new firms (6 percent of those with positive revenue) applied for patents, trademarks, or copyrights during their first few years in existence. By the fifth year of operation, surviving firms appear similar to those in the [earlier survey], with roughly 18 percent having obtained a patent, trademark, or copyright." Further, In a separate set of questions, businesses are asked directly whether they have "developed any proprietary technology, processes, or procedures." This question results in a slightly broader measure of innovation than patent, trademark, and copyright applications in that it conceivably covers a more fluid set of activities related to innovation in production or in the firm's business model. Yet only 7 or 8 percent of new businesses (depending on the sample) reported that they had developed any proprietary business practices or technology during their first few years in business. Even conditional on survival 5 years later, 80 percent of firms still reported not having developed any proprietary technology, process, or procedure.

The [survey] asks one last broad question about the potential innovation taking place within the firm. This question asks about how the product or service produced by the business compares with the products and services of other producers in the firm's market: "Right now, are there many, few, or no other businesses offering the same products or services to your [intended] customers?" The answers to this question are informative in that they indicate whether the firm is providing a new product or service to existing customers or an existing product or service to potentially new customers. Across the three samples, between 36 and 43 percent of new business owners reported providing a service similar to that of many existing firms in the market to an existing customer base; these businesses, more often than not, provide a standardized service (such as plumbing) to existing local customers. Fewer than 20 percent of respondents reported that no other business was providing their expected product or service to their expected customer base.

The responses to this question varied substantially across business owners in different industries.... For example, owners who reported starting a business in the professional, health, construction, and real estate industries were between 7.5 and 9.5 percentage points more likely to report that they were starting their business in an area where many current providers already served their expected customer base. Owners in these same industries were nearly 10 percentage points less likely to report that they were providing a new product or service or were targeting an underserved customer base.

Some further results of this survey are also shown in Table 1.

In this survey, the first round took place in 2005 before any of the 1214 subjects had started a business, and a second round took

Table 1. Responses of "Nascent Entrepreneurs".

Ex Ante Expectations and Desires of Nascent Entrepreneurs about Future
Growth and Innovation, 2006 and 2010[a]

Indicator	First year of business (2006)		Fifth year of business (2010): positive revenue only[b]
	All	Positive revenue only	
Percent reporting that they want firm to be "as large as possible"	24.3	23.0	28.3
Expected no. of employees when firm is 5 years old			
25th-percentile response	1	0	0
Median response	4	3	3
75th-percentile response	10	8	6
90th-percentile response	29	24	25
Percent expecting to develop proprietary technology, processes, or procedures in future	14.6	9.2	12.2
Percent expecting to apply for patent,copyright, or trademark in future	26.0	17.9	24.9
Percent expecting R&D spending to be a major priority for the business	25.7	19.5	22.8

a. All data are weighted using the sample weights from the indicated survey year.
Sample sizes differ slightly from those in table 7 because not all respondents
provided responses to all the questions.
b. Responses are those given in the 2006 survey.
Source: Hurst and Pugsley (2011).

place a year later when 602 of them had in fact started businesses.
These were contacted again in 2010, and 162 still had some positive
revenue in the business they had started. Table 1 reports the answers
to some of the questions they were asked in 2006. The first column
reports the answers of the whole group, the second the answers of
those who had started a business with positive revenue in 2006, and
the third column shows the 2006 responses of those who were still in
business in 2010. For example, the first column tells us that half of

all respondents did not expect their business to grow to employ more than 4 employees, 90 percent of all respondents did not expect their business to grow to employ more than 29 employees, but just over 25 percent expected to apply for a patent, copyright or trademark. These proportions do not vary much in the survivor groups.

Hurst and Pugsley went on to investigate the motivations of those who founded businesses. Once again they relied on the same questionnaire survey. The "nascent entrepreneurs" were asked to give one or two most important reasons they had for starting a business. While some gave answers like "good money," "unlimited income potential," or "to leave the business to the children," many gave "nonpecuniary reasons." For clarity, Table 2 shows the responses that were regarded as expressing "nonpecuniary motives" with the number of respondents who chose each of them. Table 3 shows the proportions of respondents who chose answers in the major categories. Once again, the first two columns show responses for all who answered the questionnaire, the next two for those who started businesses, and the last two for those who continued in business 4 years later.

There were some correlations between the motives reported and the activities planned and reported by the "nascent entrepreneurs." Their analysis shows (p. 103) "that individuals who start their business because they think they have a good business idea or because they want to create a new product are much more likely to want to grow, to want to innovate, and to actually innovate. Conversely, those who start a business for nonpecuniary reasons are less likely to want to grow, to want to innovate, and to actually innovate. ... those reporting nonpecuniary motives were much more likely to enter an already crowded market than those with a new business idea or product. Likewise, they were 5.1 percentage points less likely to report that they had already developed some proprietary technology or processes as part of their business start-up and 9.4 percentage points less likely to report expecting to get a patent, trademark, or copyright in the future. ... those who reported starting their business because they had a new business idea or product were much more likely to want the business to have a higher number

Table 2. Nonpecuniary Reasons for Starting a Business.

Reasons Reported by Nascent Entrepreneurs for Starting a Business

Reason	No. of respondents giving indicated reason	
	First response	Second response[b]
Nonpecuniary reasons		
Be own boss; tired of working for others	80	75
Flexibility; more free time; set own hours	26	22
Stay home with children; work from home	33	12
Enjoy the work, have passion for it; hobby	122	96
Job security/financial independence	34	14
Try new career; charge career; do something new	24	10
Creative; do creative work; creative outlet	9	5
Better life	3	0
Lifelong ambition	24	10
Challenge	3	3
Personal growth	2	8
To do more fulfilling work	2	3
Other lifestyle references	20	7
Other work desirability references	20	7

Source: Hurst and Pugsley (2011).

of employees in 5 years, and to want to grow their business, than those who started for nonpecuniary reasons. For example, those who started because they had a good business idea were 8.3 percentage points less likely to report wanting to keep their business to a few key employees. ... there is little statistical difference in survival rates to 2010 between those business owners who reported nonpecuniary benefits as a primary motivation and those who reported a new business idea or product as the reason they started. If anything, in some samples and specifications, those who reported nonpecuniary benefits as a primary motivation had a higher probability of survival. Second, there is no statistical difference in actual firm size in 2010

Table 3. Categories of Motives for Starting a Business.

Distribution of Reasons Offered by Nascent Entrepreneurs for Starting a Business[a]

Percent

Reason for starting business	All		Positive revenue only, 2006		Positive revenue only, 2010	
	First response	Either response[b]	First response	Either response	First response	Either response
Nonpecuniary reasons	35.3	50.5	37.6	53.9	35.0	52.4
To generate income	19.5	34.1	21.4	36.6	17.6	32.4
Had good business idea or to create new product	32.2	40.6	28.3	34.9	33.8	37.5
Lack of other employment options	2.2	3.8	2.6	4.0	2.6	4.3
Other	10.8	15.7	10.2	15.5	11.0	14.7
No.of respondents	1,214		602		162	

[a]The table uses the same data set and sample constructions as in table 7. All data are weighted using the sample weights from the indicated survey year. Respondents were asked. "Why do [or did] you want start this new business?" and could give up to two responses in their own words. All data are weighted using the sample weights from the indicated survey year.
[b]Percentages sum to less 200 percent because the about one-quarter of respondents did not provides a second response and, those who did, some provided a response that was classified in the same category as the first. See appendix table A1 for a more detailed classification of responses.
Source: Hurst and Pugsley (2011).

across the different groups. The reason is that nearly all firms had only 1 or fewer employees even 4 years after the business started."

All in all, the small businessmen studied by Hurst and Pugsley do not much resemble Schumpeter's creative entrepreneurs. But perhaps the glass is half full. Even if no more than one-fifth to one-fourth of all new business founders expect to innovate in some way, when we consider the number of new businesses formed every year, a great deal of innovation could be going on. And even if only a small proportion grow beyond 25 employees, the few that do grow large can be very important. Nevertheless, we may say that most people who start businesses start small businesses, and they are not Schumpeter's creative entrepreneurs.

3. A Model of Entrepreneurship in the Mengerian Sense

As we have seen, most businesses are small, and will remain small. We have seen that the distribution of firm sizes is extremely skewed. Nevertheless, as Alchian and Demsetz observe, every firm will have a single ultimate supervisor, who does at least some of the work that Menger describes as entrepreneurial work. (There are some exceptions in principle — worker cooperatives in which the business is run by majority rule of the employees — and they have been pretty successful, but even those almost always elect a single top supervisor.) How can we *explain* these stylized facts? Important as they are in other ways, Schumpeter's ideas will not do the job. But there are models of the sizes of businesses in economics. Nobel Laureate Robert Lucas (1978) has provided one that has influenced several other, somewhat different models since. Lucas' model will serve us as an example of the approach that most economists would adopt today. The discussion that follows is suggested by Lucas', but is of course simplified.

Lucas' model treats labor, capital and management as distinct inputs, but the management input is lumpy: each firm has just one manager (at the top level, anyway). Thus, what Lucas calls management is what we are calling entrepreneurship, as distinct from creative entrepreneurship and also from lower-level management, and the word "entrepreneurship" will be used in place of "management" from this point on. Because of this fixed input of entrepreneurship, there are diminishing returns to the variable inputs, capital and labor. For present purposes, following Lucas' outline, we will ignore the capital input, assuming that each employee comes along with an efficient lump of capital input. (In Lucas' more complicated model, this is a condition for the equilibrium.) Nevertheless, the marginal productivity of labor will decrease due to the fixed input of entrepreneurship.

But this does *not* mean that each firm gets a unit of entrepreneurship. Lucas assumes that individuals differ in their ability to supply entrepreneurship. For any individual in the population, indexed as individual i, there is a quantity θ_i of entrepreneurship input that she is able to supply, with $0 < \theta_i < 1$. Lucas calls θ_i the individual's "talent for management," though he observes that the personal characteristic that makes the person an effective business proprietor could instead be a willingness to take risk. It could also be the ability to delegate and coordinate the efficient work of others.[3] Here the word "talent" means "whatever makes the individual effective as a business manager." In any case, for any individuals i and j in the population, we may and in general will have $\theta_i \neq \theta_j$.

Now, the more entrepreneurship the proprietor can supply, the more productive labor will be at any given labor input. To illustrate what this means, let N be the employment scale of a firm and compare three individuals i, j, and k, with $\theta_i > \theta_j > \theta_k$. In Figure 1 we see the marginal productivities of labor (in money terms) for companies controlled by i, j, and k, if they all become proprietors of firms. This is a "long-run" marginal productivity of labor. The horizontal line at W is the market wage. We recall from the principles of economics that the firm will maximize profits by hiring until the marginal productivity of labor is equal to the wage. Thus, individual

---

[3]The author of this book, who is quite good at writing books, would probably be a terrible entrepreneur because he lacks this ability in particular — and doesn't much like taking risks, either.

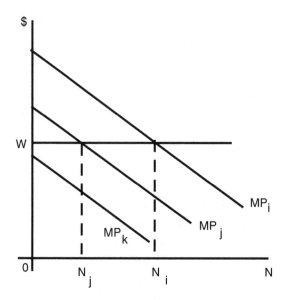

Figure 1. Employment by Individuals i, j, k.

i will form a firm of scale N_i, and individual j will form a firm of scale N_j. However, for individual k, the "profit maximizing" number of employees would be negative! Negative employees would be impossible, so the conclusion is that individual k would hire zero. Individual k will not become a proprietor of firm at all, but will instead go look for a job in somebody else's firm.

As in the example, there will be a critical value of θ, which we may call θ_0, such that an individual k with $\theta_k < \theta_0$ will not establish a firm. An individual j with $\theta_j > \theta_0$ will found a firm, and if $\theta_i > \theta_j$ then the firm headed by i will be bigger than the one headed by j. If we have a distribution function for θ, we can translate it into a distribution of the sizes of firms. For example, as Lucas observes (p. 529), if "talent" is distributed according to the Pareto distribution, the sizes of firms also will be distributed according to the Pareto distribution.

As Lucas' model shows, we can explain the skewed size distribution of firms and the fact that a majority of people do not head businesses, relying on the idea that entrepreneurship (which Lucas calls "management") is a lumpy input, that each firm gets the input of just one person, and that different individuals have different abilities to supply that lumpy input. Now, there may be more to it than that. As we have seen, Hurst and Pugsly offer evidence that "nonpecuniary motives" are important: Lucas' model, by contrast, has no place for nonpecuniary motives. Thus, Hurst and Pugsly have their own model, which is different in detail, and there are others. We will return to some of them in future chapters. Nevertheless, the broad outline of Lucas' model — the idea that the size distribution of firms can be predicted by the distribution of some characteristic of the human individuals who may or may not start businesses — is common also to the other theories.

4. Chapter Summary

Creative entrepreneurship is important, and so is small business, but they are different topics and do not overlap very much. If we understand entrepreneurship as Menger, Leibenstein, Alchian and Demsetz did, then small business and entrepreneurship are highly correlated if not quite the same thing. If we adopt some of the ideas from those authors, treating entrepreneurship as a lumpy input that cannot be purchased in markets, we can make some progress in explaining the size distribution of businesses and the choice of many people not to form businesses. Schumpeter's conception, history-making creative entrepreneurship, is exceptional in firms of any size. It is no less exceptional in small businesses than in big business. Important as it is, it is not central to the economics of small business.

Discussion Questions

(1) Compare and contrast two definitions of the word "entrepreneur."
(2) Is it possible to forecast creative developments in business? Why or why not? Explain your answer in the context of Schumpeter's concept of creative entrepreneurship.
(3) Criticize this statement: "The reason most entrepreneurs start up small businesses is to introduce innovations which, if successful, will cause the business to grow large."

(4) Criticize this statement: "Since small businesses are the source of most innovations, public policies should favor small businesses, for example by lower taxes than big businesses pay and by excluding small businesses from many regulations."

(5) Hurst and Pugsley focus on what I call VSE's–firms with 1–19 employees. Is it likely that their results would be different for a different size range of MSEs?

References

Alchian, A. A. (1950), "Uncertainty, Evolution, and Economic Theory," *The Journal of Political Economy* v. 58, no. 3 (June) pp. 211–221.

Alchian, Armen and H. Demsetz (1972), "Production, Information Costs, and Economic Organization," *American Economic Review* v. 62, no. 5 (Dec) pp. 777–795.

Hurst E. and Pugsley B., (2011), "What Do Small Businesses Do?" *Brookings Papers on Economic Activity*, Fall, pp. 73–142.

Leibenstein, H. (1969), "Organizational or Frictional Equilibria, X-Efficiency, and the Rate of Innovation," *Quarterly Journal of Economics* v. 83, no. 4, pp. 600–623.

Lucas, R. E. Jr. (1978), "On the Size Distribution of Business Firms," *The Bell Journal of Economics*, vol. 9, no. 2 , pp. 508–523.

Menger, K. (1871), *Principles of Economics*, tr. by James Dingwall and Bert F. Hoselitz (Auburn, Al: Institute for Humane Studies). All emphases are in the original.

Schumpeter, J. A. (1934), *The Theory of Economic Development*, tr. by Redvers Opie, (Cambridge, Mass: Harvard University Press).

Schumpeter, J. A. (1947), "The Creative Response in Economic History," *The Journal of Economic History* v. 7, no. 2, pp. 149–159.

Schumpeter, J. A. (1950), *Capitalism, Socialism and Democracy*, 3rd. edn. (New York: Harper).

Chapter 5

Small Business, Growth and Employment

Early research on small business was stimulated by a book by Birch (1979) that argued that small business expansion accounts for a disproportionate number of new jobs. Public policies in favor of small businesses are often justified on that basis. We will see, however, that the relation of small businesses and jobs is more complex than Birch supposed.

1. Firm Size and Jobs: Some Observations

It could be that small and medium enterprises (SMEs, or some other size category) not only open many new jobs but also eliminate many jobs through dismissals and discontinuations of the business. Then they would create many jobs on a gross basis, but many fewer, perhaps a negative number, on a net basis. Therefore, economists tend to emphasize net job creation, rather than gross job creation. Both approaches have advantages and disadvantages. Gross job creation simply ignores the fact that a sector with larger turnover (such as SMEs) will both create and destroy more jobs. Net job creation can distort the picture as the numbers do not add up in straightforward ways. Consider Table 1. Firm 3 accounts for about 2 percent of gross job creation and firm 2, 50 percent — both the same net job creation. Overall net job creation is 1; both firms 2 and 3 create 500 percent of net jobs. As this example suggests, job dynamics will require a careful approach.

Table 1. An Example of Gross and Net Job Creation

	Firm 1	Firm 2	Firm 3
Hires	200	205	**5**
Fires	209	200	0
Gross	200	205	5
Net	−9	5	5

Source: The author's numerical example.

Perhaps, though, the example may not make it clear just how problematic this issue is. As a further illustration, de Rugy (2005, p. 8) writes "Between 2000 and 2001, net total non-farm employment increased by about 41,000 jobs. Over this same period, automobile dealers experienced a net increase of about 9,000 jobs. If we characterized this data in the typical way, we would say that in 2001, automobile dealers created 21 percent of new jobs. But we would also find, for example, that legal services created 62 percent of new jobs and architectural and engineering services, 90 percent. Physician offices alone created 174 percent of new jobs! Furthermore, it seems that government created 800 percent of all new jobs — perhaps we should conclude that the government, not small businesses, is the true fountainhead of job creation.... Clearly, these statistics are meaningless — shares of a total cannot exceed 100 percent...."

2.   The Engine of Growth?

We recall that it was research by David Birch that put forward the idea that small business is the engine of employment growth in 1979. In a paper in the *Economic Perspectives* of the Federal Reserve Bank of Chicago, Erdevig (1986, pp. 15–16) summarized Birch' research as follows:

> Birch relied on a data file known as Dun's Market Identifier file (DMI) from Dun and Bradstreet. This data base contained information on 5.6 million business establishments at four different points in time-1969, 1972, 1974, and 1976. From this source he was

able to define and measure for each firm the processes by which change takes place, with emphasis on new formations, expansions, contractions, dissolutions, and movements. By aggregating firms at any given location, he was able to describe in considerable detail how economic change occurs in that location.

The results of this research were startling. Among the major findings were the following:

- Most of the variation in job growth among states and areas is due to differences in the rate of job generation (i.e., births and expansions of firms), not to differences in rates of job loss (i.e., deaths and contractions).
  . . .
- The components of job change are sensitive to the business cycle. For most states, births and expansions of firms were fewer and deaths and contractions were more numerous during an economic downturn than during a preceding upturn.
- Small firms-defined as those with 20 or fewer employees-generated 66 percent of all new jobs in the country during the early seventies. Middle-sized and large firms, on balance, provided few new jobs in relation to their size.

Birch concluded that "The job generating firm tends to be small. It tends to be dynamic (or unstable, depending on your viewpoint) — the kind of firm that banks feel very uncomfortable about. It tends to be young."

A World Bank report extends this with international data, finding (Ayyagari *et al.*, 2011, p. 3) "While small firms do not employ the largest number of people, they generate the most new jobs, across country income groups. When we look at median statistics across the sample of countries that had a net positive job creation across all firms in the country, small firms with less than 20 employees generate 45.34% of the jobs. Even in countries that had an aggregate net job loss, we find small firms with less than 20 employees to be significant job creators (36.54%)." However (p. 5), "We also find a negative association between GDP/capita and small firm contribution to employment — small firms contribute more to employment in low income countries than high income countries."

In a discussion paper for a German research institute in 2008, Neumark *et al.* (2008, pp. 2–3) summarize some of the criticisms of Birch:

> Davis *et al.* (1996) criticize the calculation used by Birch, which
> divides firms into size classes and then examines the variation
> in job growth across size classes. In particular, they argue that
> these calculations are subject to a "regression fallacy" that leads
> to upward bias in the estimated contribution of small firms to job
> growth.

Davis and his collaborators point out that (as summarized by
Neumark *et al.*, 2008)

> ...when businesses are classified by size for a given base year, two
> types of firms will 'accidentally' fall into a smaller size category:
> firms that are not small but have just experienced a transitory
> negative shock to their employment and appear to be small for
> the moment; and firms that are not small but are mistakenly
> classified as small due to random measurement errors. If such
> transitory shocks or random measurement errors are not highly
> serially correlated, both types of "small" firms will "grow" fast
> over the next year only because of regression to the mean. A reverse
> argument can be made for large firms. That is, some large firms
> are categorized as large only because of positive transitory shocks
> and random measurement errors. These firms tend to experience
> negative growth if the transitory shocks or the measurement errors
> are not strongly serially correlated, leading to a downward bias in
> the estimated growth rate of large firms.

The next section will consider this issue in more detail.

3.   The Regression Fallacy

The fallacy is that if companies tend to approach a "natural" size,
on the whole, the companies that grow will be the ones below the
natural size. They don't grow because they are small but because
they are recovering. Here is a numerical example to illustrate the
problem. For the example, there are three firms. In year zero, each
firm is at its "natural" scale. In year one, shocks shift firms 1 and 3
away from the "natural" scale. In later years, each firm makes up

Table 2. Employment Changes in Three Firms

Year	Firm 1	Firm 2	Firm 3	Average Firm Size
0	100	100	100	100
1	75	100	125	100
2	87.5	100	112.5	100
3	93.75	100	106.25	100
4	96.875	100	103.125	100
5	98.4375	100	101.5625	100
6	99.21875	100	100.78125	100
7	99.609375	100	100.390625	100
8	99.8046875	100	100.1953125	100
9	99.90234375	100	100.0976563	100
10	99.95117188	100	100.0488281	100

Source: The author's computation from his numerical example.

Table 3. Growth of Employment
and Firm Size in the Example

Scale in Year 1	Rate of Growth
75	0.166666667
100	0
125	−0.1

Source: The author's computation
from his numerical example.

half the difference of "natural" scale and the scale last year. This process is shown in Tables 2 and 3 and Figure 1.

Drawing on this point, de Rugy (2005, p. 11) argues that "while gross job creation rates are substantially higher for smaller firms, so are gross destruction rates. . . . larger employers offer greater job security. For both new jobs and the typical existing job, job durability increases with employer size. The empirical findings discredit the conventional wisdom about the job creation prowess of small business. Because of the regression fallacy and confusion between net and gross job creation, the general perception of small business job creation is distorted."

Well, then, which businesses do "create jobs?"

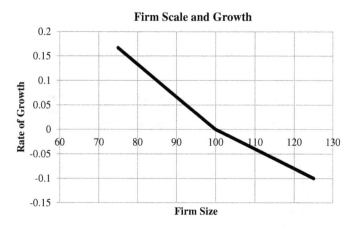

Figure 1. Fit of Growth Rate to Firm Size.
Source: The author's computation from his numerical example.

4.   Gazelles and High-Impact Companies

Companies that do grow rapidly and increase their employment have been called "Gazelles." This term seems to have originated with Birch, but in any case, as Tracy (2011, p. 17) writes "In an unlikely turn of events in 1994, Birch, a leading proponent of the small business job creation hypothesis, and Medoff, one of its earliest and most strident critics, collaborated" in a study to find common ground. This common ground was in the study of the Gazelles, or, as Tracy called them when he extended the studies in 2011, high-impact companies.

The first step in a study of high-impact companies is to identify them. What counts as "high impact?" Tracy (2011, p. 2) writes "this study examines employment and sales to classify enterprises as high-impact companies. The definition of these companies remains the same: high-impact companies are enterprises whose sales have at least doubled over a four-year period and which have an employment growth quantifier of two or more over the same period." He explains (p. 20) "The employment growth quantifier (EGQ) is the product of a firm's absolute and percent change in employment. The EGQ helps to mitigate the bias of computing change statistics solely on the basis of either absolute or percent terms."

This is a compromise, on the grounds that

— Absolute values favor bigger firms

- Consider a firm that employs 10,000, and increases its employment by 100. This is a 1 percent increase.

— Percent values favor smaller firms

- Consider a firm that employs 10 and adds 2. This is a 20 percent increase.

Figure 2 shows the minimum absolute increase in employment that will qualify the firm as a "high-impact" firm. Figure 3 shows the minimum percent increase in employment that will qualify the firm as a "high-impact" firm. Since the company must also double its sales, these limits probably affect relatively few companies — and only those that increase their productivity or price at high rates relative to their work force. By contrast, "gazelles" in previous studies were defined only by increasing sales, but must increase sales steadily at 20 percent per year or more. Table 4 gives some statistics on the distribution of high-impact firms by firm size.

Minimum Absolute Increase in Employment

Figure 2. Boundary Increase in Absolute Employment.
Source: The author's computation from the definitions.

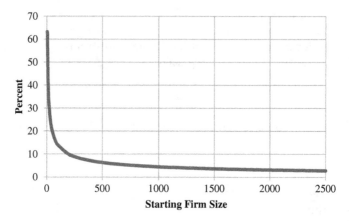

Figure 3. Boundary Percent Increase in Employment.
Source: The author's computation from the definitions.

Table 4. The Distribution of High-Impact Companies

Universe of High Impact Companies		
Number of Employees	Period	Number of HICs
1–19	1994–1998	327,397
	1998–2002	278,190
	2002–2006	359,289
	2004–2008	350,996
20–499	1994–1998	23,464
	1998–2002	20,601
	2002–2006	16,523
	2004–2008	16,424
500-plus	1994–1998	1,253
	1998–2002	1,182
	2002–2006	793
	2004–2008	842
Total	1994–1998	352,114
	1998–2002	299,973
	2002–2006	376,605
	2004–2008	368,262

Source: Tracy (2011, p. 24).

Tracy (2011) describes some of his findings as follows:

(p. 3) These companies are younger and more productive than all other firms and are found in relatively equal shares across all industries, even declining and stagnant ones.

(p. 27) In sum, there were on average about 350,000 high impact companies in the U.S. for a given period of analysis, representing on average about 6.3 percent of all companies in the economy. About 94 percent of high impact companies have 1–19 employees and about a half percent has 500 or more. ... On average, high impact companies created about 10.7 million jobs in the U.S. for each [four-year] period of analysis. Non-high impact companies shed, on average, about 4.1 million jobs in aggregate per period.

(p. 38) The average age of high impact companies in the 1–19 segment is about 17 years and is decreasing over time, though at a gradual pace. By contrast, the average age in the 500-plus segment is about double at 35 years, and is increasing at an appreciably higher rate. The average age of firms in the 20–499 segment is about halfway between the 1–19 and 500-plus segments at 25 years.

(p. 43) One might expect a disproportionate share of high impact companies to be found in high-tech industries where technological change has been rapid. But perhaps the most remarkable pattern is how evenly distributed high impact companies are across all sectors of the economy. No industry dominates consistently in its share of high impact companies, ...

(p. 46) A pattern that emerges irrespective of firm 'impact' status is enhanced productivity by firm size. For high impact firms and all other firms, revenue per employee increases with firm size. Perhaps not surprisingly, however, high impact companies are more productive than all other firms. Across all industries, employee-size segments and periods of analysis, high impact companies generate more revenue with the same share of human capital inputs.

(p. 50) ... the share of woman-owned high impact companies is virtually the same as that of woman-owned non-high impact firms.

Table 5. Overall Occurrence of High-Impact Firms

Size range	Number	% of high-impact firms
1–19	330,000	94%
20-499	20,000	5.5%
500+	1000	0.5%

Source: The author's compilation from Tracy (2011).

Thus the success rate for woman-owned firms achieving high impact status shows negligible difference from their counterparts owned by men. Women created high impact companies at virtually the same rate as men.

Table 5 shows the average distribution of high-impact firms over the entire period, in numbers and as a distribution, with the percentage of all high-impact firms in each size category. Recalling that firms with 1–19 employees are about 89 percent of all employer firms, it appears that small firms in this category are *somewhat* overrepresented among high-impact firms. But so are firms of the largest scale. It is only the residual, firms of medium size from 20 to 499 employees, which are underrepresented. (Compare Chapter 1, Table 2.)

It should be observed that this study does not correct for the regression fallacy and so may exaggerate the tendency of smaller firms to grow, and it uses the potentially confusing net job creation measure. Since the study included no start-up firms, it may have overestimated the age of high-impact firms. Nevertheless, it seems to have been successful in isolating the high-impact firms from the others, and thus the comparisons with other firms seem informative. Perhaps the most striking result is that high-impact firms are found at roughly the same *rate* in all size categories and industries, even including stagnant and declining industries.

Other studies, including studies in other countries, agree on the whole. Henrekson and Johansson (2009) surveyed 20 studies identified in a very broad literature search. Eleven countries were studied in one or more of the research projects reviewed. Henrekson and Johansson posed four hypotheses or propositions

(2009, p. 2):

> Proposition 1: In a population of firms, net employment growth is generated by a small number of high-growth firms, so-called Gazelles.
> Proposition 2: On average, Gazelles are younger than other firms.
> Proposition 3: On average, Gazelles are smaller than other firms.
> Proposition 4: Gazelles are overrepresented in high-tech industries.

Despite a wide range of definitions of terms, methods and other details, the research projects they studied supported some clear conclusions about those four propositions (pp. 15–16)

> Proposition 1 is supported. A few rapidly growing firms generate a disproportionately large share of all new net jobs compared to non high-growth firms. This is a clear-cut result. All studies find Gazelles to generate a large share, all or more than all net jobs (in the case where employment shrinks in non-Gazelle firms taken as a whole). It is noteworthy that this is particularly pronounced in recessions when Gazelles continue to grow.
> Proposition 2 is also supported. The results regarding age are unambiguous. All studies reporting on age find that Gazelles tend to be younger on average. Super Gazelles are also relatively young.
> As regards proposition 3 the results are ambiguous. Gazelles can be of all sizes, small firms are overrepresented but larger Gazelle firms are important job contributors in absolute terms, in particular a small sub-group of so-called Superstars or super Gazelles. These are both large firms and major net job creators. It appears that newness is a more important factor than small size.
> Proposition 4 is not supported. There is no evidence that Gazelles are overrepresented in high-tech industries. Gazelles exist in all industries. If anything, they appear to be overrepresented in services.

It seems that we have learned a great deal. The high-impact firms or gazelles that account for much real growth of employment and production are a small minority of all firms. They are found in all size categories, and all broad industrial sectors. On average, they are younger than other firms. Small firms may be somewhat overrepresented, though we must be somewhat cautious about that because of the regression fallacy. In any case, high-impact firms are only a small proportion of any category of firms, and in particular, most small businesses are not high-impact firms.

There also seems to be a clear policy conclusion. Public policies in support of small businesses are often justified on the basis of the supposition that this is a way of encouraging growth of production and employment. This sort of argument is invalid. This is not to say that there are no good reasons to support small business. Later chapters will suggest that there are. In particular, policies that increase the productivity of businesses of any size will have direct good consequences and, as we have seen, may well increase the number of high-impact firms. There may be particular opportunities to increase the productivity of small businesses. However, money spent on small business with the objective of increasing growth of employment will mostly be wasted, since it will go mostly to small businesses that are mature and stable or declining — most small businesses are in those categories, while gazelles are a small proportion of businesses in all size categories.

5.   A View from the JOLTS Data[1]

Since 2000, the United States Bureau of Labor Statistics has been collecting sample survey data on the number of job openings, hires, quits, layoffs and dismissals, and job turnover. This is called the JOLTS database (for Job Openings and Labor Turnover Survey). For the past few years, they have produced (tentative and experimental) data classified by establishment employment scale. For comparison with some of our other data, we will first look at job openings, in Figure 4 and Table 6. Sampled businesses are asked whether they have jobs open at the time of the survey, and how many. These data are weighted to give an estimate of the total number of jobs available by firms of that type. The data are in thousands of jobs.

But these data could be misleading. Firms in a particular size category may have more job openings because they have more

---

[1]Daniel Ripperger-Suhler, a doctoral student at Drexel University, assisted in the preparation of this section.

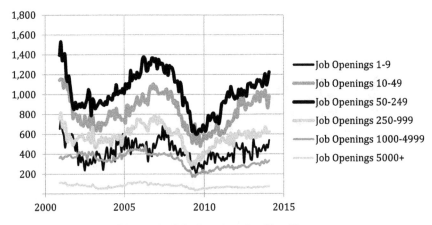

Figure 4. Job Openings by Size Class.
Source: Author's calculations from BLS data.

Table 6. Job Openings by Size Class, Average, Thousands per Month, 2001–2014

Averages					
Job Openings 1–9	Job Openings 10–49	Job Openings 50–249	Job Openings 250–999	Job Openings 1,000–4,999	Job Openings 5,000+
430	821	1,026	572	335	77

Source: Author's calculations from Bureau of Labor Statistics (BLS) data.

employees overall. Accordingly, we could look at the *rate* of job openings. The job openings rate is the job openings level divided by employment in the category plus the job openings level for the category (similar to the unemployment rate). This allows for the different overall size of employment in the different categories. Figure 5 and Table 7 show data for the rate of job openings for the same period, expressed as percentages.

In Figure 5 and Table 7, we see that (1) there is less difference than the levels suggest, (2) the smallest size category is the most volatile, (3) the second-biggest size category, 1,000–4,999, seems to lead in the overall rate of job openings and (4) all are similarly affected by macroeconomic fluctuations.

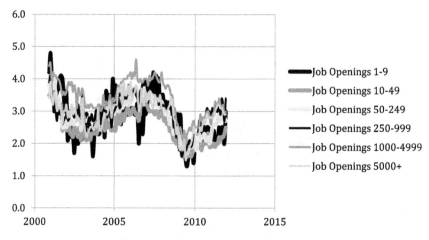

Figure 5. The Rate of Job Openings.
Source: Author's calculations from BLS data.

Table 7. The Rate of Job Openings, Average as Above

Averages					
Job Openings 1–9	Job Openings 10–49	Job Openings 50–249	Job Openings 250–999	Job Openings 1,000–4,999	Job Openings 5,000+
2.7572	2.5459	2.8629	3.0340	3.4057	2.9308

Source: Author's calculations from BLS data.

Another possible source of distortion is that some categories may have more job openings because they have lost or dismissed more employees, that is, because they have a higher rate of turnover. To what extent do these differences reflect differences in turnover? Bureau of Labor Statistics (BLS) measures labor turnover as the total number of separations, that is

- Quits
- Dismissals
- Layoffs
- "Other"

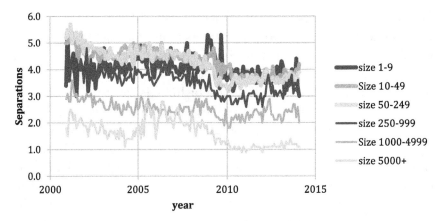

Figure 6. Labor Turnover by Firm Size Class.
Source: Author's calculations from BLS data.

The turnover "rate" is this sum divided by employment in the corresponding category. Turnover by firm size category in the BLS data is shown by Figure 6.

Job openings and labor turnover are important for labor market dynamics. If job openings are plentiful, then unemployment will tend to decline, while high labor turnover, all in all, will slow the growth of overall employment. In Figure 6, we see (1) once again, employment category 1–9 is the most volatile; (2) otherwise, bigger firms have less turnover, especially the largest categories; (3) there may be a downward trend, overall; (4) macroeconomic fluctuations have less apparent impact. (This may be because changes in quits tend to offset changes in layoffs and dismissals.) These observations seem to support the view that the smaller size categories, overall, have more labor turnover.

We have seen the employment dynamics is complex, with some signs of differences among size categories. The detailed JOLTS data enable us to look at employment dynamics more directly. Now, "hires" are probably a better indicator of job creation than "openings" are. First, an opening may remain open for several months, while the report of a hire will be reflected in the data only in the month at which the job is filled. Second, some openings may not be filled, but instead simply withdrawn. Third, sometimes an opening will be created to replace a person who has quit or been dismissed, so that the opening is not really a new job. As before, to make the data on hires comparable, we should use the "rate" of hires reported in the data. The rate of hires is the total number of hires divided by the number of people employed in the corresponding category of establishments. To obtain a "net rate," we may subtract the rate of separations (labor turnover) from the rate of hires. The rate of separations is the total number of separations divided by employment in the same category of firms, and so is expressed in comparable numbers. The difference between these rates is just the rate of growth of employment in the corresponding category of firms. Moreover, unlike other measures of net job creation, this one can be aggregated with numbers that "add up." For example, taking the six size categories in JOLTS,

$$
\frac{H - S}{N} = \frac{N_1}{N}\left(\frac{H_1 - S_1}{N_1}\right) + \frac{N_2}{N}\left(\frac{H_2 - S_2}{N_2}\right) + \frac{N_3}{N}\left(\frac{H_3 - S_3}{N_1}\right)
$$
$$
+ \frac{N_4}{N}\left(\frac{H_4 - S_4}{N_4}\right) + \frac{N_5}{N}\left(\frac{H_5 - S_5}{N_5}\right) + \frac{N_6}{N}\left(\frac{H_6 - S_6}{N_6}\right)
$$

$$(1)$$

Here, H is total hires for all categories, S is total separations, N is total employment, H_1 is hires in the smallest category, H_2 is hires in the second smallest category and so on; and S_1 is separations in the smallest category and N_1 is total employment in the smallest category and $2, 3, 4, 5, 6$, indicate the same variables for the larger categories. In Eq. (1),

$$
\frac{H_i - S_i}{N_i}, \quad i = 1, \ldots, 6 \tag{2}
$$

is the rate of growth of employment in size category i. Thus, the "weighted sum" in Eq. (1) is the weighted sum of the rates of growth of employment in the different size categories of firms. This weighted sum is also the overall rate of growth of employment in the economy as a whole, in part because the weights add up to one. We might call the weighted growth rate

$$\left(\frac{N_i}{N}\right)\left(\frac{H_i - S_i}{N_i}\right) \tag{3}$$

the "employment growth contribution" of size category i (EGC$_i$) since it allows both for the rate of growth of employment in sector i and for the number of employees in that category relative to the whole. We should keep the regression fallacy in mind —**** a firm may be shown in a smaller size category because it is below its stable scale of employment, and because such a firm would tend to grow fast, that will exaggerate the employment growth contributions of the smaller size categories somewhat. Nevertheless, taking the categories as wholes, this should not be a very large influence.

Accordingly, we may look at the EGC data for the different employment size categories. As in Figures 4–6, we find that the month-to-month data display a great deal of fluctuation, probably much of it random. Accordingly, Figure 7 shows overlapping one-year averages of the EGC$_i$ for the six firm size categories. The smallest size categories are shown by the thicker curves, with 0–9 black, 10–49 medium gray and 50–249 light gray, while the bigger size categories are shown by the thinner curves, with 250–1000 black, 1000–5000 medium gray and 5000+ dark gray. The dashed black line is the total rate of employment growth in the U.S. economy as a while. These are weighted growth rates *per month*, so that rates in the fractions of one percent are not surprising.

One thing that is suggested by the figure is that the medium-size establishment category, employment scale 50–249, shown by the thick gray curve, shows a relatively consistent large contribution to employment growth. This is reinforced by the averages in Table 8. In the period 2001–2006, in fact, the average growth contribution of this medium-size enterprise category is more than the total, being partly offset by negative average rates in other sectors, including the small-employer category with 20–49 employees. In the period 2009–2017, a period of stronger consistent overall employment growth, there are no negative averages, but the contribution of the medium-size enterprises is about one-half of the total. In 2007–2008, the period

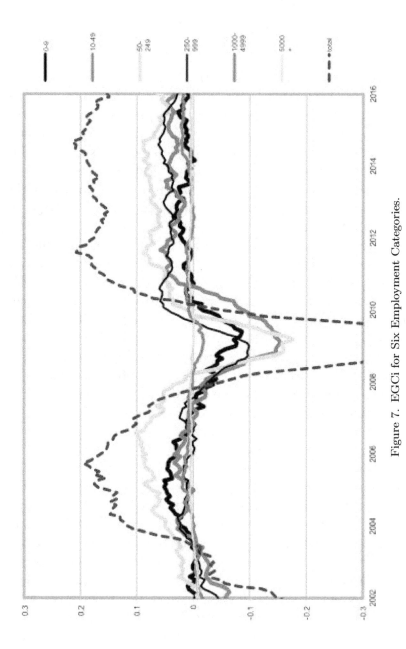

Figure 7. EGCi for Six Employment Categories.

Table 8. Average Employment Growth Contributions

Averages 2001–2006		Averages 2009–2017		Averages 2007–2008	
"1-9-"	0.0123	"1–9"	0.0038	"1–9"	−0.0249
"10–49"	−0.0105	"10.49"	0.0075	"10-49"	−0.0500
"50–249"	0.0507	"50–249"	0.0450	"50–249"	−0.0094
"250–999"	−0.0096	"250–999"	0.0309	"250–999"	−0.0223
"1000–4999"	−0.0026	"1000–4999"	0.0070	"1000–4999"	0.0031
"5000+"	0.0005	"5000+"	0.0035	5000+	0.0033
total	0.0407	total	0.0978	total	−0.1003

of the "Great Recession," the medium-size enterprise category drops with overall employment. In this period, it is the stability of the largest enterprise size categories that stands out. Even in that period, the medium size enterprise category declines less than the other four smaller size categories.

Does this conflict with the finding on Gazelles and high-impact firms? It is true that, in those studies, medium-size firms are slightly underrepresented among the high-impact firms. However, employment growth is represented in quite different ways in the two studies. The categories of firm size used in the study of high-impact firms are broader — their midsize enterprises category includes not only the 50–249 category in the JOLTS data but much of two other categories. More importantly, the measure based on the JOLTS data reflects employment growth in the category as a whole. It may be that many firms in the 50–249 employee category do not grow rapidly enough to be classed as high-impact firms but nevertheless grow consistently and persistently enough to make an important contribution to employment growth. If there are a lot of them, so that they begin with a large share of employment, this would result in a large EGC_i. Conversely, it is striking that the biggest size categories, despite employing more than half of the work force, had contributions much smaller in most years. The high-impact firms are relatively few in all size categories, but stand out as leaders in their size categories and industrial sectors. Seen in that perspective, it is not surprising to find leaders in all fields. Conversely, the field, that is the industry and size category, may have the most important role in determining the characteristics of the leaders. What the EGC_i data show us is not the performance of the leaders but the performance of the category as a whole, reflecting not only rapid growth but also consistent growth and large numbers of firms. Nor does it seem to reverse the tentative conclusion on public policy. Firms that grow consistently and persistently, at whatever size, are already established as successful firms. To increase employment growth, the objective presumably would be to shift more firms, regardless of size category, to that pattern. That requires that the policy "pick the winners" in advance, and that remains an unsolved problem.

Both the study on high-impact companies and the JOLTS data pertain to the United States and to quite limited periods, so we should in any case be cautious about generalizing them to other times and places.

6.   Conclusion

The firms that are most active in generating growth of production and employment, high-impact firms, include some firms throughout the whole population of firms, and thus, unavoidably, many of them are small businesses. High-impact firms are distributed across many industrial sectors. Small firms are more volatile, both hiring and firing more than bigger firms. That is, they have greater turnover. It may be that small businesses are overrepresented among high-impact firms. But high-impact firms are a small proportion of firms in every size category: most small businesses are not high-impact firms (and most big businesses are not high-impact firms, either.) In exploring this, we have to be careful to avoid several difficulties: net job creation is a very problematic concept, though it is the approach usually used in studies of high-impact firms; the regression fallacy also creates bias in favor of small firm growth. For these reasons, studies of high-impact firms may exaggerate the importance of small firms. A public policy designed to promote the growth of production and employment cannot be focused strictly on small businesses.

The data from JOLTS on job openings, hiring and labor turnover can give us a different perspective on small business and job creation. We can define a measure of the contribution of a sector to employment growth in such a way that the parts do add up to the whole. Nevertheless it is possible for a part to be more than the whole, if other parts are negative as they sometimes will be. This is observed, on average, in USA in the early 21st century. In USA, for the 21st century so far, we do observe some patterns. In periods of steady growth, it seems to be medium-scale enterprises, but not small employers, that lead in employment growth. But the pattern is quite different in the period of recession, when the smaller categories decline the most and the largest enterprises continue their slow employment growth. It can only remain an open question whether these patterns are more general. It is also unclear whether they have any implications for public policy. We have learned a great deal, but still have much to learn.

Discussion Questions

1. Explain the regression fallacy and its implications for small business.
2. "Job creation" by a segment of business may be discussed in terms either of gross or net job creation. Discuss the advantages and disadvantages of each.
3. Define and discuss "high-impact companies."
4. Define EGC_i and describe how JOLTS data can be used to measure the EGC_i for each firm size category i.
5. Criticize the following statement: "Since a higher proportion of SMEs are HICs than in other size categories, government policy to support SMEs would increase economic growth."
6. Criticize the following statement: "Since most small businesses do not create many jobs, government policies in support of small business should be eliminated."

References

Ayyagari, M., Demirguc-Kunt, A. and Maksimovic, V. (2011), "Small vs. Young Firms across the World: Contribution to Employment, Job Creation, and Growth," Policy Research Working Paper 5631, The World Bank, Development Research Group, Finance and Private Sector Development Team, April.

Birch, D. (1979), *The Job Generation Process* (Cambridge, MA: Center for the Study of Neighborhood and Regional Change, Massachusetts Institute of Technology).

Davis, S. J., Haltiwanger, J. C. and Schuh, S. (1996), *Job Creation and Destruction* (Cambridge, MA: The MIT Press).

de Rugy, V. (2005), "Are Small Businesses The Engine of Growth?" *American Enterprise Institute,* AEI Working Paper #123, December 8.

Erdevig, E. H. (1986), "Small Business, Big Job Growth," *Economic Perspectives* v. Nov–Dec, pp. 15–24.

Henrekson, M. and Johansson, D. (2009), "Gazelles as Job Creators – A Survey and Interpretation of the Evidence," IFN Working Paper No. 733, Research Institute of Industrial Economics, Stockholm, Sweden.

Neumark, D., Wall, B. and Zhang, J. (2008), "Do Small Businesses Create More Jobs? New Evidence for the United States from the National Establishment Time Series," Discussion Paper No. 3888, December, Forschungsinstitut zur Zukunft der Arbeit (Institute for the Study of Labor), Bonn, Germany.

Tracy, S. L., Jr. (2011), *Accelerating Job Creation in America: The Promise of High-Impact Companies* (Washington, DC: Corporate Research Board, LLC) for the Small Business Administration Office of Advocacy, under contract number SBAHQ-10-M-0144.

Chapter 6

Small Business as Family Business

Not all small businesses are family businesses, and conversely. However, there is an overlap, and family ownership and management are especially common in the smallest size range. Accordingly, this chapter will review some research on family businesses, which, in practice, are mostly small and medium enterprises (SMEs). In particular, if a small business relies a great deal on family labor, in both managerial and other activities, will this be an advantage or a disadvantage relative to other businesses that do not rely on family labor? A case can be made for both possibilities. We will not be concerned with the succession from one family manager to another in this chapter; however, that will be discussed in a later chapter.

1. Family and Non-Family Businesses and Their Performance

Like many concepts in the economics of small business, the "family firm" is a category that may have blurry boundaries. Barbera and Moores (2011) observe that "family firms have been defined as those which are either owned, controlled, and/or managed by a family unit. Such a definition allows for a wide range of 'family firms', because the extent of family ownership, control and management can differ among individual firms, ..." So "Family firm" can mean at least two things: (1) mostly owned by members of a family and (2) managed by one or more family members. Some family-owned businesses are nevertheless professionally managed. In this chapter, we are mostly concerned with firms that are family-owned and -managed, both (1) and (2).

It may be that family businesses differ from non-family businesses in ways that lead to different performance. A number of points are put forward as to the reasons.

(1) Family members benefit directly from increases in the productivity of the firm, and so may be more committed than non-family members. Family managers may be more effective and family-member employees may work harder, increasing labor productivity. This is sometimes described as "lower agency cost." In the economics of principles and agents, the principle (the owner of the enterprise) may have to take costly precautions to assure that the manager (who is an agent of the owner of the enterprise) makes a real effort to maximize the owner's profits. When the manager is the owner — or a member of the owner's family — this cost disappears or is reduced. This is true of other employees as well.

(2) On the other hand, family managers may lack professional training that a non-family manager might have.

(3) Family businesses may be more risk averse, since losses could deprive future generations of the family of its wealth. They may avoid debt or leverage for the same reason.

(4) Family managers may, however, have a more long-term perspective, and for the same reason. Future generations can benefit from decisions made today.

(5) Family managers, motivated by "nonpecuniary preferences," may divert business resources for their own consumption.

(6) Similarly, motivated by lifestyle preferences rather than money, they may not try to maximize profits but base their decisions on other, more personal reasons.

Here again, the "performance" of the firm might be measured in different ways, with or without regard for the "nonpecuniary motives" of the family. Sharma (2004, p. 6) notes "Recognition of the intertwinement of family and business in family firms has led to a definition of high-performing family firms that takes into consideration performance on both family and business dimensions. It is generally accepted that these firms aim to achieve a combination of financial and nonfinancial goals." In this chapter, we will focus on a measure that is neutral with respect to "nonpecuniary motives" but corresponds with the way that economic impacts are measured in gross national product accounting: productivity. Syverson (2011, pp. 329–330) explains

> Simply put, productivity is efficiency in production: how much output is obtained from a given set of inputs. As such, it is typically expressed as an output–input ratio. Single-factor productivity measures reflect units of output produced per unit of a particular input. Labor productivity is the most common measure of this type, though occasionally capital or even materials productivity measures are used. Of course, single factor productivity levels are affected by the intensity of use of the excluded inputs. Two producers may have quite different labor productivity levels even though they have the same production technology if one happens to use capital much more intensively, say because they face different factor prices. Because of this, researchers often use a productivity concept that is invariant to the intensity of use of observable factor inputs. This measure is called total factor productivity (TFP) (it is also sometimes called multifactor productivity).
>
> Conceptually, TFP differences reflect shifts in...a production function: variation in output produced from a fixed set of inputs.

The question for this chapter then is: does family ownership and/or management affect the total factor productivity of the firm, and if so, how, in what direction, and how much? For that purpose, we will need some background on production functions.

2. Some Useful Theory: The Cobb–Douglas Production Function

We begin from the assumptions that the output that a firm can produce is limited by the inputs it can command and the technology with which they can be used. Given technology, generally more labor will result in more output, and more capital similarly will result in more output, both subject to diminishing returns. Representing Q as output, L as labor input, and K as capital input, the production function would be $Q = f(L, K)$. This function is a mathematical rule that tells us how output increases or decreases when one or more of the inputs increases or decreases. The production function gives us the *largest* output that can be produced with the given inputs, in the given circumstances. We will digress a little to introduce some of the mathematics used in production functions. This will probably seem pretty old hat to readers who have studied mathematics, and perhaps to those who have studied macroeconomics, but they may consider it a brief refresher.

It is not likely that the production function can be closely approximated by a linear function. Most approaches to the production function rely on two kinds of nonlinear functions. Fortunately, they work together well. They are:

- The logarithmic function and
- The exponential function.

The exponential function is easier to understand. Suppose a variable grows at a constant rate, in the sense that its growth in any year is a constant proportion of the level it starts the year at. For human population, for example — if the population is P, suppose there are nP born every year and mP die every year. Then, the net increase in the population is $nP - mP = (n - m)P$. Every year, the population grows by proportion $(n - m)$ of its starting point. Thus population, over time, follows an exponential function of increase or decrease. The exponential function can be written as $y = \mu e^x$ where e is a constant with a value of approximately 2.71828 and μ is any constant. In this example, μ would be P and x would be $n - m$ times the number of years since the population was measured as P. We see that the independent variable x is in the exponent. That's why this function is called "exponential."

The logarithm of x is usually written $\ln(x)$. The logarithm function is the inverse of the exponential function in the sense that, for any x, $\ln(e^x) = x$; $e^{\ln(x)} = x$. This is usually called the "natural" logarithm. The constant e is the base of the natural logarithm system. Logarithms to base 2 and 10 are also used for specialized purposes.

Logarithms, exponents, and multiplication are all connected by rules that are put to use in the Cobb–Douglas production function. Among the rules are:

$$\ln(x \times y) = \ln(x) + \ln(y) \tag{1}$$

$$\ln(x/y) = \ln(x) - \ln(y) \tag{2}$$

$$\ln(x^z) = z\ln(x) \tag{3}$$

The Cobb–Douglas production function was developed by Professor Cobb and Professor (later Senator) Douglas to represent the determination of output by the quantities of capital and labor together, allowing for the assumption of diminishing marginal returns to a variable factor of production. It is most often written as

$$Q = AL^\alpha K^\beta \tag{4}$$

where Q represents the quantity of output, L the quantity of labor used, K the quantity of capital, and α and β are constants, each between zero and one; it is often assumed that $\alpha + \beta = 1$. Then, A is a constant that corresponds to overall or "total factor" productivity.

Without going into the mathematical details, if labor is paid its marginal product, then the wage is $w = \alpha(Q/L)$, so that the share of wages in product is $wL/Q = \alpha$. Taking logarithms on both sides of Eq. (4), we have the equivalent expression:

$$\ln Q = A + \alpha \mathrm{Ln} L + \beta \mathrm{Ln} K \tag{5}$$

(It is conventional to leave off the parentheses, writing ln Q rather than $\ln(Q)$.) This is a linear equation, and thus much easier to use. In particular, we may add a random error term:

$$\ln Q = A + \alpha \mathrm{Ln} L + \beta \mathrm{Ln} K + \varepsilon \tag{6}$$

and this equation can be estimated by very simple, well-known methods of regression analysis — provided we have the data. That was the idea that got Dr. Douglas' attention when Dr. Cobb, a mathematician, suggested it to him. In this, we assume:

(1) That labor and capital each are homogenous quantities,
(2) That land and raw materials are not important, so that in practice, Q is "value added," that is, revenue minus the cost of raw and semi-finished materials,
(3) Everyone uses the same technology.

The constants α and β are known as "factor elasticities." They can be estimated by a linear regression of $\ln Q$ on $\ln N$ and $\ln K$ — "assuming" that α and β both are constants for all the production units observed. If all firms or units observed have the same technology available, and they all use it similarly, then this should be so.

There are other ways of writing a production function. Most are more complex, especially when they are applied to statistical estimation. This *relative* simplicity is a major reason why the Cobb–Douglas approach is so widely used. But "everything should be as simple as possible, but not simpler."[1] It may be that the Cobb–Douglas approach is too simple. As things stand, nevertheless, the Cobb–Douglas function is the state of the art in the study of small business. And we will see that it can be adapted to a somewhat more complex reality.

3. Putting the Cobb–Douglas Production Function to Work

The question before us is whether family and non-family businesses have different production functions. That could be so if they do not have the same technology — perhaps because some are better educated or have more experience — or they do not use the technology in the same way, because they have different "non-pecuniary motives." In particular, we might pose the hypothesis that the total factor productivity, A, might be different in family than in non-family enterprises. Suppose we have observations for a sample

---

[1]This saying is often attributed to Albert Einstein, but seems to be a paraphrase of Einstein's expression by Roger Sessions in the *New York Times* (8 January 1950).

that includes both family and non-family firms, then we make use of a "dummy variable," D, which equals one if the observation is a family firm and zero if it is not. Then we estimate an equation written as:

$$\ln Q = A + \gamma D + \alpha \mathrm{Ln}L + \beta \mathrm{Ln}K + \varepsilon \qquad (7)$$

where γ is the estimated coefficient of the dummy variable just as α and β are the estimated coefficients of the logarithmic labor and capital variables. For family firms, D takes the value of one so that we can interpret $A + \gamma(1) = A + \gamma$ as the total factor productivity of a family firm. For non-family firms, D takes the value of 0 so that we can interpret $A + \gamma(0) = A$ as the total factor productivity of a non-family firm. If γ is positive, then, family firms have greater productivity than non-family firms, and if γ is negative, family firms have less productivity than non-family firms. All this is subject to the usual qualifications about statistical significance.

But it has been argued that this is still too simple. Barbera and Moores (2011, p. 2) observe "Despite the importance of unique resources and capabilities on firm productivity, one of the more curious aspects of previous investigations is that those utilising a Cobb–Douglas framework have assumed fixed factor elasticities in the production process for both family and non-family firms. In other words, it is assumed that labour and capital output contributions for both types of firm are homogeneous." Notice that they use the term "output contribution" as a synonym for the factor elasticities, i.e., α and β. They also use a Cobb–Douglas approach with a dummy variable that is one if the observation is a family firm and zero if it is not. However, it enters the equation three times, and in different ways. In place of Eq. (7), we have:

$$\mathrm{Ln}\, Q = A + \gamma D + \alpha \mathrm{Ln}L + \zeta_1 D^* \mathrm{Ln}L$$
$$+ \beta \mathrm{Ln}K + \zeta_2 D^* \mathrm{Ln}K + \varepsilon \qquad (8)$$

The product variables $D^*\mathrm{Ln}L$ and $D^*\mathrm{Ln}K$ are called "interactive dummy variables." Then ζ_1 and ζ_2 are their estimated coefficients. Barbera and Moores (2011) use a slightly different terminology.

Notice that $\alpha \mathrm{Ln} L + \zeta_1 D^* \mathrm{Ln} L = (\alpha + \xi_1 D)^* \mathrm{Ln} L$. Thus, the sum $\alpha + \zeta_1 D$ is the estimated coefficient for $\ln N$, estimated in such a way that it can be different for family firms and for non-family firms. Similarly, the sum $\beta + \zeta_2 D$ is the estimated coefficient for $\ln K$, with differences for family and non-family firms. Barbera and Moores (2011, p. 7) write $\alpha_{i,j} = \alpha + \zeta_1 D$, where i denotes the firm observed in the study and $j = 1$ if it is a family firm (so that $D = 1$) and $j = 0$ if it is not, so that $D = 0$ and thus $\alpha_{i,2} = \alpha$ Similarly they write $\beta_{i,j} = \beta + \zeta_2 D$ with the parallel interpretation, and they write $A_{i,j} = A + \gamma D$. Thus, they are able to estimate the difference for a family firm with respect to total factor productivity, that is γ, and the difference with respect to the output elasticity of labor, ζ_1, and with respect to the output elasticity of capital, ζ_2. Notice that Eq. (7) is a special case of Eq. (8): if we begin with Eq. (8) and assume $\zeta_1 = \zeta_2 = 0$, we have Eq. (7). Thus, if Eq. (7) is the correct specification, we may estimate Eq. (8) and we expect to find that the estimates of ζ_1 and ζ_2 are both approximately zero. If we do not find that they are approximately zero, then Eq. (7) is shown to be a mistake.

4.   Taking It to the Data

This is a clear, if not simple, approach to answering the question whether family firms have different production possibilities than non-family firms — if we can find the data to do the statistical analysis. Unfortunately appropriate data are hard to find, and that is one reason why there have been relatively few studies on this question. Several studies have relied on data on companies that are listed on stock exchanges or publically traded or both. (See Barbera and Moores 2011, p. 4 for a list of some earlier studies with these details) However, while some small businesses may be primarily family owned and nonetheless listed or publically traded, these data are not very representative of small family businesses in general.

As we have seen, the distinction between family and non-family firms is not always quite clear. The only real way to solve this problem is to ask them. Wall (1988), for example, studies a set of small enterprises in Western New York, using a data base developed at

Canisius College in Buffalo, New York, for the purpose. He writes (p. 25) "A survey on family business was distributed to the entire database.... Our intention was to permit companies to classify themselves as family or non-family firms using Question One: 'Do you consider yourself a family business?"' Barth *et al.* (2005, p. 111) write "Our information on ownership (whether the firm is family-owned or not) is based on response to the following question: 'Are at least 33% of the shares in the firm, owned by one person or by one family?' If the respondent answers 'yes,' the firm is classified as family-owned. Owner-management is measured by response to the following question: 'Does the manager come from the owner family?"' Barbera and Moores (2011) have access to a more complex questionnaire study. They report (p. 10) that it asked:

(1) Do you consider the business to be a family business? Yes/No.
(2) If yes, why do you consider this a family business? Family members are:
  (i) Working directors or proprietors. Yes/No.
  (ii) Employed in the business. Yes/No.
  (iii) Not working, but contribute to decisions. Yes/No.
  (iv) Business acquired from parents. Yes/No.
  (v) Close working relationship between management and staff. Yes/No.
  (vi) Other. Yes/No.

Barbera and Moores (2011) rely mainly on question (1), arguing that, after all, it is the attitude of the family more than anything else that would cause it to operate differently than a non-family business.

Further, data on capital inputs are often harder to find than those for labor inputs. Wall (1988, p. 27) noting "the limitations of the data available, especially the lack of direct data on physical capital for privately held firms," uses the age of the firm instead of a measure of capital. Some other studies used data sets with some financial information and they used the sum of equity and liabilities as the measure of capital (Barbera and Moores, 2011, p. 11, Barth *et al.*, 2005, p. 111). Barbera and Moores (2011) use a database of over

3,000 Australian firms with 200 or fewer employees, which includes observations on equity and liabilities among other measures.

Finally, there is an issue for any regression study: correlation is not causation. If we observe, for example, that family businesses are less productive than other small businesses, it may be because family businesses choose lines of business that are less productive, though they may have other advantages from a family point of view, such as industries in which increasing returns to scale are less important. There are two steps that can be taken to limit this problem. One is to allow, in the estimation, for differences from one industry to another. All of the studies discussed in the next section do this to some extent. The other is to use a statistical technique that treats some variables as "endogenous," that is, as being partly determined by the dependent variable. If family businesses tend to choose less productive fields, then the dummy variable for family business is "endogenous," that is, partly determined by productivity, the dependent variable. Without going into detail, a method that is often used to allow for an endogenous variable is called two-stage least squares. Barbera and Moores (2011, p. 15) double-check their simpler estimates by doing an estimate using two-stage least squares as well.

5. Results

In 2011, Barbera and Moores (2011, p. 5) write "the literature to date has largely assumed that capital output contributions [that is, factor elasticities] between family and non-family firms are the same" and (p. 6) "... are there any differences in total factor productivity for family firms? Previous studies have suggested that there are." In particular, Wall (1988, p. 29) writes "family firms in Western New York produce 18 percent less in sales than their privately held, small non-family counterparts." That is, the estimate for γ in Eq. (7) is -0.18, with a t-ratio of -2.14. The t-ratio tells us that: IF the actual value of γ is zero THEN the probability of an estimate of -0.18 is less than 5 percent, and this is interpreted as saying that the estimate is significantly less than zero.

Barth *et al.* (2005, pp. 113–114) write "The results in Model 1 show that on an average, family-owned firms are less productive than non-family-owned firms. The difference is estimated to be −0.102 or approximately 10%. Model 2 controls for the importance of owner-management. Family-owned firms with a manager from the owner family are less productive than non-family-owned firms. These results suggest that difference in management regime is the driving force behind the productivity gap of Model 1." They check this result by estimating models that include capital input and a dummy variable for firms that are listed on the stock exchange. "The results indicate that firms with family management are about 14% less productive than nonfamily-owned firms." However, the data set used by Barth *et al.* (2005, p. 111) includes only firms with 10 or more employees, and so excludes the smallest category of small businesses.

As Barbera and Moores (2011) note, these studies use Eq. (7), which may be a specification error, and specification errors can result in bias. Accordingly, they estimate both Eqs. (7) and (8). When they estimate Eq. (7) (p. 10), their results are similar to those of Wall (1988) and Barth *et al.* (2005): estimates of γ are negative and between −0.1 and −0.2, and are statistically significant at the 1% level: that is, if the true value of γ is zero, the probability of obtaining their estimates is less than 1 percent. That is, of course, assuming that Eq. (7) is the correct specification. When they estimate Eq. (8), allowing for differences in the factor elasticities, however, the results are different. Estimates of γ are always very close to zero. Barth *et al.* (2005, p. 11) write "Also apparent . . . is the positive and consistent interaction between family firms and labour employed in the production process. Depending on the time period and estimation technique, we find differences in the output contribution [factor elasticity] of family firm labour . . . are significant in that it is greater than the output contribution of non-family firm labour; this difference ranges from as little as 6% to as large as 15%. This estimate can be interpreted as for all labour employed, . . ." On the other hand (Barth *et al.*, 2005, p. 10), "family capital contributes less to output than non-family-firm capital by approximately 2–8%, depending on time period and estimation technique." That is, family firms use the total capital of the firm somewhat less efficiently than non-family firms. Looking at Table 10 in Barth *et al.* (2005, p. 14) where the authors check for differences by firm size, we find that this result is almost completely limited to firms with 10 or fewer employees. (They are by far most of the firms observed, because of the skewness of the distribution of firm size.) Thus, we had best say that very small enterprise (VSE) family firms make better use of labor and less effective use of capital — this may not be applicable to small employers with more than 10 employees and medium-size enterprises (MSEs). When Barbera and Moores (2011) check their estimates by using the two-stage least-squares method, they find that it does not make very much difference, having already allowed for differences in productivity among different industries.

Using the overall estimate by Barbera and Moores (2011), we could write the estimate for the production function of a small Australian family firm as

$$Q = 1.32 L^{0.867} K^{0.176} \tag{9}$$

while for a small non-family firm it is

$$Q = 1.27 L^{0.802} K^{0.24}. \tag{10}$$

Barbera and Moores (2011), then, draw quite different conclusions than do Wall (1988) and Barth *et al.* (2005). What are we to make of that? There is no doubt that Barbera and Moores (2011) have used a better method, so that their results are more reliable. There is good reason to think that, if Barth *et al.* (2005) were to re-estimate using Eq. (8), they would get quite different results — though we cannot know for sure unless the experiment is done. The data available to Wall would not allow this, since he has no data for firm capital. On the whole, our best evidence suggests that differences along the lines of Eqs. (9) and (10) probably apply to small firms in other industrialized countries and for other periods of time.

6. Summary

We can begin the summary with a phrase often seen in economics research: we need more research on this question, and especially more and better data. Nevertheless, the research we have supports definite conclusions. We have some reasons to think that family firms, especially in the VSE category, may make different use of inputs than non-family firms. The Cobb–Douglas production function approach provides a way to test that, if we have the data. We do now have some sources of data on firms that we can put to work in statistical studies on this issue. Earlier research suggests family firms may make less effective use of resources. But this earlier research is based on the simplifying assumption that the factor elasticities of capital and labor are the same in family and non-family firms. When we allow for differences in the factor elasticities, the case appears more complex. At least in very small enterprises:

- There seem to be little or no differences in overall efficiency.
- Labor seems more effectively used.
- Capital less so.

Discussion Questions

(1) How might we distinguish between family firms and non-family firms? Could there be more than one criterion?
(2) Explain the Cobb–Douglas production function.
(3) What is a dummy variable? How can it be used in statistical analysis with a qualitative variable such as "either a family firm or not?"
(4) Discuss some differences between family and non-family firms that might result in differences in the productivity of inputs.
(5) According to the Barbera and Moores (2011) study, do family and non-family SMEs differ in their overall or "total factor productivity?" Why or why not?
(6) The Barbera and Moores (2011) study used data for Australia. Would we expect different results if the study used data from another country? Why or why not?

References

Barbera, F. and Moores, K. (2011), "Firm Ownership and Productivity: A Study of Family and Non-family SMEs," *Small Business Economics*, October.

Barth, E., Gulbrandsen, T. and Schøne, P. (2005), "Family Ownership and Productivity: The Role of Owner-Management," *Journal of Corporate Finance*, v. 11, pp. 107–127.

Sharma, P. (March 2004), "An Overview of the Field of Family Business Studies: Current Status and Directions for the Future," *Family Business Review*, v. XVII, no. 1, pp. 1–35.

Syverson, C. (June 2011), "What Determines Productivity?" *Journal of Economic Literature*, v. XLIX, pp. 326–365.

Wall, R. A. (April 1988), "An Empirical Investigation of the Production Function of the Family Firm," *Journal of Small Business Management*, pp. 24–32.

Chapter 7

The Life Cycle of Small Business, Part 1: "Spawning"

In this chapter, we focus on the life cycle of small businesses. A key question is: what is the role of experience and formal learning in the founding of small businesses? In particular, is the probability of a start-up, and the success of the start-up, influenced by earlier employment in larger businesses? What sort of businesses are most likely to "spawn" small-business start-ups?

In the latter half of the 20th century, economists gave new attention to "human capital." As an example, consider a student who studies full time in a college of business to qualify as an accountant. This is costly: in addition to the cost of tuition and books, the student gives up the alternative of instead working full time at a job she can qualify for, and the wages she could otherwise earn. This sacrifice is the opportunity cost of her time, and is usually the largest cost she bears. She expects that the increased salary she will earn as a qualified accountant will more than repay those costs. Thus, she is investing in training, and this is an example of a human capital investment. The same idea can be extended to most other educational activities, to activities to maintain health and many expenditures on raising children. It seems certain that human capital plays a role in small business as in other businesses. But is formal education the only source of productive knowledge, or can human capital be formed by experience on the job? In this chapter, we review some theory and evidence relevant to the role of human capital, experience and training in small businesses.

1. Some Useful Theory: Human Capital and Learning by Doing

Much of our understanding of the concept of human capital is traceable to the Nobel Laureate (1979) economist Theodore Schultz. In his 1961 Presidential Address[1] to the American Economic Association, Schultz introduced human capital as follows (Schultz, 1961, p. 1)

> Although it is obvious that people acquire useful skills and knowledge, it is not obvious that these skills and knowledge are a form of capital, that this capital is in substantial part a product of deliberate investment, that it has grown in Western societies at a much faster rate than conventional (nonhuman) capital, and that its growth may well be the most distinctive feature of the economic system. It has been widely observed that increases in national output have been large compared with the increases of land, man-hours, and physical reproducible capital. Investment in human capital is probably the major explanation for this difference.
>
> Much of what we call consumption constitutes investment in human capital. Direct expenditures on education, health, and internal migration to take advantage of better job opportunities are clear examples. Earnings foregone by mature students attending school and by workers acquiring on-the-job training are equally clear examples. Yet nowhere do these enter into our national accounts. The use of leisure time to improve skills and knowledge is widespread and it too is unrecorded. In these and similar ways the quality of human effort can be greatly improved and its productivity enhanced. I shall contend that such investment in human capital accounts for most of the impressive rise in the real earnings per worker.

No modern economist would deny the importance of human capital in this sense. But people may also acquire "useful skills and knowledge" by direct on-the-job experience, without "deliberate

---

[1]The address was given in December, 1960, but not published until March of the following year.

investment," and without the cost of forgoing the opportunity to earn a wage while learning. Not long after Schultz' address, Nobel Laureate (1972) Arrow (1962) argued[2] that learning by doing on the job is the fundamental source of new "useful skills and knowledge." He wrote (Arrow, 1962, p. 156)

> I advance the hypothesis here that technical change in general can be ascribed to experience, that it is the very activity of production which gives rise to problems for which favorable responses are selected over time.

He offered two examples:

> It was early observed by aeronautical engineers, . . . that the number of labor-hours expended in the production of an airframe (airplane body without engines) is a decreasing function of the total number of airframes of the same type previously produced. Indeed, the relation is remarkably precise; to produce the Nth airframe of a given type, counting from the inception of production, the amount of labor required is proportional to $N^{-1/3}$.
>
> The Horndal iron works in Sweden had no new investment (and therefore presumably no significant change in its methods of production) for a period of 15 years, yet productivity (output per manhour) rose on the average close to 2% per annum. We find again steadily increasing performance which can only be imputed to learning from experience.

Even if learning by doing does not require a "deliberate investment," it can be anticipated, and we can plan for it. Students will be familiar with this possibility if they consider internships or cooperative jobs or choose a job early in their career in part for the experience they can gain from it. Thus, the distinction between human capital and learning by doing is perhaps a little less strict than these two great Nobel Laureates might lead us to believe. In the rest of this chapter we will use the term "human capital" for "useful skills and knowledge" acquired either through formal training or learning by doing.

---

[2]I have rearranged the order of the quotations.

The focus on technology in the ideas of Schultz and Arrow may also be too narrow. Hayek (1945) — yet another Nobel Laureate! (1974) — has warned us about this:

> The knowledge...of which we must make use never exists in concentrated or integrated form, but solely as the dispersed bits of incomplete and frequently contradictory knowledge which all the separate individuals possess. The economic problem of society is thus...a problem of how to secure the best use of resources known to any of the members of society, for ends whose relative importance only these individuals know. Or, to put it briefly, it is a problem of the utilization of knowledge not given to anyone in its totality.
>
> Today it is almost heresy to suggest that scientific knowledge is not the sum of all knowledge. But a little reflection will show that there is beyond question a body of very important but unorganized knowledge which cannot possibly be called scientific in the sense of knowledge of general rules: the knowledge of the particular circumstances of time and place. It is with respect to this that practically every individual has some advantage over all others in that he possesses unique information of which beneficial use might be made, but of which use can be made only if the decisions depending on it are left to him or are made with his active cooperation. We need to remember only how much we have to learn in any occupation after we have completed our theoretical training, how big a part of our working life we spend learning particular jobs, and how valuable an asset in all walks of life is knowledge of people, of local conditions, and special circumstances. To know of and put to use a machine not fully employed, or somebody's skill which could be better utilized, or to be aware of a surplus stock which can be drawn upon during an interruption of supplies, is socially quite as useful as the knowledge of better alternative techniques.

Speaking particularly of family businesses, Bjuggren and Sund (2002) go a bit further still. Bjuggren and Sund (2002, p. 125) write "two key elements are knowledge idiosyncrasy...and uncertainty/complexity.... Special attention will be paid to knowledge idiosyncrasy as the central explanatory variable.... In many trades of a more craftsmanship character this knowledge is, to a large extent, tacit. It is acquired over time by observing and listening to the older generation and by practising what thereby has been learned." Idiosyncratic knowledge of small business proprietors will play an important part in coming chapters.

Idiosyncratic knowledge of the "particular circumstances of time and place" may be essential for the entrepreneur who owns and directs a small company, and this knowledge will often be gained more by experience on the job than by formal training. Jovanovic (1982) has built a theory of small business around the idea that each entrepreneur must learn one key "particular circumstance of time and place:" just how able she or he is as an entrepreneur.

Jovanovic begins from a model much like that of Lucas, discussed in Chapter 4, Section C of this book. As in that model, potential entrepreneurs differ in their capacity for successful management or entrepreneurship. Individuals differ in some parameter that we might interpret as "ability" or, as Jovanovic suggests, "a favorable location." But Jovanovic differs from Lucas in that he assumed that, at the beginning, a potential entrepreneur does not know his own effectiveness. Jovanovic writes[3]

> Costs are random, and different among firms. For each firm, the mean of its costs may be thought of as the firm's "true cost." The distribution of true costs among the potential firms is known to all, but no firm knows what its true cost is. All firms have the same prior beliefs, and each firm regards itself as a random draw from the population distribution of true costs. This "prior" distribution is then updated as evidence comes in.
>
> If the firm has low true costs, it is likely that the evidence will be favorable, and the firm will survive. If its costs are high and the evidence adverse, the firm may not wait too long before withdrawing from the industry.
>
> Efficient firms grow and survive; inefficient firms decline and fail. Firms differ in size not because of the fixity of capital, but because some discover that they are more efficient than others. The model gives rise to entry, growth, and exit behavior that agrees, broadly, with the evidence.

---

[3] Again, I have changed the order of the quotations.

Jovanovic's theory is consistent with the observation that younger firms grow faster, on average, than mature firms but are also more likely to fail. It is also consistent with the idea that, more generally, learning from experience may be a particularly important source of human capital for a small business entrepreneur. We will next discuss a study that provides some specific evidence on that point.

2. Spawning

When a proprietor or partners start up a business, they may be able to benefit from their earlier experience as employees. But can they gain valuable human capital by working for a successful larger business? If so, what sorts of businesses are most likely to give rise to new foundations by their ex-employees? How does the previous experience influence the success of the start-up? These issues are addressed by Dick *et al.* (2011, p. 1) who write "several academic studies argue that many entrepreneurs make use of business ideas encountered through previous employment ... [this] process, by which former employees create new, independent ventures, is referred to as 'entrepreneurial spawning.'" They elaborate (Dick *et al.*, 2011, p. 2)

> Especially large firms are often argued to have high spawning rates. An explanation could be that employees start new ventures because they become frustrated that the entrepreneurial opportunities they identify are constantly rejected by their employers.... Small firms, in contrast, are assumed to equip their employees with the necessary skills for founding new ventures which is reflected in increased spawning rates.... Regarding firm performance, two opposing views can be brought forward as well. Whereas less successful firms could spawn more new ventures because the opportunity costs for employees to leave the firm are low, well performing firms might have high spawning rates as employees become exposed to more entrepreneurial opportunities....
>
> A shortcoming in the current literature on entrepreneurial spawning, however, is that the link between the characteristics of the spawning firms (the former employers) and the success of the newly spawned ventures is insufficiently discussed.... Of particular interest is the question whether successful firms also spawn

successful ventures. It can be assumed that better performing firms provide an excellent learning environment for their employees, resulting in the creation of more successful ventures....

Dick *et al.* (2011) were able to use a dataset for the Netherlands. This data is very unusual in that it allows employees to be linked to the firm they work for, year by year. Thus, it is possible to extract a sample in which an employee or employees of firm A have founded firm Z a year or two or three later. If so, then A is said to have "spawned" Z. Of about 300,000 firms just 20,000 "spawned." The study found that almost 20,000 firms had "spawned" start-ups, and 24,000 start-ups were "spawned," 1999–2004. Many more firms did *not* spawn start-ups. Accordingly, they chose as a control group a sample of 10 percent of non-spawning firms, comprising 28,000 firms, for comparison with the firms that did "spawn." For the pre-existing firms that may or may not have spawned start-ups, firm size was measured by the logarithm of total assets; success was measured by sales growth and by return on assets; "Control" variables included the average wage as a proxy for the "quality" of the labor input. Control variables are variables included in the regression to avoid specification error and resulting bias. Other control variables were: "focus" on one industry, the age of the company, and location in one of the 12 official regions of the Netherlands.

Their research confirmed some earlier studies (Dick *et al.*, 2011, p. 2) in finding that larger firms spawned more start-ups, but that financially successful firms were less likely to spawn start-ups than unsuccessful ones. Simply comparing the spawners and the control sample, they observe (Dick *et al.*, 2011, p. 7) that

> The descriptive statistics reveal that, on average, a spawning firm breeds roughly 2.21 ventures over the analyzed period of 6 years. This corresponds to an average of 0.39 spawned ventures per year. Comparing spawners with non-spawners shows that the former are, on average, almost four years older than the latter. Spawning firms are also much larger than non-spawning firms. This is reflected in the significantly higher average asset level. However, non-spawning firms significantly outperform spawning firms in terms of ROA (return on assets). There is no significant difference regarding

the sales growth of spawning and non-spawning firms. Finally, spawning companies pay significantly higher average wages than non-spawning companies and are also less likely to be diversified.

To refine this judgement, Dick *et al.* (2011) estimate a regression model with the number of start-ups spawned as the dependent variable and the characteristics of the spawning or non-spawning firms as the independent variables. Since the number of start-ups spawned cannot be a fraction, the study used a model that estimates the probability of $0, 1, \ldots$ positives. The probability was assumed to be distributed as a "negative binomial" product. This is a model that assigns different probabilities to an event that can only have two results — "success" or "failure," and in this case "spawn" or "don't spawn" — but is repeated in such a way that the number of "successes" or "spawns" may be zero, one, two, and so forth. The model assigns probabilities to zero, one, two, $\ldots$ according to a single parameter r. Figure 1 shows the way that the probabilities vary with r. Then, r is the dependent variable of the regression. Thus, it is the probabilities that vary according to the independent variables.

The question then is, how does r change as the independent variables change? Since the data include a very large number of zeros, that would imply a very small r. That might be right, but hard to estimate. To adjust, Dick *et al.* (2011) add one to every count of start-ups spawned. This is a "zero-inflated" estimate. On this basis, they verify that: (1) Bigger companies spawn more start-ups. This is not surprising, since, after all, they will generally have more employees who might found new businesses. (2) Financially *unsuccessful* firms spawn more start-ups, but this has relatively small impact. (3) Younger companies spawn more start-ups. (4) Firms that pay higher average wages spawn more start-ups. (5) The tendency to spawn varies in a complicated way from industry to industry and region to region.

To judge the success of the start-ups, Dick *et al.* (2011) rely on corporate tax data. Since non-employer businesses are not subject to corporate taxes in the Netherlands, and many of the spawned firms are self-employed individuals, they limit their study of the success of

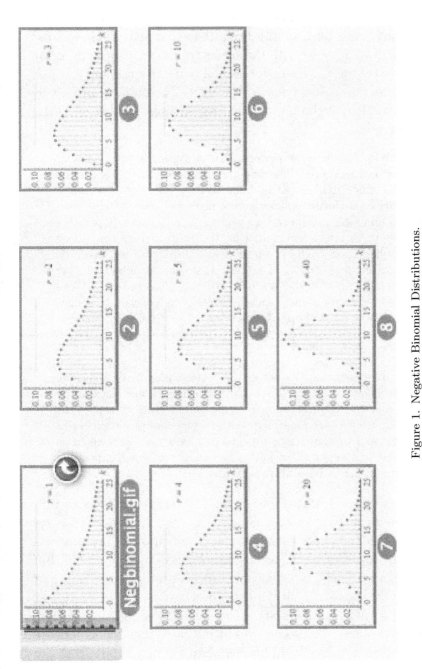

Figure 1. Negative Binomial Distributions.

Source: Wikipedia. The pictures shown in Wikipedia are an animated GIF file. Available at https://en.wikipedia.org/wiki/ Negative_binomial_distribution (accessed on 28/12/2015).

the spawned ventures to 438 ventures that did pay corporate taxes. They linked these back to the firms that spawned them, and did another regression study with the success of the venture firms as the dependent variable and characteristics of both the spawning firm and the new start-up as independent variables. These are estimated by the most familiar method, ordinary least squares. Dick *et al.* (2011, p. 8) write,

> We examine the ventures' performance by considering two different performance measures. The first one is the ventures' returns on assets.... Since ROA could be influenced by differences in capital structure or dividend policies across firms, we also use operating returns on assets ... as a second performance measure. [Operating returns on assets] is calculated as the ratio of earnings before interest and taxes (EBIT) to total assets and is a widely accepted performance measure.... The fact that our sample is highly unbalanced (most of the ventures are only observed once) does not allow us to use growth measures as dependent variables since we would lose most of our observations.

The key findings are

> ...it can be seen that the better the performance of the spawning companies (in terms of ROA), the better the performance of the ventures ... the financial success of the parent firms influences the financial success of the spawned ventures. One interpretation of this finding could be that venture founders who worked at such firms were able to access and exploit more valuable knowledge, possibly resulting in increased venture performance.

There is a good deal of insight here about the conditions that lead to the formation and success of new small businesses. We see that the founders' experience of employment in other businesses is important: Unsuccessful larger businesses spawn more start-ups, but successful larger businesses spawn more successful start-ups. The first of these results is consistent with the idea that the opportunity cost of leaving employment to start a new business is higher in a more successful business. The second result indicates that the experience of employment in a successful business forms human capital that can contribute to a successful start-up.

3. Summary

This chapter has explored the founding of a small business, with a view to the role of human capital at the stage of the founding. Human capital is a familiar concept but often exemplified by formal education. For our purposes, we are more interested in human capital formed by learning by doing and that corresponds to knowledge of the particular circumstances of time and place, of the individual's own capabilities and the opportunities that are idiosyncratic to a particular business, or tacit (unspoken) knowledge of the routines and attitudes that can make a business successful. Thus, we observe that entrepreneurs who leave relatively successful large firms to begin their own enterprises tend to be more successful than many others. This is probably not surprising, but it reinforces the understanding that experience is a key source of the human capital that can make a small business successful.

Discussion Questions

(1) More profitable businesses spawn fewer start-ups, but on average the ones they spawn are themselves more profitable. Explain this dichotomy.
(2) What is the meaning of "learning by doing" in the formation of human capital? Contrast "learning by doing" with other forms of human capital formation.
(3) Discuss the role of experience in the life cycle of small business.
(4) The study by Dick *et al.* (2011) used data for Dutch firms. Would we expect different results if the study used data from another country? Why or why not?

References

Arrow, K. J. (1962), "The Economic Implications of Learning by Doing," *The Review of Economic Studies*, v. 29, no. 3 (June) pp. 155–173.

Bjuggren, P.-O. and Sund, L.-G. (2002), "A Transaction Cost Rationale for Transition of the Firm within the Family," *Small Business Economics*, v. 19, no. 2, pp. 123–133.

Dick, J. M. H., Hussinger, K., Blumberg, B. and Hagedoorn, J. (2011), "Is Success Hereditary? Evidence on the Performance of Spawned Ventures," *Small Business Economics*, October.

Hayek, F. A. (1945), "The Use of Knowledge in Society," *The American Economic Review*, v. 35, no. 4, pp. 519–520.

Jovanovic, B. (1982), "Selection and the Evolution of Industry," *Econometrica*, v. 50, no. 3, pp. 649–670.

Schultz, T. W. (March 1961), "Investment in Human Capital," *The American Economic Review*, v. LI, no. 1.

Chapter 8

Small Business and Liquidity Constraint

Small businesses differ from bigger businesses in important ways. One of the "stylized facts" mentioned in Chapter 2 is that "efficient markets" hypothesis does not seem to apply to small businesses. On the other hand, it is often said that small businesses sometimes cannot get access to capital funds even though their business plans could be profitable. Some research on small business has observed that small closely-held businesses often have definite preferences as to how they might raise capital. This is called the "Pecking Order Hypothesis" (e.g. Koropp *et al.*, 2012). The Pecking Order Hypothesis is that a closely held firm will predictably prefer internal finance to borrowing but prefer borrowing to share issues that would dilute the close control. Thus, where internal finance is insufficient, borrowing may play a strategic role, and limits to the firm's access to loan capital may be a particular strategic handicap.

The limits on loan capital and the apparent failure of the efficient markets hypothesis for small firms are sometimes linked and explained by the idea that many small businesses are "liquidity constrained." Discussions of liquidity constraint can involve complex mathematics. This chapter will introduce the idea of liquidity constraint, making it "as simple as possible, but not simpler." But we will first need to return to the mathematics of probability.

1.   More Useful Theory: Expected Value

We recall that when we throw a single die, the probability of a particular number, 1, 2,..., 6, is in each case one-sixth, if the die is "fair." McCain (2014, pp. 157–159) writes

> Throwing a single die is a pretty simple event,... In applications of probability we often have to deal with much more complicated events. As an example, suppose someone were to offer you a bet. You can throw a single die, and he will pay $10 if the die shows six, but nothing otherwise. How much is this a gamble worth to you? If he would ask you to pay a dollar to play the game, would it be worthwhile? What if he asked for two?
>
> One way to approach this is to think what would happen if you played the game a large number of times — let's say that you played it hundred times. Since we know that the probability of a six on each throw is one sixth, you can expect to see approximately 1/6 of 100 sixes in the 100 throws. One sixth of 100 is between 16 and 17. So you could expect to win roughly 16 or 17 times. If you paid $1 for each game, so it you paid a total of $100, and you would win approximately 10 dollars times 16 or 17 wins, that is, approximately $160 or $170, you would be pretty certain to come out ahead. But if you paid $2 per game, for a total of $200, it doesn't look so good.
>
> But we really want the value of a single play. Each play has two possible outcomes–a six, which pays $10, and any other number, which pays nothing. The probability of the ten dollar payoff is 1/6, and the probability of nothing is 5/6. Multiply each of the payoffs by its probability and add the two together. We have 1/6*10+5/6*0 for a total of 1.67. Thus, $1.67 is the value of an individual gamble.
>
> This is an example of the "mathematical expectation" or "expected value" of an uncertain payoff. **The expected value is a weighted average of all the possible payoffs, where the weights are the probabilities of those payoffs.** Thus, in the game of throwing one die, the payoffs of one and zero are weighted by the probabilities of 1/6 and 5/6 and added together to give the weighted average or expected value.
>
> Let's try another example of expected value. Joe Cool is taking a three-credit course in Game Theory, and his grade is uncertain. He is pretty sure that it will be an A, B, or C, with probabilities 0.4, 0.4, and 0.2. His college calculates grade point averages by assigning 4 "quality points" per credit for an A, 3 for a B, 2 for a

C and 1 for a D. What is the expected value of the quality points Joe will get from Game Theory? If he gets an A he gets $3*4 = 12$ quality points, if a B, 9, and if a C, 6. So we have an expected value of $0.4*12 + 0.4*9 + 0.2*6 = 9.6$ quality points.

Expected values are important whenever people have to make decisions without certain knowledge of the results, and thus play an important role in any discussion of business decisions — including the decisions of small businessmen and entrepreneurs — and in game theory. Every business has to make decisions without certain knowledge of the results, and so the expected value plays a part in many aspects of business economics. It is central to the idea of liquidity constraint.

2.   Liquidity Constraint

This section will introduce the economic concept of "liquidity constraint" and its implications for the economics of small business, primarily by means of a numerical and spreadsheet example.[1] For our example, we have two interested parties: a small businessperson and a banker. The small businessperson has an opportunity to invest in a new startup business. In order to get started, the businessperson will have to invest one million dollars, $1,000,000. The result of the startup is uncertain, because one of three events may occur, as shown in Table 1.

Table 1. Business Startup Outcomes and Values

Event	Value of Business	Probability
1. Excellent prospects for business	$1,400,000	0.7
2. Poor prospects for business	$500,000	0.25
3. Very poor prospects for business	0	0.05

Source: The author's numerical example.

---

[1]The example follows an outline suggested by Kalecki (1937), Baumol (1953), and Sirkin (1970). Some details of the spreadsheet will be given in Appendix A.

We may compute the expected value of the business, using the numbers in columns 2 and 3 (Table 1). It is

$$0.7(1400000) + 0.25(500000) + 0.05(0) = 1105000 \qquad (1)$$

so the investment of \$1,000,000 gives an expected value of \$1,105,000. Despite the risk of Events 2 and 3, the expected value rate of return of 10.5 percent looks pretty attractive.

But here's the catch. In order to make the \$1,000,000 investment, the businessperson will have to borrow some money from the banker. But the banker will in turn face some risk that the businessperson will become bankrupt. In Event 3, the businessperson certainly will be bankrupt and the bank will lose its entire loan. In Event 2, if the bank has lent more than \$463,415, the businessperson will be bankrupt and the bank will lose some part of its loan. (We will see later why exactly \$463,415 is the breakpoint.) The bank will have to take these risks into account. We will suppose that the bank, like the businessperson, makes its decisions on the basis of the mathematical expectations of the payments it receives. The bank pays its depositors interest at 2.5 percent, so that it must charge the businessperson a rate high enough so that the mathematical expectation of its payments from the businessperson will cover at least that cost of 2.5 percent. That, in turn, will depend on how much the businessperson borrows. Let r be the rate of interest specified in the loan contract, and B be the amount borrowed. Suppose that $B < \$463,415$. Then the bank receives its full repayment of $(1 + r)B$ in Events 1 and 2 and the expected value payment to the bank is

$$0.95(1 + r)B \qquad (2)$$

and to earn at least its cost this must be at least $(1 + 0.025)B$, so that

$$r \geq \frac{1.025}{0.95} - 1 = 0.0789 \qquad (3)$$

the bank must charge the businessperson an interest rate of at least 7.89 percent. The difference between 7.89 percent and 2.5 percent in a case such as this is called a "risk premium."

Although the bank could profitably charge interest of more than 7.89 percent, we will assume that competition among banks is strong enough that the bank never charges more than the minimum that covers its costs of interest to depositors. This may not be realistic, but it is a "best case" assumption: the point is that even in the best case of perfectly competitive banks with negligible overhead costs, the businessperson may not be able to raise the capital she needs.

To see why $463,415 is the upper limit, let us suppose that the bank loans exactly that amount. Suppose that Event 2 occurs. Then the businessperson has just $500,000 to repay the loan of $463,415 plus the interest due, which is $(0.0789)(463,415) = \$36585$. The sum of the two, $\$463,415 + \$36585$, is exactly $500,000 — so in this case the bank gets its full repayment with interest.

However, if it had lent any more than $463,415, it would lose some of its interest, and perhaps some of the principle, in a case of Event 2.

If the loan is more than $463,415, then the repayments to the bank are as shown in Table 2.

Using these data, the bank's expected value repayment with $B > \$463,415$ is

$$0.7(1 + r)B + 0.25(500000) \tag{4}$$

and in order for this to cover the bank's cost of $0.025B$, r must be at least

$$r \geq \frac{1.025}{0.7} - \frac{500000}{B}\frac{0.25}{0.7} - 1$$
$$= 1.46 - 0.35\frac{500000}{B} - 1 = 0.46 - \frac{178571.4}{B} \tag{5}$$

Table 2. Bank Repayments If $B > \$463,415$

Event	Repayment	Probability
1.	$(1+r)B$	0.7
2.	$500,000	0.25
3.	0	0.05

Source: The author's computations based on the numerical example.

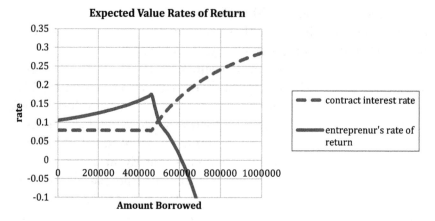

Figure 1. Interest Rate and Net Rate of Return.
Source: The author's computations from the numerical example.

This is a bit complex, and as we see it depends on the amount loaned B. If B is just \$463,415, then r is once again 7.89 percent, and that is what we would expect at the boundary. As B rises above \$463,415, the bank's contract interest rate increases as shown in Figure 1. The contract interest rate is shown by the dashed line.

As B rises from \$463,415 without any upper limit, r approaches 46 percent as an upper limit. For a loan of the entire \$1,000,000 to start up the business, the contract interest rate r would be 28.6 percent. In reality, a banker would probably "ration capital" by refusing to loan the entire amount, rather than raising the contract interest rate smoothly; and a real-world case would probably be more complex in ways that would make the bank's decision to ration its capital a reasonable one. Even for this simplified example, we can be sure that the whole \$1,000,000 will not be lent. To see why, we need to change perspective and look at the results for the borrower, the small businessperson.

As long as she borrows less than \$463,415, the businessperson can repay the loan with a profit if Event 1 occurs, and if Event 2 occurs, she will lose a great deal but walk away with something left after she has repaid the loan with interest. In that case, the expected value of profit for the businessperson is

$$\Pi = (0.7)(1,400,000) + (0.25)(500,000)$$
$$- 1,000,000 - (0.95)(1+r)B \qquad (6)$$

In Eq. (6), the first two products on the right-hand side give the expected value of the firm's value, the third term is the million dollars that has to be committed to the startup, and the last term is the expected value of interest payments on the amount borrowed. These interest payments will be made in both Events 1 and 2, provided less than \$463,415 was borrowed, and so the probability is the total of the probabilities of those two events, $0.7 + 0.25 = 0.95$. To calculate the businessperson's rate of return, we divide the profit by the amount put up by the businessperson rather than the bank, that is, $\$1,000,000 - B$. Thus the businessperson's rate of return is

$$\left[\frac{(0.7)(1,400,000) + (0.25)(500,000) - 1,000,000 - (0.95)(1+r)B}{1,00,000 - B}\right]$$
$$(7)$$

If more than \$463,415 was borrowed, and Event 2 occurs, then the businessperson will be bankrupt and will leave with nothing in Event 2 as also in Event 3. Thus, in that case, the expected value of the profit is

$$\Pi = (0.7)(1,400,000) - 1,000,000 - (0.7)(1+r)B \qquad (8)$$

and in that case the rate of return is

$$\left[\frac{(0.7)(1,400,000) - 1,000,000 - (0.7)(1+r)B}{1,000,000 - B}\right] \qquad (9)$$

These changes are visualized by the solid curve in Figure 1. As the amount borrowed increases from zero toward \$463,415, we see that the rate of return increases modestly from 10.5 percent to about 17 percent. This occurs because increased borrowing increases the businessperson's leverage — she is collecting all of the profits above the contract rate of interest but investing less of her own money, so that while the numerator of Eq. (7) decreases somewhat, the denominator decreases even more rapidly. Beyond $463,415, however, the contract rate of interest increases along with B, and the increase of both together results in a steady decrease in the businessperson's expected value profits and rate of return, with the profits and the rate of return negative if a bit more than $600,000 is borrowed.

If she can, the businessperson will probably want to borrow the largest amount she can before interest rates start to go up, that is, again, $463,415. This maximizes the expected value of profits. This involves some risk (leverage always does), so she might prefer to borrow less, trading off somewhat lower profits for somewhat less risk. In order to do either of these things, however, she must put up at least $536,585 of her own money. But what if she *doesn't have* $536,585? Say, for example, that she can put up at most $450,000. Then she will face a contract interest rate of 14 percent, and the expected value of her profits will be $28,214 for a rate of return of 6.2 percent. This may be sufficient so that the startup will go forward, but is significantly less than the overall expected rate of return for the project at 10.5 percent. Suppose instead that she can put up at most $400,000. Then she will face a contract interest rate of 16.6 percent, and the expected value of her profits will be $5,000 for a rate of return of 1.5 percent. Rather than invest in business, she would probably choose to invest in financial securities for a better rate of return. Indeed, she could simply deposit her money in the bank for a 2.5 percent rate of return and far less risk. Suppose yet again that she can put up at most $300,000. In that case, she would have to borrow $700,000, would face a contract interest rate of 21 percent, and face an expected value loss of over $40,000, a rate of return of minus 14 percent. In that case, her profit-maximizing decision definitely is not to invest in the start-up. In the first case, she is unable to borrow for maximum profits, and in the other two cases unable to borrow profitably at all, because she does not have enough *liquid assets* to invest in the project. A person in that situation is said to be *liquidity constrained* — constrained or limited by the lack of sufficient liquid assets.

What is a "liquid asset?" It is an asset that can be readily sold at a predictable price and at a very low transaction cost. An asset that is not liquid is said to be illiquid. Liquid assets are suitable for collateral because the bank can sell them to recover some of its loan. For example, the money working capital of the business is liquid at 100 percent of its nominal value, but working capital will usually be only a small part of the assets of a nonfinancial business. The stock in trade of a store will probably be liquid, but only at a fraction of its wholesale cost, since there will be a cost of transaction in reselling it. According to a report in the *New York Times* (Frank, 2015), wine can be a liquid asset. Some wine collectors borrow money to buy more wine, or in one case to open a restaurant, using the wine already in their cellars as collateral. "A new crop of wine lenders has started offering collectors cash for up to 60 percent of the value of their collections, with relatively low interest rates." On the other hand, as we have seen in Chapter 7, idiosyncratic human capital is an important asset of many small businesses, and it must be almost completely illiquid. Now, idiosyncratic human capital may also be important in larger businesses, but as an organizational asset that can be valued in capital markets; in contrast, the cost of valuing the idiosyncratic human capital of a small business will often be prohibitive. These, at least, are assumptions we make going forward, and we will find that they are consistent with the evidence.

In the numerical example, the start-up is itself efficient. It carries some risk of failure, but in a real case, it would be one of many thousands of such small-business opportunities in the economy. If the rule were that these opportunities should be realized when the expected value exceeds the cost (including the opportunity cost rate of return on invested capital), then the gains from the successful startups would more than repay the losses from the failures. This will not comfort the losers — no individual is an average — but rules have to do with averages, and "take the risk when the expected value exceeds the costs" seems to be a good rule.[2] What we have seen in this

---

[2]This was the view of A. C. Pigou, an important founder of the modern economics of public policy. See *Economics of Welfare*, 1920, p. 915.

example is that a start-up that should occur, according to the rule, may not occur because the businessperson is liquidity constrained. Now, it might be that some other entrepreneur, with more money, would step in and carry the start-up forward, but (1) this might not be feasible if the start-up depends on some complementary human capital (knowledge or creative product or personal contacts) accessible only to the liquidity constrained businessperson, and in any case (2) in the United States, at least, it is an objective of public policy to open small-business opportunities to the population as widely as feasible. For these reasons, liquidity constraint is a problem for public policy. We may say that the access of small businesses (and potential small businesses) to capital is limited by liquidity constraint. Some important policies of the Small Business Administration are intended specifically to increase the access of small businesses and small business startups to capital, despite liquidity constraint, as we will see in Chapter 14.

Liquidity constraint is also important in some other branches of economics. In the period following the crash of 2007–2008, many banks were much more reluctant to lend money, in part because they saw risks as increased and in part because their capital had been impaired by past losses. As a result, liquidity constraint seems to have become much more widespread, both for businesses and consumers. The further result was that their spending was reduced and the number of start-ups and small business expansions declined, and this seems to have resulted in a "multiplier effect" that made the decline even worse. Thus, liquidity constraint could be an important aspect of macroeconomics, but we have a great deal to learn here.

In summary, liquidity constraint means that a businessperson or small business may be unable to borrow sufficient funds for efficient operation because the businessperson has too little liquid assets to match the funds that are borrowed. This can occur because the risk of failure is shared between the businessperson and the lender, and it is not shared symmetrically. For that reason, the bank may require that a minimum proportion of the investment come from the liquid assets of the businessperson, and if not, charge a higher interest rate or even refuse to loan. Thus, one objective of public policy toward small business may be to increase the access to capital in the presence of liquidity constraint.

3.　Some Evidence

There have been a number of studies of the importance of liquidity constraint as a determinant of the formation or survival of small businesses. While there is still some controversy, both as to results and their interpretation, an early study by Evans and Jovanovic (1989, p. 810) sets a baseline, and their conclusion is clear "... we find that a person cannot use more than 1.5 times his or her initial assets for starting a new venture. Thus ... most individuals who enter self-employment face a binding liquidity constraint and as a result use a suboptimal amount of capital to start up their businesses." They begin by assuming (Evans and Jovanovic, 1989, p. 810) "People have endowments of entrepreneurial ability and assets that may be correlated. The financial capital that they can devote to a business is a multiple of these assets. This multiple is a measure of the degree of liquidity constraints." Thus, they begin from the Lucas model of the distribution of business size, adding the possibility of liquidity constraint, which Lucas had not taken into account. Thus, like Lucas, they assume that a talent for management (or for entrepreneurship in the broader sense) is distributed at random in the population, and (p. 810) "To our knowledge, this paper reports the first structural estimates of the distribution of this key parameter."

Evans and Jovanovic (1989, p. 811) write "At the start of the period, the individual must decide whether to work for himself (i.e., become an entrepreneur) or continue to work for someone else (i.e., remain a wage worker). At the end of the period, self-employment opportunity will yield him a gross payoff equal to y, while wage work will yield him a wage of w.... A person takes up self-employment if his expected net income is higher there. Otherwise he chooses wage work." The wage depends on the individual's experience, education, and a random variate. The business earnings, y, depend on the person's "talent for management," the amount invested and (again) a random variate. But the businessperson's income will also have a wealth component, which may be negative if she has borrowed money to start-up the business and must pay it back. Further Evans and Jovanovic (1989, p. 812) write "We shall assume that each person can borrow up to an amount that is proportional to his wealth; the factor of proportionality is denoted by $\lambda - 1$. Since the amount borrowed cannot exceed $(\lambda - 1)z$, the most that a person can invest in the business is $z + (\lambda - 1)z = \lambda z$."

Then (Evans and Jovanovic, 1989, p. 810), "The model is estimated with data on roughly 1,500 white males who were wage workers in 1976 and either wage workers or self-employed workers in 1978. The data were drawn from the National Longitudinal Survey of Young Men." "Of these individuals, 89 (4.5 percent) entered self-employment" (p. 817). They summarize the results as follows:

> (p. 822) The estimated correlation between entrepreneurial ability and assets is negative and statistically significant. Thus we can reject the hypothesis that assets are a positive proxy for entrepreneurial ability. The key finding is that there are binding capital constraints. In the second column, which constrains [the correlation of ability and assets] to be zero, the point estimate of λ is 1.44 with a 99 percent (plus or minus three standard deviations) confidence interval of (1.31, 1.59).

> p. (824) Using the estimated structural parameters, we can calculate the fraction of the population that has values of [the parameters such that they would face liquidity constraint.] The average probability of being a constrained entrepreneur ... is 3.75 percent, and the average probability of being an unconstrained entrepreneur ... is 0.06 percent. Thus the liquidity constraint is binding for virtually all the individuals who are likely to start a business.

Several subsequent studies have found correlations between wealth and new business success that are consistent with an important role for liquidity constraint. For example, Holtz-Eakin *et al.* (1994) found that companies owned by proprietors who received inheritances were more likely to survive in the period studied. The inheritances would enable the proprietors to reduce their borrowing or increase their collateral, relaxing the liquidity constraint. In

Germany, Schäfer and Talayera (2009) reported similar results. In a study of Italy, Sarno (2006, p. 133) argues that "investment appears to be excessively sensitive to fluctuations in cash flow. This would indicate that access to capital markets is limited and that the firms face financial constraints." He finds that this is so, and that the limitation is more pronounced in Southern than Central and Northern Italy (p. 140). In a study of Tunisia, a less-developed country, Mesnard and Ravallion (2006, p. 381), following broadly the approach of Evans and Jovanovic (1989), find that Tunisian outmigrants who return to the country are more likely to become self-employed if they return with greater wealth, but that this effect is nonlinear, in that beyond some limit the increasing wealth of the potential entrepreneur has less or no effect on the probability of self-employment. This is consistent with the idea a returning migrant with a smaller "nest egg" is more likely to be liquidity-constrained. For Sweden, Nykvist (2008) also found a nonlinear relationship between wealth and the probability that an individual would start a business. Nyquist follows the example of Hurst and Lusardi (2004) in estimating the relationship between wealth and the probability of starting a business as a high-order polynomial. That is, the independent variables include the square, cube, fourth and higher powers of wealth. Figure 2 shows their result.

In the figure, the dashed line is the sixth-order polynomial (with all powers of wealth through the sixth power), the dotted line is first-order[3] polynomial, and the solid line gives the estimates for each range of 100,000 Swedish Kronor. Nyquist (2008) offers this as evidence that liquidity constraint is an important influence on entrepreneurship in Sweden.

In a study of Portugal, Cabral and Mata (2003) extended the Evans and Jovanovic (1989) approach to model the growth of small businesses. Examining a dataset for businesses all founded in 1984, their results were consistent with the hypothesis that the size at founding and the growth and survival of the firms was influenced

---

[3]Since the dependent variable is a probability, and cannot be greater than one, this cannot be a straight line.

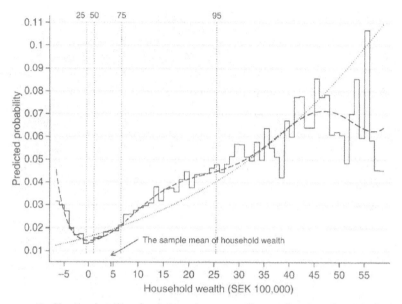

Predicted probability of entering entrepreneurship as a function of wealth; first-order polynomial in wealth (dotted line), sixth-order polynomial in wealth (dashed line) and wealth dummy variables (solid line). The dotted verticle lines indicate the 25th, 50th, 75th and 95th percentile of the wealth distribution.

Figure 2. Wealth and the Probability of a Business Startup in Sweden.
Source: Nykvist (2008, p. 31).

by liquidity constraint. Their discussion of the growth of small businesses in Portugal will be revisited in a later chapter.

We see that there is a considerable range of evidence in favor of the conclusion that liquidity constraint is an important influence on small businesses, both on the founding and on the survival of small businesses. This is not to say that the issue is settled. There is still some controversy. Models[4] based on other assumptions, without liquidity constraint, can often account for the same data without postulating liquidity constraint. In other cases, the same results may be differently interpreted. For example, Hurst and Lusardi (2004), in the paper mentioned earlier, presented evidence of a nonlinear relationship between wealth and the probability of

---

[4] An example is Hurst and Pugsley (2011).

starting a business in the United States, but argued that this is evidence *against* a liquidity constraint, since the probability of starting a business is roughly constant up to a wealth level of about $140,000 (in 1996 dollars) and (p. 326) "It is only at the very top of the wealth distribution — above the ninety-fifth percentile (approximately $300,000 of wealth) — that the probability of starting a business becomes large. The positive association between wealth and business entry found in the linear model is thus driven solely by households at the top of the wealth distribution." Contrast this with the interpretation Evans and Jovanovic (1989) give for results in a model that is, to be sure, quite different in detail: "Only high-ability/low-asset people are affected by the wealth constraint. But it is precisely these people who are most likely to want to switch to self-employment.... Thus the liquidity constraint is binding for virtually all the individuals who are likely to start a business." It seems that a good deal can depend on interpretation.

Thus, while the hypothesis of liquidity constraint is consistent with the evidence, the evidence does not compel us to draw that conclusion. There are other possibilities. What can one do in these circumstances? One can only make one's best judgment based on the balance of the evidence. The author's judgment, for what it is worth, is that liquidity constraint is a real and important factor in the founding and operation of small businesses in almost all real situations, and this judgment will be reflected in the remainder of the book.

4. Conclusion

We have noted an alleged "stylized fact" that many small businesses do not have efficient access to capital markets, and the "efficient markets" hypothesis may fail for them, because of "liquidity constraint." We have seen that, using the probability concept of the expected value, and using the idea that important small-business assets (including "idiosyncratic knowledge") often are illiquid, we can construct a theory that shows how a liquidity constraint can arise — at least as an example. We have also seen that there is a good deal of evidence consistent with such a theory, although some controversy continues on the subject. While it is in part a matter of judgment, at this stage in the discussion, it is concluded that liquidity constraint is an important influence on small business in general.

Discussion Questions

(1) When a lender and a borrower agree on a loan, what risks are there for the lender? For the borrower?
(2) How is the concept of expected value used to analyze the risks to the lender and, respectively, the risks to the borrower?
(3) Define liquidity constraint. How does the liquidity constraint for the *borrower* depend on the risks assumed by the *lender*?
(4) Criticize the following statement: "Since markets are efficient and people are rational, any business that is profitable in expected value terms will be started up by somebody."
(5) Propose a government policy that might increase efficiency in an economy in which many small businesses are affected by liquidity constraint.

References

Baumol, W. (1953), "Firms with Limited Money Capital," *Kyklos,* v. 6, no. 2, pp. 119–131.

Cabral, L. M. B. and Mata, J. (2003), "On the Evolution of the Firm Size Distribution: Facts and Theory", *The American Economic Review*, v. 93, no. 4, pp. 1075–1090.

Evans, D. S. and Jovanovic, B. (1989), "An Estimated Model of Entrepreneurial Choice under Liquidity Constraints," *Journal of Political Economy*, v. 97, no. 4, pp. 808–827.

Frank, R. (2015) "A Cellar Full of Collateral, by the Bottle or the Case," *New York Times Business Day*, July 25, available at http://www.nytimes.com/2015/07/26/business/a-cellar-full-of-collateral-by-the-bottle-or-the-case.html?_r=0, (accessed on 29/12/2015).

Holtz-Eakin, D., Joulfaian, D. and Rosen, H. S. (1994), "Sticking It Out: Entrepreneurial Survival and Liquidity Constraints," *Journal of Political Economy*, v. 102, no. 1, pp. 53–75.

Hurst, E. and Lusardi, A. (2004), "Liquidity Constraints, Household Wealth, and Entrepreneurship," *Journal of Political Economy*, v. 112, no. 2, pp. 319–347.

Hurst, E. G. and Pugsley, B. W. (2011), "Non Pecuniary Benefits of Small Business Ownership," *Brookings Papers on Economic Activity* (Fall) pp. 73–142.

Kalecki, M. (1937), "The Principle of Increasing Risk," *Economica,* New Series, v. 4, no. 16 (Nov) pp. 440–447.

Koropp, C., Grichnik, D. and Gygax, A. F. (2012), "Succession Financing in Family Firms," *Small Business Economics,* v. 41, pp. 315–334.

McCain, R. A. (2014), *Game Theory: A Nontechnical Introduction to the Analysis of Strategy,* 3rd Edition (World Scientific).

Mesnard, A. and Ravallion, M. (2006), "The Wealth Effect on New Business Startups in a Developing Economy," *Economica,* New Series, v. 73, no. 291, pp. 367–392.

Nykvist, J. (2008), "Entrepreneurship and Liquidity Constraints: Evidence from Sweden," *The Scandinavian Journal of Economics,* v. 110, no. 1, pp. 23–43.

Sarno, D. (2006), "Liquidity Constraint on the Production of Firms in Southern Italy," *Small Business Economics,* v. 25, no. 2, pp. 133–146.

Schäfer, D. and Talayera, O. (2009) "Small Business Survival and Inheritance: Evidence from Germany," *Small Business Economics* v. 32, no. 1, pp. 95–109.

Sirkin, G. (1970), *Introduction to Macroeconomic Theory* (Homewood, IL: Irwin).

Appendix A. The Spreadsheet Example

Liquidity constraint example

Case 1 return	Case1	1400000
Case 2 return	Case2	500000
Case 3 return is zero.		
Case 1 prob	Pone	0.7
Case 2 prob	Ptwo	0.25
Bank alternative cost	Ratecost	0.025

Amount borrowed	Contract interest rate	Entrepreneur's expected value	Entrepreneur's rate of return
0	0.078947368	105,000	0.105
50,000	0.078947368	103,750	0.109210526
100,000	0.078947368	102,500	0.113888889

(*Continued*)

(*Continued*)

Amount borrowed	Contract interest rate	Entrepreneur's expected value	Entrepreneur's rate of return
150,000	0.078947368	101,250	0.119117647
200,000	0.078947368	100,000	0.125
250,000	0.078947368	98,750	0.131666667
300,000	0.078947368	97,500	0.139285714
350,000	0.078947368	96,250	0.148076923
400,000	0.078947368	95,000	0.158333333
450,000	0.078947368	93,750	0.170454545
463,415	0.078947368	93,414.625	0.174091011
500,000	0.107142857	51,428.57143	0.102857143
550,000	0.13961039	28,214.28571	0.062698413
600,000	0.166666667	5,000	0.0125
650,000	0.18956044	−18,214.28571	−0.052040816
700,000	0.209183673	−41,428.57143	−0.138095238
750,000	0.226190476	−64,642.85714	−0.258571429
800,000	0.241071429	−87,857.14286	−0.439285714
850,000	0.254201681	−111,071.4286	−0.74047619
900,000	0.265873016	−134,285.7143	−1.342857143
950,000	0.276315789	−157,500	−3.15
1,000,000	0.285714286	−180,714.2857	

Selected formulae follow:

Amount borrowed	contract interest rate	entrepreneur's expected value	entrepreneur's rate of return
0	=IF(A12 < case2,(1+ratecost)/(pone+ptwo)-1,(1+ratecost)/pone-(case2/A12)*(ptwo/pone)-1)	=pone*case1+ptwo*case2+A12-(1000000+(pone+ptwo)*(1+B12)*A12)	=C12/(1000000-A12)
=A12+50000	=IF(A13<case2,(1+ratecost)/(pone+ptwo)-1,(1+ratecost)/pone-(case2/A13)*(ptwo/pone)-1)	=pone*case1+ptwo*case2+A13-(1000000+(pone+ptwo)*(1+B13)*A13)	=C13/(1000000-A13)
=A13+50000	=IF(A14<case2,(1+ratecost)/(pone+ptwo)-1,(1+ratecost)/pone-(case2/A14)*(ptwo/pone)-1)	=pone*case1+ptwo*case2+A14-(1000000+(pone+ptwo)*(1+B14)*A14)	=C14/(1000000-A14)
=A14+50000	=IF(A15<case2,(1+ratecost)/(pone+ptwo)-1,(1+ratecost)/pone-(case2/A15)*(ptwo/pone)-1)	=pone*case1+ptwo*case2+A15-(1000000+(pone+ptwo)*(1+B15)*A15)	=C15/(1000000-A15)
=A15+50000	=IF(A16<case2,(1+ratecost)/(pone+ptwo)-1,(1+ratecost)/pone-(case2/A16)*(ptwo/pone)-1)	=pone*case1+ptwo*case2+A16-(1000000+(pone+ptwo)*(1+B16)*A16)	=C16/(1000000-A16)
=A16+50000	=IF(A17<case2,(1+ratecost)/(pone+ptwo)-1,(1+ratecost)/pone-(case2/A17)*(ptwo/pone)-1)	=pone*case1+ptwo*case2+A17-(1000000+(pone+ptwo)*(1+B17)*A17)	=C17/(1000000-A17)
=A17+50000	=IF(A18<case2,(1+ratecost)/(pone+ptwo)-1,(1+ratecost)/pone-(case2/A18)*(ptwo/pone)-1)	=pone*case1+ptwo*case2+A18-(1000000+(pone+ptwo)*(1+B18)*A18)	=C18/(1000000-A18)
=A18+50000	=IF(A19<case2,(1+ratecost)/(pone+ptwo)-1,(1+ratecost)/pone-(case2/A19)*(ptwo/pone)-1)	=pone*case1+ptwo*case2+A19-(1000000+(pone+ptwo)*(1+B19)*A19)	=C19/(1000000-A19)

(*Continued*)

(*Continued*)

Amount borrowed	contract interest rate	entrepreneur's expected value	entrepreneur's rate of return
=A19+50000	=IF(A20<case2,(1+ratecost)/(pone+ptwo)-1,(1+ratecost)/pone-(case2/A20)*(ptwo/pone)-1)	=pone*case1+ptwo*case2+A20-(1000000+(pone+ptwo)*(1+B20)*A20)	=C20/(1000000-A20)
=A20+50000	=IF(A21<case2,(1+ratecost)/(pone+ptwo)-1,(1+ratecost)/pone-(case2/A21)*(ptwo/pone)-1)	=pone*case1+ptwo*case2+A21-(1000000+(pone+ptwo)*(1+B21)*A21)	=C21/(1000000-A21)
463415	=IF(A22<case2,(1+ratecost)/(pone+ptwo)-1,(1+ratecost)/pone-(case2/A22)*(ptwo/pone)-1)	=pone*case1+ptwo*case2+A22-(1000000+(pone+ptwo)*(1+B22)*A22)	=C22/(1000000-A22)
=A21+50000	=IF(A23<case2,(1+ratecost)/(pone+ptwo)-1,(1+ratecost)/pone-(case2/A23)*(ptwo/pone)-1)	=pone*case1+ptwo*case2-(1000000-A23)-(1+B23)*A23	=C23/(1000000-A23)
=A23+50000	=IF(A24<case2,(1+ratecost)/(pone+ptwo)-1,(1+ratecost)/pone-(case2/A24)*(ptwo/pone)-1)	=pone*case1+ptwo*case2-(1000000-A24)-(1+B24)*A24	=C24/(1000000-A24)

Chapter 9

The Life Cycle of Small Business, Part 2: Succession

In a previous chapter, we discussed the founding of small businesses, but now we turn to a later stage in the life cycle. The typical small business relies on a single individual for the entrepreneurial input — management and initiative — or at most on a compact group. The entrepreneur will often be the proprietor or owner of a significant proportion of the firm. A key manager may also be an important owner. In a family business, the chief or key manager is likely to be a family member. What happens when the chief or a key manager does not continue — due to retirement, ill health or death? This is the *succession problem*, and it has two aspects. First, a retiring proprietor, or his heirs, will often want to take their capital out of the business: as a retirement fund, for example. This may create a problem in that the transition to new ownership will have to be financed. If small businesses have limited access to capital, this may present a particular obstacle. Second, it will be necessary to choose a new chief manager. If the business is a family business, the new chief may be chosen from among the departing chief's relatives. Even if the business has not been run as a family business, the heirs of the proprietor will have a particular interest in the choice of the new chief manager. In fact, it is common the world around for the chief manager of a family-owned firm to be a member of

the owner family. But why so? Wouldn't the owners be better off
to appoint the best manager available, regardless whether she is a
family member or not? If not, why not? Those topics will be taken
in reverse order.

1. Succession and Opportunism

Why should a family, as owners, choose a family member as manager?
There are at least two reasons. One is preference. The family, or the
retiring founder-owner, may simply prefer to have a family member
succeed. There was a case of this in my family: my Uncle Jim started
a mobile-home and motorhome park, and left it to his younger son.
The elder son had a pension, but the younger son, who had assisted
his father over the years, had no other income. The brothers are still
speaking, but not on very good terms.

When a founder or owner-family chooses a family member as
the successor, some economists use the term "nepotism" for the
motivation. This seems unfair, since "nepotism" is understood as
misuse of authority. When a corporate executive appoints his nephew
to a no-show job in the corporation, this is a fraud against the
shareholders — and so properly called nepotism. However, when the
family are the owners, there seems no reason why their preferences
should not determine the decision. Where small business operation is
a lifestyle choice, it should not be surprising if the family-as-owners
might prefer to preserve that lifestyle by appointing one of their own
as manager.

This has to be qualified in two ways. First, if the company is
mainly family-owned but there are outside minority shareholders or
partners, appointment of a family member might be seen as a fraud
on the minority owners. This clearly does occur sometimes, and the
law on this point varies from country to country, and in the United
States, from state to state. On the whole, the United States has
pretty strong protection of minority shareholders. Second, in some
countries, economic development policy calls for the substitution
of professional management for traditional family management, on
the grounds that professional management may be more efficient.

To that extent, within-family succession may be against public policy.

But there is a second reason why the family might choose to appoint a family member. The jargon phrase for this reason is "appropriation risk." This will require a more extensive explanation — and more theory.

1.1. *Some Useful Theory: Idiosyncratic Human Capital*

For many small businesses, a crucial business asset is knowledge — the kind of human capital that arises from learning by doing, from the experience of running the business day to day. In Hayek's terminology, this is "knowledge of the particular circumstances of time and place." Bjuggren and Sund (2002) and Lee *et al.* (2003), among others, see this as a key aspect of the choice of a successor. Bjuggren and Sund (2002, p. 125) write

> In all family firms the problem of succession has to be faced at some point. When that time comes, the decision to let a younger generation of family members take over or sell to new non-family owners has to be made. A lot of different factors of a pecuniary and non-pecuniary character may be influential in the choice between these alternatives. To simplify matters, we will here make the assumption that the objective in a succession decision is to maximise wealth. Decision factors of a more sentimental character will thus be disregarded. The decision problem in successions then boils down to a question of under which circumstances is it likely that the present value of a firm is higher in a succession of a firm to heirs than what can be received in a sale to non-family owners. In a micro-explanation two key elements are knowledge idiosyncrasy of a family character and uncertainty/complexity.... Special attention will be paid to knowledge idiosyncrasy as the central explanatory variable. Knowledge idiosyncrasy possessed by a family member is . . . the basic reason for transition within the family to be a wealth maximising strategy.... Family idiosyncratic knowledge is acquired in a learning by watching and doing fashion.... In many trades of a more craftsmanship character this knowledge is, to a large extent, tacit. It is acquired over time by observing and listening to the older generation and by practising what thereby has been learned.

Lee *et al.* (2003) base their reasoning on

> ...(1) the effects of specific human capital in the form of idiosyncratic knowledge and (2) the ability of prospective successors on families' successor choice for their businesses.

These studies argue that a family member may often be chosen as the successor manager of a family business because family members are less likely to act opportunistically and take advantage of the idiosyncratic human capital of the family enterprise in ways that go against the interests of the family. But what do we mean by "opportunism?" Is "opportunism" anything more than rational self-interest? A bit of game theory can help to clarify that.

1.2.   *More Useful Theory: Opportunism and Subgame Perfect Equilibrium*

Noncooperative game theory discusses rational choices by self-interested agents who may sometimes be opportunistic. Here is a simple example (not necessarily to do with small or family business) just to illustrate the idea. It will be a game between a landlord and the tenant. The apartment occupied by the tenant needs painting. The tenant is a skilled painter. The landlord could put up the money and the tenant do the painting and they would both be better off. However, the tenant might then take the money to gamble in Atlantic City and leave the apartment unpainted. It is easy to see that this would be opportunistic.

Because one "player," the landlord, must make a commitment first, we cannot represent this as a table, as in the Prisoner's Dilemma, a well-known example in game theory. Instead, it will be better represented as a decision tree. In game theory, we call this a "game in extensive form." Figure 1 shows the painting game in extensive form. At node 1, the landlord makes the decision to advance money or not. At node 2, the tenant makes his decision whether to go to Atlantic City or do the painting as agreed. The numbers at the end of the arrows are payoffs to the two "players." The first payoff is to the landlord, the second to the tenant, on an arbitrary scale up to 10 for both.

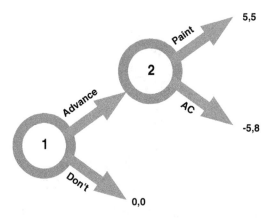

Figure 1. The Painting Game.

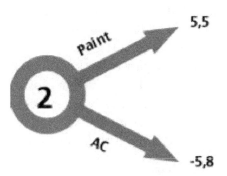

Figure 2. The Last Stage of the Game.

We have a method for solving this sort of game to determine the "rational" equilibrium. It is called "backward induction." Assume both players are ruthlessly self-interested. First, solve the last stage, then work backward. The first stage of the solution is focused on the last stage of the game, shown in Figure 2. At the last stage (assuming the tenant is ruthlessly self-interested), the tenant will choose Atlantic City for 8 rather than paint the apartment for 5. Thus the landlord expects a payoff of −5 if he advances the money.

Thus, in effect, the landlord is playing the one-person game shown in Figure 3. This is called the "reduced game." In the reduced game, his best choice is: don't advance the money. By this decision, he

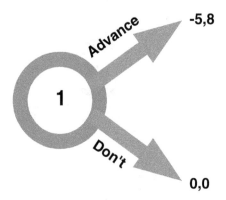

Figure 3. The Reduced Game for the Painting Game.

avoids being a victim of opportunism. Thus, the rational and self-interested solution is that the landlord does not advance the money, knowing that the tenant will not honor his agreement to do the painting. The solution we have obtained is called a "subgame perfect Nash equilibrium." It is a particular kind of Nash equilibrium — and there are other kinds. It is different, for example, from the more familiar "Prisoner's Dilemma." In any case, it does seem to capture the idea of opportunism. We will apply it to an example with idiosyncratic knowledge as a result of learning by doing.

1.3.   *Appropriation Risk*

The specific case of opportunism we are concerned with here is "appropriation risk." It will be illustrated here by a fictional example.

Smythe and Company is a B2B business services company owned by the Kovaks family in Bloomingarden, Ind. It has been managed for decades by Uncle Laszlo, but the company is now owned by a family-held corporation. Uncle Laszlo wants to retire. When Uncle Laszlo was in charge, the company's most important asset was "goodwill" in the form of his idiosyncratic knowledge of the company's past and probable future clients. To keep the company profitable, Uncle Laszlo will remain for a few years as executive director of the company, in order to pass his idiosyncratic knowledge on to his successor.

The family are considering whether to appoint Cousin James as the successor manager. Cousin James has a BBA degree from Podunk U, with a C- average, and is only a fair manager. As an alternative, they could hire Kevin, a first-rate professional manager. (Kevin has a bachelor's degree in business from a very distinguished school with straight A's and an excellent record in his previous job.) Kevin's alternative salary is 10, and so he can be hired for a salary of 10 or more. Because of the relative capabilities of the two candidates, the family, acting as the board of directors, expect that if Cousin James is appointed, the gross profits of Smythe and Company will be 80, but if Kevin is appointed and manages the company for the future, the gross profits will be 100. As before, the payoffs are on an arbitrary scale of 100. The reader may mentally add as many zeros as may make the example "realistic." (All payoffs are discounted to present value.)

However, if Kevin acts opportunistically, after he has gained Uncle Laszlo's idiosyncratic knowledge, he can leave Smythe and Company, set up his own company, and take away half of their business. Their decision is illustrated by the following decision tree, Figure 4. This decision tree is again what would be called a "game in extensive form" in game theory. The payoffs are first for the family and second for Kevin, s is Kevin's salary, and Kevin will not accept the position if his salary is less than 10. Thus, the best the family can do is a payoff of 90, if Kevin accepts and does not act opportunistically. But once he has been appointed to the position, Kevin is better off leaving the company if his salary is less than 50. In a world of capable opportunists, this is what the Kovaks family will expect that Kevin will do, so they appoint James for a family payoff of 80.

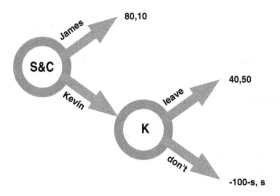

Figure 4. Appropriation Risk.

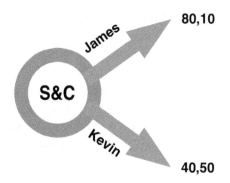

Figure 5. Reduced Game of Appropriation Risk.

The decision of the Kovaks family is rational, in the terms of noncooperative game theory. To see this, we again solve Figure 4 backward. Looking first at the last step, then, we see that for any salary less than 50, Kevin's best response is to leave. This leaves the Kovaks family playing the reduced game shown as Figure 5. Their best response is to appoint James, for a family payoff of 80, rather than Kevin, for a family payoff of 40. If they pay Kevin 50 or more, their payoff at the second stage can be no more than 50, which again is less than 80, leaving it as their best response to appoint James. In game theory, a sequence of decisions is *subgame perfect* if each player chooses her or his best response, in self-interested terms, in each subgame and in the game as a whole. In this example, Kevin's decision whether leave Smythe and Company and form his own company or not to do that is a subgame, and his best response is to leave. Thus, anticipating this, the best response for the Kovaks family is to appoint Cousin James.

If Kevin leaves Smythe and Company after learning their idiosyncratic knowledge, Kevin is *appropriating*, that is, making his own property, an asset that was created by the family business. That is the origin of the term *appropriation risk*. The Kovaks family has appointed Cousin James, a relatively poor manager, in order to avoid appropriation risk. It is a central idea of the economics of organization that many business practices and contract forms are adopted in order to avoid or minimize the risk of losses due to opportunism. The practice of appointing a family member as a successor manager would then be a case in point.

Of course, in this example, we are assuming that Cousin James, as a family member, will not act opportunistically at the expense of the rest of the family. Perhaps even Cousin James could profit by leaving Smythe and Company and taking half the customers with him. We are assuming that his warm family feelings toward his relatives will dissuade him from this. Of course, this is not always true — treachery among family members is as old a story as Cain and Abel — but these stories are shocking just because they go so much against our common human sentiment. Opportunism against family members seems uncommon enough, especially in societies in which family honor is highly valued, that family-managed enterprise remains common worldwide. Preference and trust will reinforce one another. The preference to appoint a relative will arise from the same warm family feelings that deter opportunism. Conversely, if I were to suspect that a relative would act opportunistically at my expense, that suspicion would probably cancel any warm feelings I might have toward that relative, so that I would prefer *not* to see her appointed as manager.

For a conclusion, we may concur with the conclusion of Lee *et al.* (2003, p. 664) on their more complex model: "we suggest here that observations of the appointment of family members as successors to family firms are not necessarily evidence of nepotism. Rather, this could be a rational response by families to the appropriation risk and the agency paradox that they encounter in engaging agents as heads of their businesses, given that family businesses are highly idiosyncratic in general."

2. Succession, Finance and Planning

There are three major aspects of succession that have been studied:

1. Transition of management
2. Transition of ownership
3. Succession planning

The latter two will be discussed in this section.

2.1.   *Liquidity Constraint, Again*

On the transition of management, we have seen that there are good reasons why a family member may be chosen as the successor management. This may not be possible — there may be no family member who can take charge. However, there will be a succession of ownership. The firm may be sold, or a professional manager may be appointed while the heirs retain ownership. Even when there is a family member available to succeed as chief manager, that person is likely to be only one of the heirs, and ownership is likely to be shared among them. Kimhi (1997, p. 130) writes

> Even if people seek to equalize the amounts they bequeath to each of their children, owners of family businesses will prefer to choose only one child as a successor, provided that enough nonbusiness resources are available to compensate other children. This is because joint ownership of a family business often leads to conflicts and power struggles that eventually cause the collapse of the business and loss to all parties.... However, nonbusiness resources are generally insufficient at the point in time at which succession decisions are made, and hence other heirs claim a share in the family business. This can be solved by breaking the linkage between ownership and operation of the business, so that each child gets a share of ownership but one child gets sole responsibility for the operation of the family business.

Any of these approaches will require a financial adjustment that may be limited by liquidity constraint.

Assuming the business is to be sold to a new owner-manager, one possible solution is suggested by Koropp *et al.* (2012, p. 318):

> To deal with unforeseen events the manager-owner could buy an insurance policy that would provide funds to a family trust. The family trust would then provide a loan to the successor and a reasonable income to the spouse.

This assumes, of course, that succession results from the death or disability of the principle. However, it provides an example of the sort of financial arrangements that may facilitate succession, and it provides also an example of succession planning, which has itself been a topic of research to which we will return. (It also seems to be a smart move for many small businessmen.)

Succession of ownership and management need not take place at the same time. Transition of ownership may be delayed for a considerable time after the transition of management, as in the example of Smythe and Company in the previous section. For this purpose, again, financial adjustments may be needed and may be limited by liquidity constraint. Kimhi (1997, p. 314) writes

> A common obstacle to the growth of small family businesses is the lack of sufficient capital. The family has limited resources so that self-financing of the business is limited, and this fact in turn limits the ability of the family to borrow against collateral.... However, the ability to borrow increases over time as the family accumulates assets that can serve as collateral. This of course also depends on the consumption behavior of the family. Eventually the constraints may not be binding after a certain period of business operation and asset accumulation. The effects of borrowing constraints on the optimal timing of succession depend on whether they are still binding at the optimal time of succession without the constraints. Things are different when the borrowing constraints are still binding at... the optimal time of succession....

There is no universal solution to this problem. Some businesses will choose one solution, and others another. But there seem to be some common patterns. In the paper previously mentioned, Koropp *et al.* (2012, p. 318) write

> Typically, the top management of a family firm prefers internal financing to external financing... because it imposes fewer restrictions on the management team.... In addition, in situations that require substantial amounts of financing, such as for a family business succession transaction, internally generated funds might not be sufficient.... According to Pecking Order Theory, the family firm will prefer debt to equity.... Using debt financing also provides a cost advantage over using equity capital, and this advantage is even higher for private firms, compared to public ones....

"Common sense" suggests that a succession plan is likely to give rise to a more satisfactory succession and may improve firm performance before the succession, since it provides certainty. The research literature is inconclusive on this conjecture. However, where a succession plan exists, it can tell us something about the different ways that small businesses approach the financing of succession.

2.2. Succession Planning

Koropp *et al.* (2012), in a paper previously quoted, studied succession plans in Germany. They *assume* that the objective is to transfer both management and ownership within the family. This (especially ownership transition) can impose financial costs that require some outside finance. The paper explores this decision largely from an organization behavior (management) perspective, but there are some important economic aspects considered as well. A questionnaire method is used, and the questionnaire responses are analyzed by a regression. The dependent variable is the proprietor's *intent* to use debt to finance succession. This is a yes-or-no variable, so the study uses a *logistic* regression. This is a regression that predicts the probability of a yes. They write (Koropp *et al.*, 2012, p. 323)

> The data of this study were gathered via a mailed survey in 2008, which is a common method for obtaining data in family firm research. The initial sample was drawn from the Hoppenstedt database, the largest database on German companies.... We...included only firms with minimum sales of EUR 700,000 in 2007 (approximately U.S. $1 million) in our sample.... To determine whether a firm is a family firm,...we analyzed the family's ownership, family management, and family board positions for the firms.... We randomly selected 2,200 firms and sent them a questionnaire with a personalized cover letter to the owner-manager and an addressed return envelope. After three reminders, a total of 362 questionnaires were received. The response rate of 16.5% is similar to that of other recent studies on family firms in Germany.... However, because some questionnaires were deemed unusable due to missing data, our final sample included 187 German family firms.

The predictor variables are

- *Personal* factors of the proprietor,
- *Process* factors of the transition itself and

- *Firm* factors that may influence the raising of capital or the transition itself.

Under the heading of personal factors, they considered answers on the questionnaire that indicated the proprietor's attitude toward debt, risk aversion and experience with debt. Under process factors, they used indices developed from questionnaire responses for need for family control, succession planning and prior experience with succession. Some control variables were also self-reported on the questionnaire. They included profitability, size, growth, whether or not there is an advisory board and ownership dispersion. The questionnaires also asked about the intention to use financial sources other than debt in the succession. These resources were family wealth, retained earnings and equity. There are some possibilities of bias, arising (e.g.) from the fact that some questionnaire responses may be more accurate than others. Diagnostic tests indicated no problem on this score.

Summarizing their analysis, they write (Koropp *et al.*, 2012, p. 330)

> Consistent with the arguments developed earlier, we found that attitudes toward debt and financial knowledge are significant predictors of the owner-manager's intention to use debt financing... succession experience was found to be a strong determinant. Previous succession experience generates knowledge that allows the owner-manager to foresee potential problems and related expenditures that will arise with the succession.... Finally, three of our firm-specific controls were found to significantly influence the owner-manager's intention to use debt for succession financing. In particular, a firm's growth and profitability affect succession-financing decisions. Both higher growth and lower profitability are likely to force the owner-manager to use external debt financing because of limited self-generated financial capacity.... Accordingly, firm variables affect the feasibility of certain financial behaviors. In addition, our findings suggest that family firms exhibit financial behavior that is consistent with the Pecking Order hypothesis.... However, when adopting a broader perspective on our findings, we find that individual-level factors (including financial intentions) are the most important determinants of succession financing decisions,

accounting for approximately 75% of the conceptual model's explained variance.

They also find that when there is a succession plan, the business person is more likely to intend to use debt than when there is no plan. But perhaps this is not surprising — those who do not have a plan may simply not have considered the decision. In any case, this evidence reinforces the impression that, even if they are not liquidity constrained, many small businesses prefer to avoid raising capital outside the company. The "pecking order hypothesis" can probably be applied at all stages of a small firm's life cycle.

3.   Employee Stock Ownership Plans (ESOPS)

If there is no intention to continue the small- or medium-scale business as a family firm — perhaps because the founder's heirs have their own careers and do not want to give them up to manage the firm, or because the owners want to diversify their investments — there is another solution to the problem of ownership transition in the United States and some European countries: sell it to the employees. If the business is sold to one or two key employees, this is likely to be a loan-and-sale deal such as has already been mentioned. But another option is to sell the business to the employees as a group, through an employee stock ownership plan, an ESOP. This has some tax advantages in the United States, and that is true to some extent in some other industrialized countries. The National Center for Employee Ownership (2016), an academic institute located at Rutgers University, explains as follows:

> An ESOP is a kind of employee benefit plan, similar in some ways to a profit-sharing plan. In an ESOP, a company sets up a trust fund, into which it contributes new shares of its own stock or cash to buy existing shares. Alternatively, the ESOP can borrow money to buy new or existing shares, with the company making cash contributions to the plan to enable it to repay the loan. Regardless of how the plan acquires stock, company contributions to the trust are tax-deductible, within certain limits.
>
> Shares in the trust are allocated to individual employee accounts. Although there are some exceptions, generally all full-time

employees over 21 participate in the plan. Allocations are made either on the basis of relative pay or some more equal formula. As employees accumulate seniority with the company, they acquire an increasing right to the shares in their account, a process known as vesting. Employees must be 100% vested within three to six years, depending on whether vesting is all at once (cliff vesting) or gradual.

When employees leave the company, they receive their stock, which the company must buy back from them at its fair market value (unless there is a public market for the shares). Private companies must have an annual outside valuation to determine the price of their shares. In private companies, employees must be able to vote their allocated shares on major issues, such as closing or relocating, but the company can choose whether to pass through voting rights (such as for the board of directors) on other issues. In public companies, employees must be able to vote all issues.

The same source tells us that ESOPs are "by far the most common form of employee ownership in the U.S.... Almost unknown until 1974, by 2014 7,000 companies had ESOPs covering 13.5 million employees." Further, "Companies can use ESOPs for a variety of purposes.... ESOPs are most commonly used to provide a market for the shares of departing owners of successful closely held companies, to motivate and reward employees, or to take advantage of incentives to borrow money for acquiring new assets in pretax dollars." ESOPs are somewhat complicated, however, and they are applicable only where the business has a corporate form, so they will probably be more useful as a succession strategy for a business of medium employment scale than to those at the smallest scale.

For our purposes, this is the key point: an owner-manager of a small- or medium-scale business may be able to use an ESOP to solve or facilitate the ownership transition at succession. It would be wrong, however, to overlook the influence of an ESOP on employee motivation, since this is a major reason for the public support of ESOPs. In testimony in favor of ESOPs, Professor Douglas Kruse (2002) an associate of the National Center for Employee Ownership, reports that "Studies are split between favorable and neutral findings on the relationship between employee ownership and firm performance." He goes on to report on an analysis of 32 research studies, using statistical methods (called meta-analysis) to balance their results. The report is that

> Productivity improves by an extra 4–5% on average in the year an ESOP is adopted, and the higher productivity level is maintained in subsequent years. This one-time jump is more than twice the average annual productivity growth of the U.S. economy over the past 20 years.
>
> The average estimated productivity difference between ESOP and non-ESOP firms is 6.2%, and the average estimated additional increase in productivity following adoption is 4.4% (relative to the increase among otherwise-similar firms in the same period)...
> This roughly corresponds to the productivity increase associated with a 25% increase in capital stock, and is more than twice the economy-wide annual productivity growth rate of 2.0% from 1980–2000.

On this account, then, an ESOP could not only facilitate the transition of ownership, but could improve the performance of the firm in the meantime. The student should keep in mind that these favorable reports all come from one source, and while the mission of the National Center for Employee Ownership is *unbiased* study of employee ownership, other economists would draw other conclusions. Another criticism of ESOPs from a financial point of view is that the *employees* would be better off if their wealth were diversified rather than invested in one company. (This can be said of all small-business proprietors, and simply has to be balanced against the advantages of concentrated ownership, in this case against the motivational benefits of an ESOP.) In any case, the controversy is between neutral and favorable findings on firm performance with an ESOP. What is clear is that the entrepreneur who establishes an ESOP as part of a succession plan need not be concerned that firm performance will deteriorate as a result.

4. Summary

Succession, we have seen, has two aspects: who shall be the successor, and how will this be financed. On one hand, we observe that worldwide, companies largely owned by a family tend to appoint family members to succeed to leadership, even when the family members are less qualified in terms of formal schooling and expertise. This seems to arise from the danger of appropriation risk, that is, the risk that the idiosyncratic knowledge of the small business could be appropriated and used in competition with it. On the other hand, financing succession may require the use of debt or the issue of equity. The "pecking order hypothesis" tells us that equity issue is the lowest choice on the pecking order, and the use of debt may be limited by liquidity constraint, which is also very much associated with the importance of human capital, idiosyncratic knowledge, as an illiquid asset in many small firms. For a firm that already has a corporate form, and where there is no family succession of management, ESOPs may facilitate the transition of ownership.

Discussion Questions

(1) Discuss some of the pros and cons of the choice of a successor manager within the family. Give examples if possible.
(2) What is the relation of subgame perfect equilibrium to opportunism?
(3) What is the pecking order hypothesis?
(4) Criticize this statement: "Because family businessmen are very risk-averse, they will not make efficient use of capital markets, and for this reason family business should be discouraged as a matter of public policy."
(5) The study of succession planning used data for German firms. Would we expect different results if the study used data from another country? Why or why not?

References

Bjuggren, P.-O. and Sund, L.-G. (2002), "A Transaction Cost Rationale for Transition of the Firm within the Family," *Small Business Economics* v. 19, no. 2, pp. 123–133.

Kimhi, A. (1997), "Intergenerational Succession in Small Family Businesses: Borrowing Constraints and Optimal Timing of Succession," *Small Business Economics* v. 9, pp. 309–318.

Kruse, D. (2002), "Research Evidence on Prevalence and Effects of Employee Ownership: 2002 Report by Douglas Kruse, Rutgers University," National Center for Employee Ownership, available at https://www.nceo.org/articles/research-prevalence-effects-employee-ownership (accessed on 1/1/2016).

Lee, K. S., Lim, G. H. and Lim, W. S. (2003), "Family Business Succession: Appropriation Risk and Choice of Successor," *The Academy of Management Review* v. 28, no. 4, pp. 657–666.

National Center for Employee Ownership. (2016), "How an Employee Stock Ownership Plan (ESOP) Works," available at https://www.nceo.org/articles/esop-employee-stock-ownership-plan (accessed on 1/1/2016).

Chapter 10

Franchising

A large number of small businesses benefit from long-term relationships with bigger businesses through contracts of franchising. In the United States, there are approximately one million business establishments involved in franchising.[1] This chapter will consider some research on small businesses in franchising. A franchise is a long-term relation between two businesses that is aimed at their mutual benefit. To the extent that it is successful, the relationship will generate a surplus, which economists call a "quasi-rent" and others might designate as value creation. This poses at least two questions. First, how can the governance of the relation be arranged so as to yield the largest surplus? Second, how is the surplus divided between the participants? The answer to both questions, but especially the second, will depend on the bargaining power of the participants. These questions will be taken up in turn, but first we will expand on the definition of franchising.

1. What is a Franchise?

Franchising is a way of doing business in association with another business. A franchise is a relationship between businesses whereby one business, the franchisor, permits another business, the franchisee,

---

[1]In 2005, the number reported was 909,253, according to Pricewaterhouse-Coopers (n.d.).

to use the trademark and name of the franchisor in return for some fees and on certain conditions. This will ordinarily be a one-to-many relationship, with a single franchisor granting franchises to a number of franchisees, and the franchisees will commonly be small businesses.

A distinction may be made between product distribution franchises and business format franchises. In a product-distribution franchise, the franchisee sells the franchisor's product. In this case, the franchisor licenses the use of its trademark but most other aspects of the business are determined by the franchisee. Some examples are gasoline stations, automobile dealerships and soft drink distributors. In a business format franchise, the franchisee operates the business along the lines prescribed by the franchisor. Commonly, they are selling the franchisor's product, but in addition the franchisor provides training, marketing services and guidelines such as an operations manual. Examples include "fast-food" restaurants, tax preparation services, some convenience stores and some hotel chains (PricewaterhouseCoopers, n.d.).

Benefits to the franchisor include the ability to increase turnover and extend the territory of the business without proportionate increases in capital assets (*The Economist*, 2009). Benefits to the franchisee include large-scale marketing and savings from bulk buying, a brand with a widespread reputation and assistance in many aspects of the start-up and conduct of the business, including, in many cases, financial assistances as well as assistance in the choice of a site along with consultation and training. There are also hazards on both sides. The franchisor may, for example, sell competing franchises too close to existing ones, impairing the profits of the existing franchises. This may or may not be limited by the franchising contract or by legislation. On the other hand, the franchisee may fail to maintain the quality standards of the franchisor or may fail to honor commitments made by the franchisor on the behalf of the franchisee. Here is an example from my own experience. Franchisors of hotels may operate a centralized reservation service. This could bring the franchisees customers they would not get otherwise, but when there is a surge of local demand, the franchisee might find it profitable to raise the price and refuse to honor reservations at

> **Elements of the Economics of Organization.**
>
> 1. Transaction Costs
> 2. Incomplete Contracts
> 3. Opportunism
> 4. Principal-Agent Problems
> 5. The Problem of Corporate Governance
> 6. Agency Cost

customary rates made through the reservation service. This injures both the franchisor's brand name and the opportunity for other franchisees to benefit from the central reservation service and might thus be grounds for cancellation of the franchise.

A franchise, then, is a long-term business-to-business relationship that may accommodate economies of scale in some, but not all, business processes. Business processes that display strong economies of scale, such as national or international branding and advertising and quality control, can be carried out on a large scale by the franchisor; other processes, where there are less economies of scale or perhaps even diseconomies of scale, will be carried out by the franchisee. It is, in other more general terms, an organization among a number of firms. To better understand this way of doing business, we will make use of the economics of organization.

2. Some Useful Theory: A Brief Introduction to the Economics of Organization

In recent economics, the phrase "the economics of organization" refers to a branch of economic research that attempts to answer some questions that arise due to the presence of hierarchical business organizations in the economy. It is also known as "transaction cost economics," and while that term is a bit old-fashioned, it expresses a key point: that transaction costs influence the role and presence of hierarchical business organizations. (This is one reason why this subfield of economics has applications in the economics of small business.) "The economics of organization" is not simply the study of organizations in the economy, but a study that relies on a particular perspective, in which transaction costs are important.

"Organization" does not necessarily mean the kind of hierarchical organization that we visualize with a table of organization. In fact, market relations are a form of organization, though it is relatively unconscious self-organization. Adam Smith writes "Observe the accommodation of the most common artificer or day-labourer in a civilised and thriving country, and you will perceive that the number of people of whose industry a part, though but a small part, has been employed in procuring him this accommodation, exceeds all computation. The woollen coat, for example, which covers the day-labourer, as coarse and rough as it may appear, is the produce of the joint labour of a great multitude of workmen. The shepherd, the sorter of the wool, the wool-comber or carder, the dyer, the scribbler, the spinner, the weaver, the fuller, the dresser, with many others, must all join their different arts in order to complete even this homely production." And Smith goes on for a long paragraph in this way. The point is that the market equilibrium assigns these different people their tasks, assures them of the materials and tools that they need for their work and coordinates all this to produce "The woollen coat ... which covers the day-labourer, ..." This is organization of a very high order, even though there is no overall boss nor hierarchy to make these decisions. Let us make this our definition of organization:

Definition: An organization is a social system that assigns specialized tasks in a coordinated way.

We can conceive of a society in which all organization is by market relations, a society of self-employed persons each of whom lives by selling his or her products, not by selling his or her labor for a wage or salary. (In that world, the economics of small business would just be economics!) This is the first question the economics of organization tries to answer: why do we not in fact rely on non-hierarchical market relations to organize all of our economic activity? In the 1930s, economist Dennis Robertson wrote that firms with hierarchical organization were "Islands of conscious power in this ocean of unconscious co-operation like lumps of butter coagulating in a pail of buttermilk." Why do they exist? In 1937, Ronald Coase quoted this and responded that the answer was to be found in transaction costs. Businesses balance the cost of market transactions against the costs of hierarchical organization. The hierarchical organizations will expand so long as the marginal cost of hierarchy is less than the marginal cost of transactions. But they will expand no further. Thus, instead of a market economy in which the activities of individual people are coordinated by market relations, we see an economy in which (to a considerable extent) market relations coordinate the activities of hierarchical business firms that use relations of authority and direction for their internal coordination. More than 50 years later, in 1991, Coase was awarded the Nobel Memorial prize for that idea. It took a long time, but Coase' idea eventually had widespread influence in economics. (Coase passed away in 2013 at the age of 102.)

What are the costs of transaction? To carry on market transactions, the transactors have to contact one another, which may require search and the consideration of alternative matches with other transactors. These activities require resources and are risky. Negotiation to arrive at a deal also requires some resources and, again, is risky. It may be necessary to draft a contract and see to its enforcement, and these activities also demand costly resources. On the other hand, hierarchically organized businesses also face some of these costs, as they much search for and match employees, find customers, and draft and enforce contracts. However, these costs will evolve differently. Since relations within the organization are durable, the search for new employees and other internal partners will be less frequent. As the hierarchical enterprise gets larger, the contracts get more complex and costly, more than in proportion to size. Contracts will be more complex than contracts for market transactions, and so more costly to draft and implement. On the other hand, the hierarchical organization has means of enforcement not available for market transactions. The employee may be rewarded with promotion or bonuses, or may be punished by withholding these or by direct sanction that stops short of firing. For market transactions, enforcement will often be a very costly lawsuit. Thus, if a hierarchical firm is considering expanding its hierarchy — that is, making a make-or-buy or merger decision — it will balance those costs and choose the less costly alternative, according to Coase.

The greater complexity of contracts for hierarchically organized firms points to another key fact for the economics of organizations: contracts are typically incomplete. After all, drafting a contract is a costly process, and the longer and more complex the costlier. Thus, a contract will, not as a rule, not cover every possible contingency that might arise. For example, I have a family share in some forest land in Louisiana. If I were to form a contract for a specialist to manage the forest, our contract will probably include some guidelines as to how we will handle exploration and drilling for hydrocarbons — "fracking" — which might or might not occur during the course of the contract. If the land were in Washington State, the contract probably would not include anything about drilling, since it is so unlikely in Washington State that it would not be worth the cost to write the contract to deal with it. But if the land were in Washington State, we probably would have the contract provide guidelines for dealing with a landslide, whereas the probability of a landslide in northwestern Louisiana is small enough that it would not be worthwhile to deal with it.

Prior to the 1960s, economists treated incomplete contracts as "friction" that could be ignored, and, for purposes of theory, assumed that all contracts were complete and could be enforced without cost. However, beginning in the 1960s, Oliver Williamson (Nobel 2009) began to explore the implications of incomplete contracts for the economics of organization, and his work was the foundation of the subfield of economics of organization. He posed the question why these incomplete contracts took the form that they did, and his answer centered on opportunism. The incompleteness of contracts, together with costs of transaction, create occasions for opportunism, and reasonable employers and employees would prefer contracts that protect them from opportunism. (Although Williamson did not use game theory, we recall that opportunism can be understood in terms of game theory, using the concept of subgame perfect equilibrium.)

Now, market relations are mutually beneficial, and so have some tendency to increase efficiency, while there is no such tendency in hierarchical relations of authority and direction, since they are not, in abstract, mutually beneficial. Thus we pose a second question: can hierarchical economic organizations be controlled approximately efficiently? We can find an answer in the ideas of Alchian and Demsetz, which have already been discussed in the chapter on entrepreneurship: if the top-level supervisor is the proprietor, and so receives the net revenue of the firm, the top-level supervisor will have an incentive to make the organization as efficient as possible, and to assure that mid-level supervisors do not shirk but do their own work effectively, in turn reinforcing the productivity of the employees at the line. This is an important result for small employer firms.

But what about corporations? In a corporation, the owners are the shareholders, and the top-level supervisor is an employee. This is *the problem of corporate governance*. The corporate CEO is an *agent* of the stockholders, who are the *principal* owners of the firm, so that the problem of corporate governance is a particular instance of the *principal-agent problem*. There is a large literature on this topic, and one of the leaders has been the French economist Jean Tirole (Nobel 2014). Adam Smith thought that the problem of corporate governance could not be solved, writing "Negligence and profusion, therefore, must always prevail, more or less, in the management of the affairs of such a company." Most modern economists believe, however, that it is possible for the principal to write a contract establishing contingent payments such as profit-sharing, bonuses and stock options that will motivate the agent to act in the interest of the principal. But the contracts will be complex and the contingent payments are a cost to the principal. These are known as *agency costs*.

Of course, the problem of corporate governance is mostly a problem for big business, but we have already seen applications of principal-agent problems, agency cost and opportunism in the economics of small business, when we consider the role of family members in the management of small family firms and succession. In the discussion of family, recall, it was observed that employment of family members and family management reduces agency cost. In the discussion of succession, we saw that avoiding opportunism was a key reason for appointing family members to manage family-owned firms, in succession and in general. These are applications of the economics of organization to small business. We will see that the economics of organization is also helpful in understanding franchising.

3.   The Economics of Organization Perspective on Franchising

Much of the economic research on franchises has relied on the economics of organization. Williamson (1979, p. 234) writes "Among the factors on which there appears to be developing a general consensus are: (1) opportunism is a central concept in the study of transaction costs; (2) opportunism is especially important for economic activity that involves transaction-specific investments in human and physical capital; . . ." An investment is transaction-specific if it has value only on the condition that the transaction takes place or is continued. For example, a franchisee's investment in promotion of her business using the national brand owned by the franchisor is transaction-specific in that it is of value only if the franchise relationship is continued. Transaction-specific investments will be particularly important for franchises. For example, Hussain *et al.* (2013, p. 161) "examine the impact of transaction-specific investments, intangible system-specific assets and brand name assets on the franchisor's . . . strategy."

Michael (2000) is particularly concerned with the potential problem of free riding on the part of the franchisee. In economics "free riding" refers to a case in which a good result requires efforts or resources from two or more participants. If one of the participants then relies on the efforts or resources of others, without committing her own resources or efforts, that participant is a "free rider." Generally free riding is inefficient, but the "free rider" may nevertheless benefit on net.

A franchisor may directly operate some proportion of her locations. This is called "tapered integration" (Michael, 2000, p. 499). This comes from the term "vertical integration," in which a single firm both produces and sells a product, or otherwise operates at more than one stage of the supply chain. "Tapered integration" is tapered in that it combines a degree of vertical integration (the franchisor operating some of its locations) with its opposite, in the form of the independently owned franchisees. At the same time, a franchisee may operate just one or more than one establishment. When the franchisee operates more than one establishment, it is called a multi-unit franchisee. Thus, a franchise chain may be a complex collection of ownership forms ranging from very small through medium-scale to large international businesses. Both tapered integration and multi-unit franchises may impact the performance of the businesses, as we will see. We first consider multi-unit franchises and later (in the following subsection) tapered integration, in both cases using the economics of organization perspective.

3.1. *Multi-unit Franchises*

Hussain *et al.* (2013) argue that ideas from the economics of organization can explain the franchisor's decision between single-unit and multi-unit franchises. Among those economics of organization variables are transaction-specific investments, intangible capital and free-riding. In effect, the multi-unit franchise is a mini-chain, but the consolidation of franchise units will modify the impact of transaction-specific investments, intangible capital and free-riding, so that franchisors will adopt these different approaches in circumstances more favorable to each. These circumstances in turn will include differences in transaction costs among the three arrangements.

With respect to free-riding, Hussain *et al.* (2013, p. 163) explain "...free-riding refers to franchisees' propensity to reduce product quality in order to maximize unit profits, which ultimately results in a reduction of brand name value.... If a franchisor has a strong brand name, there is a higher risk of free-riding by franchisees. The franchisor can reduce the free-riding risk by increasing franchisees' incentives through allocating additional residual income rights under a multi-unit franchising contract... [Further,] larger multi-unit franchisees earn higher economic rents compared with single-unit franchisees, which reduces their incentive to free-ride on the brand name."

With respect to intangible assets, Hussain *et al.* (2013, p. 162) observe that "...system-specific and brand name assets are the main components of the franchisor's know-how. The development of a strong brand name is based on the franchisor's investments in intangible system-specific know-how.... Under a given proportion of company-owned outlets, multi-unit franchising enables the franchisor to exercise more control over the use of system-specific know-how (e.g. because of more standardized operational routines between the headquarters and the outlets) and simultaneously mitigates the free-riding risk, especially under a strong brand name, through bundling multi-unit outlet rights. Second, highly intangible system-specific know-how and brand name assets require high transaction-specific investments by the franchisees to realize high quasi-rents. Hence, multi-unit franchising increases the quasi-rent stream for both partners by strengthening the bonding effect of transaction-specific investments." This reasoning is summarized in a schematic shown as Figure 1.

This leads them to form three hypotheses (Hussain *et al.*, 2013, pp. 163–164):

> H1 Franchisees' transaction-specific investments are positively related to the percentage of multi-unit franchisees within the chain.
> H2 Intangible chain-specific assets are positively related to the percentage of multi-unit franchisees within the chain.
> H3 The brand name value of the chain is positively related to the percentage of multi-unit franchisees within the chain.

They "test the hypotheses with data from 138 franchise chains in France in the retail and service industries" (Hussain *et al.*, 2013, p. 162). Hussain *et al.* (2013, pp. 164–165) report "a questionnaire including measures on the percentage of multi-unit franchisees within the chain and brand name value and a postage-paid reply envelope. We received 138 usable questionnaires from chains covering all industries, for a response rate of 24.4%.... Percentage of multi-unit franchisees was measured by a single item in the questionnaire: 'What is the percentage of your franchisees that have more than one unit?' Franchisee transaction-specific investments were operationalized by using the cost of setting up a unit, and intangibility of system-specific

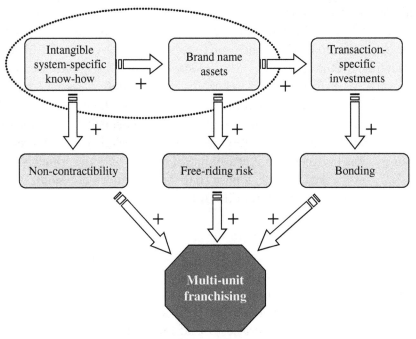

Figure 1. A Schematic of the Economics of Organization as Applied to Franchising.

Source: Hussain *et al.* (2013, p. 162).

assets was measured by the number of days for initial training.... Brand name value was measured with a 4-item scale ..., The items were: 'Compared with our competitors, our brand recognition is strong,' 'Compared with our competitors, our chain has a good reputation for quality and service,' 'Our brand name is one of our most precious assets,' and 'Compared with our competitors, our chain is well respected.' ... Chain age, chain size, proportion of franchised units (vs company-owned ones) and industry were used as control variables.... We used ordinary least squares regression to test the hypotheses." Some of the variables were expressed in logarithmic terms.

In their regression estimates, the coefficients for the measures of set-up costs, initial training and brand value were positive and statistically significant by the conventional standard, and they take this as evidence that their three hypotheses were correct. Hussain *et al.* (2013, p. 167) conclude, "The results indicate that multi-unit franchising enables the franchisor to better control the use of highly intangible system-specific assets in local markets and simultaneously mitigates the franchisor's free-riding risk under a strong brand name. In addition, highly intangible system-specific know-how and a strong brand name require high transaction-specific investments by the franchisees that function as bonding mechanisms to increase cooperation between the multi-unit franchisees and the franchisor." We may also take this as evidence that the economics of organization is a good basis for understanding franchising.

3.2. *Bargaining Power*

Investments that are transaction-specific, we recall, are investments that have value only within a particular transaction or ongoing relationship. One example is the human capital that makes an employee productive in a particular task in a particular company, but a task that is idiosyncratic to that employee and that company (Ravenna and Walsh, 2013). Another, as we have seen, is the investment of a franchisee in promoting her own business on the basis of a brand owned by the franchisor. Now, any transaction-specific investment creates a surplus, relative to the alternatives available to the parties, since the value of the transaction-specific asset cannot be realized by selling it to outside parties. This surplus is the reason the investment is worthwhile, but it poses the question: how is the surplus to be divided? That can only be determined by negotiation, by bargaining. Bargaining power is still not especially well understood in economics: there are several theories of bargaining. However, some things are common to just about all theories and so are pretty clearly known. First, bargaining power is greater if the bargainer has better alternatives to turn to if the bargaining breaks down. Second, bargaining power can be increased by threats, and this will be more effective if the threats are greater and if they are more credible.

Michael, in the paper cited above, explores the implications of tapered integration for bargaining power. Recall, tapered integration means that the franchisor operates some locations while granting others to franchisees. Michael (2000, p. 499) argues that this increases the franchisor's bargaining power : "Gains in bargaining power from tapered integration come from two sources, incentives and information, ..." On one hand, by operating some of the franchises, the franchisor obtains experience and knowledge of the costs and other conditions faced by the franchisee, and this knowledge enhances the franchisor's bargaining power. (It might also improve the service provided by the franchisor to the franchisee, increasing the surplus from their joint activity, a point that Michael does not mention.) On the other hand, the fact that the franchisor operates some units makes their threat to terminate the franchise relationship in a particular case more credible than it might be otherwise. Some franchisors routinely replace poor performers with company-owned locations, at least for some period, in order to rebuild their local market.

Nor does negotiation occur only at the beginning of the relationship. We recall, as Williamson and others have stressed, that contracts cannot in practice be complete. That being so, in the words of Michael (2000, p. 499) "Rather than specifying explicit and formal terms for all conditions, the . . . contract creates an 'adaptive range,' a framework and a set of boundaries, within which conflicts are resolved through negotiation between the parties. . . . Negotiation within the adaptive range rather than literal adherence to contract terms facilitates adaptation to change and the preservation of the relationship. Such a negotiation is always carried out in the shadow of the law; when the parties cannot agree within the adaptive range, they resort to the courts. . . ." Thus, when negotiations break down, we are likely to see a lawsuit. Since most lawsuits for termination are initiated by franchisors, Michael assumes that measures that increase the franchisor's bargaining power reduce the likelihood of litigation.

Returning to the problem of free riding by franchisees, Michael (2000, p. 498) writes "If any single franchisee relaxes his effort to produce high quality, customers will still patronize his unit, assuming that his quality is identical to others sharing the trademark. The franchisee can avoid the cost of quality while gaining from the investments in quality of the franchisor and of other franchisees.... This conflict must be resolved through negotiations or legal remedies under the contract." He continues (Michael, 2009, p. 499) "By employing tapered integration, the franchisor would be likely to raise bargaining power and become more likely to be able to reach agreement with the franchisee within the adaptive range of the contract. Litigation and termination become less likely." Thus, (Michael, 2009, p. 500) "Hypothesis 1: As tapered integration rises, litigation falls, all other things equal." An increase in the surplus, consequent on the knowledge that the franchisor gains by operating some locations, might reinforce this tendency.

A relatively long training period could also increase the franchisor's bargaining power, Michael (2000, p. 500) observes: "...franchisees...have less bargaining power when faced with high fixed costs of switching, including investments in training.... Training is likely to raise switching costs for the franchisee, because franchisees frequently rely on training to learn the specifics of the business and the industry and by increasing the system specific human capital the franchisee develops." Thus (Michael, 2000, p. 501) "Hypothesis 2: As the length of the training program rises, litigation falls, all other things equal."

Further, somewhat surprisingly, "Selecting less informed partners is likely to raise bargaining power.... A prospective franchisee's industry experience is likely to be useful in operations, but...Such a franchisee may be more demanding of the franchisor and less willing to follow the franchisor's system.... In addition, a more experienced franchisee may have additional resources to bring to the franchise relationship, and also have more outside alternatives to operating the franchise, thus creating bargaining power for the franchisee.... Therefore industry experience would appear to enhance franchisee bargaining power,...and inhibit agreement within the adaptive range. Therefore: Hypothesis 3: Systems that require previous industry experience of their franchisees will experience higher litigation, all other things equal" (Michael, 2000, p. 501). Michael also assumes that tying — that is, requiring the franchisee to purchase inputs from the franchisor — will increase the probability of litigation, while a grant of an exclusive territory to the franchisee will reduce it.

Michael tested his hypotheses using data on franchises in the restaurant industry. The data were taken from the Uniform Franchise Offering Circular of each company. The Uniform Franchise Offering Circular is a document prescribed by the Federal Trade Commission and so gives a uniform basis for comparison. There were 99 companies in the sample. The dependent variable was the probability of litigation: "Litigation is measured as all lawsuits with franchisees in which the franchisor has engaged in the last three years" (Michael, 2000, p. 502). Since the dependent variable can only take nonnegative whole number values, Michael used a negative binomial distribution function for his study. We have seen this before: if you do not remember, review Chapter 7. Independent variables include the (log of the) number of franchisees, the proportion of locations that are franchisor-owned, the length of the franchisor's training program, a dummy variable that is one if industry experience is required of franchisees, and zero otherwise, the age and growth rate of the franchisor.

Recall, the negative binomial distribution is characterized by a single parameter so that the probability of a larger overall count increases with that parameter. Thus, Michael finds that the coefficients of the proportion of locations that are franchisor-owned and the length of the franchisor's training program are negative and significantly different from zero, these results confirm his hypotheses 1 and 2. With respect to these hypotheses, though, both of these effects could result from the formation of human capital that increases the surplus. Michael finds that the coefficient of the dummy variable that represents a requirement that franchisees have industry experience is positive, significantly different from zero, and quite large by comparison with the two just considered. Thus, this requirement increases the probability of a lawsuit, other things equal. In this case, if human capital were the mechanism, we would expect the franchisee's experience human capital to increase the surplus and thus reduce the probability of a lawsuit! Thus, this finding is unambiguous evidence for the bargaining power hypothesis. The estimates are shown as Table 1. The second column, dispersion, is an estimate of the variability of the respective independent

Table 1. Estimates of the Probability of a Lawsuit

Negative Binomial Estimation of Litigation in Franchise Systems

	Conditional Mean of Litigation (1)	Dispersion (2)
Log (Franchised units)	0.4014***	−0.8862***
	(0.1110)	(0.2133)
Owned units	−0.0013***	−0.0026***
	(0.0003)	(0.0009)
Training weeks	−0.0699***	−0.1296**
	(0.0178)	(0.0602)
Experience required?	0.9444***	1.082*
	(0.3110)	(0.5854)
Percent tied	0.0358*	−0.019
	(0.0187)	(0.0463)
Exclusive territory granted?	−0.9192***	−1.019*
	(0.2715)	(0.5507)
Years franchising	0.0429***	0.0332*
	(0.0162)	(0.0192)
Three year growth rate	−0.0076	−0.0448**
	(0.0054)	(0.0214)
Constant	−0.8379	5.842***
	(0.8314)	(1.264)
Chi-sqnared test (df = 16) for all coefficients zero	70.3***	

Notes: (1) Sample size is 99. (2) Standard error is in parentheses under coefficient estimate, (3) Significance levels are noted with asterisks: *** is 1%; ** is 5%; * is 10%; all in two tailed tests. (4) Likelihood ratio test of this model versus Poisson equals 234 (1 df), significant at p < 0.001.

Source: Michael (2000, p. 505).

variables, which may depend on some of the other independent variables.

Clearly, Michael's findings are consistent with his hypotheses as to how decisions by the franchisor can influence the relative bargaining power of the parties, and the relation of bargaining power to the likelihood of a lawsuit. Human capital might explain part of these results, but a human capital explanation would be inconsistent with some. More generally, Michael's research shows the importance of bargaining power and thus, indirectly, the value of the economics of organization perspective in understanding franchising.

4. Summary

Franchising is a way of doing business, a partnership between large and small businesses, that can open opportunities for small business, but every opportunity comes with its costs and risks. It enables the big business partner to increase their turnover without increasing their assets, and enables the small business partner to benefit from a national brand and other activities in which there are economies of scale, that might as a consequence be too costly otherwise. This relationship will create transaction-specific assets, both of tangible and intangible capital. The partnership generates a surplus, but like any such coalition, it presents two kinds of challenges to the partners. First, how can the partnership be governed so as to make the surplus as large as possible, preserving the value of the national brand while assuring that the small business partner can make effective use of her idiosyncratic local knowledge and the transaction-specific resources? Second, how will the gains from this joint activity be distributed? Both depend on bargaining power, and we may expect that the franchisor, as the leader in the relationship, will determine their strategies, with respect for example to multi-unit franchisees and to tapered integration, with a view to increasing their own payoff, both by increasing the surplus and by increasing their bargaining power. What the studies we have discussed tell us is that there are opportunities for both.

Discussion Questions

(1) Define a franchising business and give an example.
(2) Give three examples of the application of the economics of organization to the economics of small business.
(3) Why would bargaining and bargaining power play a role in franchising?
(4) Define "tapered integration" and give an example.

(5) Why would the number of lawsuits filed by franchisors or franchisees depend on tapered integration and training? What about tied sales and exclusive territories?

References

Hussain, D., Perrigot, R., Mignonac, K., El Akremi, A. and Herrbach, O. (2013), "Determinants of Multi-unit Franchising: An Organizational Economics Framework," *Managerial and Decision Economics*, v. 34, pp. 161–169.

Michael, S. C. (2000), "Investments to Create Bargaining Power: The Case of Franchising, *Strategic Management Journal*, v. 21, no. 4, pp. 497–514.

PricewaterhouseCoopers (n.d.), *Economic Impact of Franchised Businesses*, v. 2, prepared for the International Franchise Association.

Ravenna, F. and Walsh, C. (2013), "Screening and Labor Market Flows in a Model with Heterogeneous Workers," (Paper presented in the Research Seminar at the Drexel University Department of Economics and International Business, May, 2013).

Smith, Adam (1994), The Wealth of Nations (New York: The Modern Library).

The Economist (2009), "Idea: Franchising," available at http://www.economist.com/node/14298990 (accessed on 14/1/2014).

Williamson, O. E. (1979), "Transaction-Cost Economics: The Governance of Contractual Relations," *Journal of Law and Economics*, v. 22, no. 2.

Chapter 11

The Controversy Over "Gibrat's Law"

In this chapter, we consider one of the oldest research topics in the economics of small business, and a very long-running controversy. The earliest research in this area was done by a French engineer, Robert Gibrat, and has to do with the general rule he proposed and which is known as "Gibrat's law." But this is not a purely intellectual exercise. To understand "Gibrat's law," and to determine whether it is a good approximation to the truth, we need to understand how small businesses grow, and that is a key issue for economic policy with respect to small business.

1. Pareto and Gibrat

In the economics of small business, we have made a great deal of use of skewed distribution functions, right from the start. In doing so, we were following a tradition begun by the great Italian economist, Vilfredo Pareto (1848–1923). Pareto is better known for clarifying the concept of economic efficiency, defining what economists still call "Pareto Optimality." However, Pareto was also interested in the distribution of income, and investigating this distribution in several different countries, he found that incomes tended to be distributed according to the same kind of skewed distribution, a power law that is called the Pareto distribution. (It has also been discovered by some other scholars in other fields and is also known is the Zipf distribution and as the Bradford distribution.) The Pareto distribution can be written as

$$\log N = \log A + m \log x \tag{1}$$

where N is the number of income earners who earn incomes larger than x, and A is a positive constant and m a negative constant. Notice that there is a large family of Pareto distributions, since the constants A and m can differ from one application to another. Figures 1 and 2 show two instances of Pareto distributions and illustrate how the distribution can be different for different values of the coefficients A and m. Notice also that the incomes are on a logarithmic scale to make the curves (especially the curve in Figure 1) more visible.

Pareto's discovery that income distributions in different countries follow similar patterns was well known in the early 20th century, when Robert Gibrat (1904–1980) did his work in economics. Gibrat, an engineer, followed Pareto's example and studied the size distribution of business firms. Using the data available to him then, Gibrat found that distribution of the sizes of firms is highly skewed, and he seems to have been the first to make that observation. Gibrat went further and proposed an explanation for this highly skewed distribution.

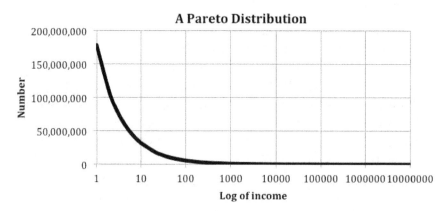

Figure 1. A Pareto Distribution with $A = 19$ and $m = -0.75$.

Source: The author's numerical example.

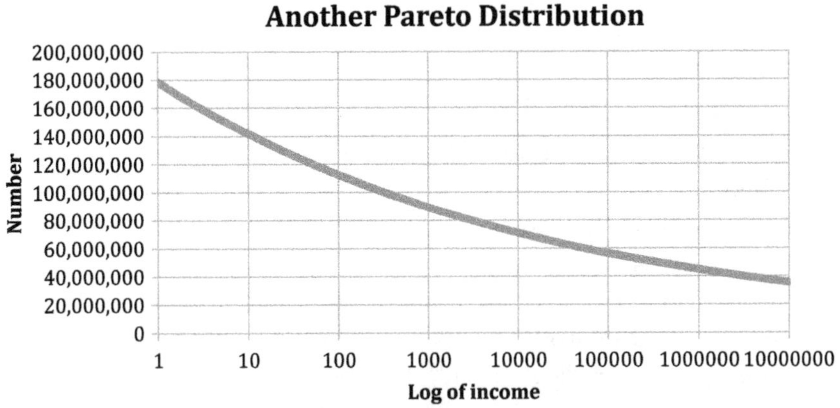

Another Pareto Distribution

Figure 2. A Pareto Distribution with $m = -0.1$.

Source: The author's numerical example.

Gibrat's explanation for the skewness of the size distribution of firms began from a hypothesis about the dynamics of firm growth. It was an extremely simple — in some ways negative — hypothesis. According to Sutton (1997),

> Gibrat's book presented the first formal model of the dynamics of firm size and industry structure, and its lengthy subtitle confidently announced a "new law": the Law of Proportional Effect.
>
> Gibrat traced the origins of his thinking to the work of Jacobus Kapteyn, an astronomer who had become interested in the widespread appearance of skew distributions in various settings, especially in biology. Kapteyn's approach was to assume that underlying such distributions was a simple Gaussian process: a large number of small additive influences, operating independently of each other, would generate a normally distributed variate z (the "Law of Laplace" in Kapteyn's book). An observed skew distribution of some variate x could be modeled by positing that some underlying function of x was normally distributed.... In his book, Gibrat postulated the "simplest" such process, suggesting that the logarithm of x developed in such a fashion. This amounts to saying that the expected value of the increment to a firm's size in each period is proportional to the current size of the firm.

That is, letting x_t be the size of the firm in period t, and x_{t+1} be the size of the firm in period $t + 1$, assuming that the difference from t to $t + 1$ is "small," then the growth rate of the firm

$$\frac{x_{t+1} - x_t}{x_t} = \varepsilon_t \tag{2}$$

is a normal random variate. That is, the growth rate of the firm, ε_t, is independent of the size of the firm. This is Gibrat's law of proportional effect, or just Gibrat's law.

That does *not* mean that the distribution of firm sizes does not change. A firm that (randomly) grows faster in one period will have a larger base, and so grow more in absolute terms, in the next period. This will approach a "lognormal" distribution

$$X = e^{\mu + \sigma Z} \tag{3}$$

in the limit as time goes on. Here, as we recall from Chapter 2, Z denotes a draw from a normal distribution with mean zero and standard deviation 1, so $\mu + \sigma Z$ is a draw from a normal distribution with mean μ and standard deviation σ. The normal distribution is, of course, the familiar symmetrical bell curve. Taking the logarithms of Eq. (3), we have

$$Ln(X) = \mu + \sigma Z \tag{4}$$

That is, the logarithm of the variable X is distributed as a random variable with mean μ and standard deviation σ — thus, it is called a logarithmic-normal (lognormal) distribution. Like some other distributions we have discussed, this distribution is highly skewed. Figure 3 shows a lognormal distribution of firm sizes out of 10,000 firms, with three-fourths of no-employee firms. (This is zero-inflated; that is, X is the size of the firm plus one — since the lognormal would never show a value of zero.)

As evidence for his hypothesis, Gibrat showed that the distribution of firm sizes fit the lognormal distribution very well, in the data available to him. Figure 4 shows data from Gibrat's study of the sizes of French manufacturing establishments in 1920 and 1921. On the horizontal axis is the logarithm of the number of employees in an establishment plus one, and on the vertical axis the number of firms with at least that number of employees. That is, x is the value

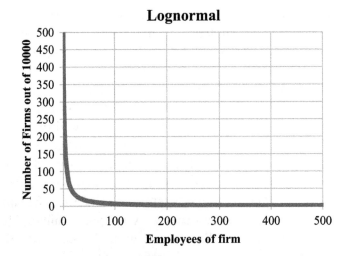

Figure 3. A Lognormal Distribution.

Source: The author's numerical example.

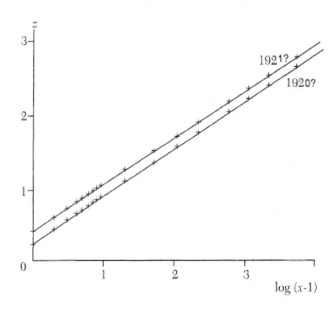

Figure 4. Gibrat's Data.

Source: Sutton (1997, p. 41).
Due to an error in the text, it is not quite clear which is 1920 and which 1921.

on the horizontal axis and $x - 1$ is the number of employees. Thus the size measure is zero-inflated — as it must be, since the logarithm of zero is undefined. For a lognormal distribution this would be a straight line — and as we see, it is very close.

As we saw in Chapter 2, it is very difficult to distinguish between the lognormal distribution and the Pareto distribution, or between either of them and some other highly skewed distributions, such as the negative binomial distribution. This is one possible criticism of Gibrat's argument. Figure 5 shows a Pareto distribution computed with the same constants as the lognormal distribution in Figure 3. Like Figures 3 and 4, it is zero-inflated. Comparison between Figures 3 and 5 shows that they are very similar. Figure 6 shows a negative binomial distribution with the same parameters, that is, 10,000 firms and three-fourths of no-employee firms, for further comparison. The data for Figure 6 are not zero-inflated since the negative binomial distribution can take a zero value.

We see that the lognormal distribution, the Pareto and negative binomial distributions look very similar. Thus, evidence that the distribution of firm sizes is approximately lognormal may not give very strong evidence for "Gibrat's law." Which distribution are we

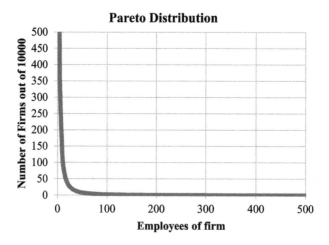

Figure 5. A Pareto Distribution of Firm Size.

Source: The author's numerical example.

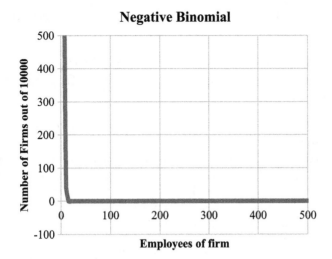

Figure 6. A Negative Binomial Distribution.
Source: The author's numerical example.

observing? On the other hand, taking the perspective of "positive economics," when Gibrat examined the statistics of French business establishment sizes, he put "Gibrat's law" to a test it might have failed — but it didn't fail. Gibrat was ahead of his time in taking this approach. We can say at least that this evidence made "Gibrat's law" more probable, and with no contrary evidence, it was reasonable to conclude that Gibrat's law was probably right. The problem is that the data he had was very limited. In the later 20th century, "Gibrat's law" was revisited, with much more and better data, with mixed results. It is true that a large component of the rate of growth of firms is random. However, in more recent studies, with better data, there is a good deal of evidence that "Gibrat's law" is not true in general. Sutton (1997, p. 44) writes

> The goodness of fit of the size distribution provides only indirect evidence for Gibrat's Law. A second strand of the literature of the 1950s and 60s focused on the direct investigation of Gibrat's Law, by looking at the relation between firm size and growth over successive years in a panel of firms. While various studies of this kind cast doubt on the idea that proportional growth rates

were independent of firm size, no clear alternative characterization emerged.

An early study by Edwin Mansfield (1962) pointed to an ambiguity in the interpretation of Gibrat's law. To quote Santarelli *et al.* (2006),

> Mansfield (1962)...shows that Gibrat's Law can be empirically tested in at least three different ways.
>
> (a) One can assume that it holds for all firms in a given industry, including those which have exited the industry during the period examined (setting the proportional growth rate of disappearing firms equal to minus one).
>
> (b) One can postulate that it holds only for firms that survive over the entire time period. If survival is not independent of firm's initial size — that is, if smaller firms are more likely to exit than their larger counterparts — this empirical test can be affected by a sample selection bias and estimates must take account of this possibility. This observation applies in particular to new and small firms, for which the hazard rate is generally high.
>
> (c) One can state that Gibrat's Law only applies to firms large enough to have overcome the minimum efficient scale (MES) of a given industry....

The first of these interpretations is problematic — both because it implies statistical properties for growth rates that are difficult to deal with and because the "death rate" of firms is not independent of their size and age. This understanding is not new. Mansfield (1962, p. 1031) wrote "Why does this version of the law fail to hold? Even a quick inspection of the [data] shows one principal reason. The probability that a firm will die is certainly not independent of its size. In every industry and time interval, the smaller firms were more likely than the larger ones to leave the industry. For this reason..., this version of the law seems to be incorrect."

It seems that "Gibrat's law" may be applicable to relatively large and mature businesses, which are the sort of businesses Gibrat studied — the only ones for which data was available in the early 20th century. But a good deal of evidence indicates that it does not apply to small businesses and new startups. Thanks to the studies and controversy on Gibrat's law, we have learned a great deal about the dynamics of the growth of small businesses and startup firms.

2.   Evidence on the Dynamics of Firm Growth

With some exceptions, studies of various industries in various countries, and internationally, tend to show that

(1) Smaller firms tend to grow faster than larger (but recall the regression fallacy).
(2) Younger firms tend to grow faster than older.
(3) There is some autocorrelation — firms that grow faster in one year are likely also to grow faster in the following year.
(4) Growth is more predictable — with a smaller standard deviation — in larger firms.

Each of these points contradicts "Gibrat's law." However, for the most part, the deviations are small. The deviations will be taken up in turn in the following sections.

2.1.   *Smaller Firms Tend to Grow Faster than Larger Ones*

On this point, we recall the "fallacy of regression," that it may seem that smaller firms grow faster than larger firms when in fact firms *that are smaller than their stable or normal scale* grow faster than an average firm, as they approach that scale, while *firms that are above their normal scale* grow more slowly, indeed at a negative rate, as they approach the stable scale. This is called "regression to the mean," since the mean or average size of firms of a particular kind does not change, but the firms "regress" toward that mean. Even if that is the explanation for the apparent faster growth of smaller firms, it is a deviation from Gibrat's law. Indeed, if there is a "stable or normal scale" toward which firms of a particular type tend to move, this is itself a contradiction of Gibrat's law. Perhaps we should rewrite the title of this subsection to say instead "firms smaller than their stable scale grow faster than firms in general." That is what the evidence suggests. Mansfield (1962, p. 1034), found that, among firms that survived from one period to the next "the smaller firms tend to have higher and more variable growth rates than the larger ones."

Over the subsequent years, many studies have revisited the evidence on Gibrat's law with more or less similar conclusions, while a few have made the case for Gibrat's Law, usually in a slightly modified form. Santarelli *et al.* (2006) listed over 50 studies since Mansfield's, and most found deviations from Gibrat's law, especially for small and young firms. Some of these studies were limited to large firms, and some supported Gibrat's law, usually with some limitation; but a common conclusion was that Gibrat's law is a good approximation for large, mature firms but that smaller and newer firms tend to have somewhat higher but more volatile rates of growth than bigger firms. These studies included data from the United States, United Kingdom, Spain, the Netherlands, Italy, Germany, Sweden, Greece, Japan, Portugal, Taiwan, Austria, Scotland, several Eastern European countries and some international studies. Research that focused specifically on regression to the mean tended to find it in smaller but not in large enterprises; one (Hart and Oulton, 1999) found regression to the mean only in firms with eight or fewer employees, in a study of United Kingdom data.

Subsequent research has, mostly, reinforced this conclusion. Studies of data from Canada (Petrunia, 2008), Taiwan (Yang and Huang, 2005), Spain (Calvo, 2006) and Greece (Fotopoulos and Giotopoulos, 2010), also find that smaller firms have some tendency to grow faster. A very few studies, including relatively recent studies of data from Denmark (Bentzen *et al.*, 2012) and the United States (Mukhopadhyay and AmirKhalkhali, 2010) find some evidence that, to the contrary, the tendency is for larger firms to grow more rapidly. The Danish study measured firm size as the money turnover, rather than employment, while the study of US data was limited to the largest firms, chosen from the Fortune 500. These differences may explain their different findings.

2.2. *Younger Firms Tend to Grow Faster than Older Ones*

Many of the studies that are referenced in the Section 2.1 had no data on the age of the firms they studied, and for that or a similar reason could say nothing about the influence of the age of a firm on its growth. However, those that did use data on firm age have tended to find that newer firms have faster growth on average. This was Evans' (1987) finding, for example. Drawing on a detailed dataset for the United States, including small as well as large firms, he writes (Evans, 1987, p. 575) "The estimates...imply that over a ten year period, a 1 percent increase in beginning-period age leads to a 1.42 percent decrease in ending-period size. Thus firm growth is smaller for older firms." Evans suggests an explanation in terms of learning, writing (p. 568) "Notably, the age relationships found are broadly consistent with the predictions of Jovanovic's theory of firm growth in which entrepreneurs learn about their abilities over time." While this learning process continues, the new entrepreneurs are able to put their learning to work in ways that produce rapid growth, or, in some other cases, exit from the business. For more experienced entrepreneurs, this learning and growing process is more nearly complete.

In a study of Portuguese data focused particularly on the impact of firm age on the growth of SMEs, Nunes *et al.* (2013) drew similar conclusions. They also distinguish between high-tech and other SMEs. Their findings (Nunes *et al.*, 2013, pp. 2–3) provide a good summary of the findings of most studies in this area:

> The empirical evidence obtained in this study lets us conclude that age is fundamental in explaining the relationships between determinants and growth in young and old SMEs: (1) the negative relationships between age and growth, and between size and growth are more relevant in the case of young SMEs than in the case of old SMEs; (2) internal financing and external financing are of greater importance for growth in young SMEs than in old SMEs; (3) R&D intensity and labour productivity are more important determinants for growth in old SMEs than in young SMEs; (4) interest on debt is of greater relative importance for diminished growth in young

SMEs than in old SMEs; and (5) R&D intensity in situations of financial deficit is of greater importance for diminished growth in young SMEs than in old SMEs, but only when the subject of analysis is high-tech SMEs.

Except for R&D intensity in situations of financial deficit, the empirical evidence indicates that the relative importance of the growth determinants of young and old SMEs in general is identical to that found when the specific subject of analysis is young and old high-tech SMEs.

Finally, the empirical evidence indicates there are significant differences in the survival determinants of young and old SMEs, irrespective of considering young and old SMEs in general or young and old high-tech SMEs as the subject of analysis.

2.3.   *There is Some Autocorrelation*

If the data are available, Gibrat's law could be directly tested by estimating a time series equation such as

$$G_t = \alpha + \gamma G_{t-1} + \beta_1 Z_1 + \beta_2 Z_2 + \cdots + \beta_m Z_m + \varepsilon_t \qquad (5)$$

where G_t is the growth rate of a firm in period t, G_{t-1} is growth in the previous period, $Z_1, \ldots, Z_m$ are other variables that might influence growth, such as the age and size of the firm, characteristics of the proprietor, etc. α, γ, and $\beta_1, \ldots, \beta_m$ are constants to be estimated. Then "Gibrat's law" says that the coefficients α, γ and $\beta_1, \ldots, \beta_m$ are all zero. In particular, if $\gamma > 0$, we say that growth is autocorrelated, and expressing the same thing in different words, we say that the firm's growth is persistent. This suggests that a higher growth rate may reflect some characteristic of the firm that itself persists over more than one period. Few of the studies to date have investigated this — often because the data are not detailed enough to allow such a study — but the few that have estimated γ find evidence that it is positive, that is, that growth is autocorrelated or persistent.

This autocorrelation raises some questions about the appropriate statistical procedures to be used. It could be argued that some of the estimates in some studies that do not allow for autocorrelation are inaccurate, in that some of the estimates of β_i are wrong. However, this probably will not change the conclusions with respect to Gibrat's law and the growth of small firms, because (1) autocorrelation is itself a deviation from Gibrat's law, and (2) while simple estimates may overestimate some of the β_i constants, it seems pretty certain that those estimates will deviate from Gibrat's law in the correct direction (Chesher, 1979, p. 407). The issue is that some of the influence attributed to the size or age of a firm may actually be better attributed to the distinct unobserved characteristics of the firm that make for persistent rapid growth.

2.4. *Growth is More Predictable in Larger Firms*

In his early work, Mansfield (previously cited, 1962, p. 1033) found that contrary to Gibrat's Law, "smaller firms often tend to have higher and more variable growth rates than larger firms." The variability is measured statistically by the *variance*[1] of the growth rates of the firms: when he compared the variance for groups of larger and smaller firms in different industries, he found the variance greater for the small firms. A number of subsequent studies found the same thing. Hart and Oulton (1996, p. 1245) wrote, summarizing a number of studies, that "it is often the case that the variance of growth decreases with increases in the size of firm." In a more extensive study by Hart and Oulton (2001), they write

> Do large firms have smaller variations in growth rates than do small and medium-sized firms? Gibrat's (1931) law of proportionate effect implies that the mean and variance of growth is independent of size, which conflicts with the widespread belief that larger firms have smaller variance of growth because they have greater scope for offsetting favourable economic shocks against unfavourable shocks. A large firm may be regarded as a portfolio of small firms and if it can acquire two firms with negatively correlated sales (e.g. sausages and ice-cream) the variance of growth of both together is less than that of each of them. At the other extreme, if a parent company grows by acquiring other companies similar to itself with positively correlated sales, the variance of growth of the whole group will be much the same as that of the individual constituent firms.

---

[1]For those whose statistics is rusty, the variance is the expected value of the squared deviations of the observations from their average.

What are the facts? There have been many reports on the relationship between the variance of growth and size of firm.... Different measures of size were used but the usual result was that the variance of growth decreased with increases in size of firm, contrary to Gibrat (1931). Over time the volume of data and the power of computers have increased remarkably so that it is now possible to examine the relationship between variations of growth and size for over 29 thousand companies,...

The variance of growth for each size class is plotted in Figure 7.

In the UK over the period 1989–93, it was found that the variance of growth varied widely across size classes of company. In the very smallest and very largest size classes it declined with increases in size of company. But for most size classes it increased with increases in size of company.... there is no simple relationship between size of company and variance of growth,...

In the period studied by Hart and Oulton (p. 7), 1989–1993, some large British firms had "downsized" in response to changing circumstances, an experience that might not be observed in other periods. They speculate that the large variances of growth rates

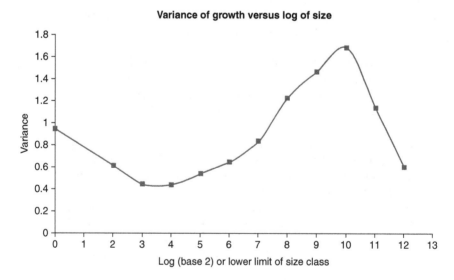

Figure 7. Firm Size and Variance.

Source: Hart and Oulton (2001, Figure 1, p. 8).

for some large firms reflect this. In any case, their evidence, and much other evidence, indicates that within the smaller size classes of firms, an increase in firm size is likely to be associated with a more predictable rate of firm growth.

3. An Example of Recent Research on Deviations from Gibrat's Law

In a paper published in 2003, based on Portuguese data, Cabral and Mata (2003) present and estimate a model of the growth of small firms that seems to capture many of the ideas that have arisen from the study of firm growth dynamics over the previous 40 years, and which is still at the state-of-the-art. Their study contrasts data on a group of larger, more mature firms (that are legally required to report financial data) with data for all employers, including the smaller. For the mature firms, the distribution appears lognormal; but for the bigger set, it deviates from the lognormal. The distributions are shown in Figure 8.

They do not have a measure of firm age. However, they have the tenure of the longest-employed employee. This sets a lower bound to the age of the firm. They use this to group firms in approximate age categories. Using this, they offer further evidence that the age of

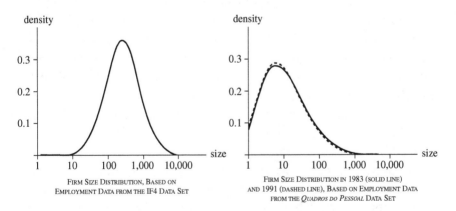

FIRM SIZE DISTRIBUTION, BASED ON
EMPLOYMENT DATA FROM THE IF4 DATA SET

FIRM SIZE DISTRIBUTION IN 1983 (SOLID LINE)
AND 1991 (DASHED LINE), BASED ON EMPLOYMENT DATA
FROM THE *QUADROS DO PESSOAL* DATA SET

Figure 8. Distributions of Firm Size in Two Portuguese Datasets.
Source: Cabral and Mata (2003, p. 1077, Figures 1 and 2).

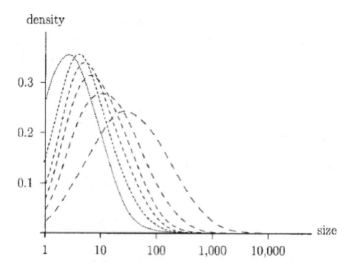

Figure 9. Age and Size Distribution.

Source: Cabral and Mata (2003, p. 1078, Figure 3).

the firm makes a difference. Consider Figure 9. We see that none of
the distributions of firm size is lognormal, but the deviations are less
extreme for the older firms. This could be interpreted in two ways.
First, it may be that the size distribution changes as the firms get
older, because of the dynamics of their growth, in that some grow
faster than others and so rise in the distribution. Second, it might be
that there are different size distributions for different kinds of firms,
but that firms that survive are the ones with the characteristics that
make for a more nearly lognormal distribution.

Cabral and Mata (2003) argue that the first of those interpretations is the correct one. In support of their argument, they use
data from their more detailed dataset, in which they can compare
the distribution for *the same group of firms*, firms founded in 1984
that survive in 1991. This is shown in Figure 10, where we see a
similar shift in the distribution of sizes of the surviving firms. These

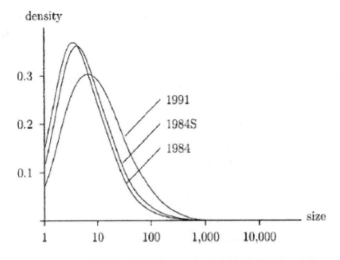

SIZE DISTRIBUTION OF THE 1984 COHORT OF
ENTRANTS: DENSITIES BASED ON 1984 AND 1991 DATA AS
WELL AS 1984 DATA FOR THE FIRMS THAT SURVIVED
THROUGH 1991

Figure 10. Size Distributions for a Group of Firms When Newly Founded and 7 Years Later.

Source: Cabral and Mata (2003, p. 1079, Figure 4).

curves are computed from the data on the number of firms *near* each size measure, smoothed in a pretty simple way. Since Figure 10 only looked at survivor firms, we can be sure that the changing shape of the distribution is *not* a consequence of one kind of firms dropping out, but of different changes in the size of the surviving firms.

Cabral and Mata (2003) propose a model to explain the data they observe. They borrow part of a model due to Nobel Laureate Robert Lucas (1978), which was discussed in Chapter 4. That model assumes that business founders are not all alike, but instead are heterogeneous. Each individual is characterized by a measure of her or his managerial efficiency, θ. Lucas tells us that if θ is less than some lower limit, the person will not start a business but instead look for a job. If θ is larger, then the person will find it profitable to start a business, and the larger that the person's θ parameter is, the larger the business will be. The Cabral and Mata (2003) paper uses this in a slightly different way. Like Lucas, they assume that the "optimal" firm size for a founder depends on her or his efficiency θ. Thus it is written as $s^*(\theta)$. Probably more efficient managers prefer larger firms, *ceteris paribus*. The distribution of *optimum* firm sizes is presumably approximately lognormal.

Thus the size of a firm founded by an individual with managerial talent θ will be no greater than $s^*(\theta)$. However, Cabral and Mata (2003) assume that the size of a new firm will also be limited by the founder's wealth (both as direct investment and collateral for loans.) If the wealth is small relative to $s^*(\theta)$, the business founder will be liquidity constrained. (Cabral and Mata 2003 use the term "asset constrained" with the same meaning.) The wealth of a potential business founder is represented by $w(\mathbf{z}, \varepsilon)$. The vector $\mathbf{z}$ represents the observable characteristics of the founder, and ε is a random variable.

Thus, at the time of founding, the size of the firm is the minimum of $s^*(\theta)$ and the limit set by the founder's wealth, $w(\mathbf{z}, \varepsilon)$. As time goes on, however, successful firms accumulate retained earnings that increase the wealth of the proprietor. They grow larger and thus relax the limit. Thus, fewer and fewer of the surviving firms are limited by the proprietor's assets $w(\mathbf{z}, \varepsilon)$, and grow to the efficient scale. Meanwhile less-successful firms will in many cases exit. Thus, the long-run distribution is the distribution of optimal sizes — approximately lognormal.

Unfortunately, Cabral and Mata (2003) did not have data on wealth. They considered age and education as proxies for wealth. Their statistical analysis suggested age is better: consistently with their model, founders' age seemed to impact younger firms but not older. Older founders may have more wealth because they have had more time to save. We also have evidence from another source that persons who have received cash gifts or inheritances are more likely to start businesses than others. Inheritance, at least, is likely to be correlated with age. To model this, they assume

(1) That the wealth limit increases with the square of the founder's age,

(2) And is lognormally distributed, for a given age,

(3) That the scale of the business after 7 years is the optimal scale and

(4) That the probability of asset constraint is *inversely* proportional to the founder's age.

Notice that age enters into this model in two ways. Their estimate does not tell us *whether* a particular firm is liquidity constrained at founding or not, but gives an estimated *probability* that it is liquidity constrained, and estimates of the scale at which it opens in both of the two cases. The role of age in assumption 1 is to determine the scale *if it is liquidity constrained*, and the role of age in assumption 4 is to determine the probability of liquidity constraint. The data used by Cabral and Meta (2003) are for firms founded in 1984 that survived until 1991, and the significance of assumption 3 is that, in 1991, each firm is at (approximately) its optimal scale.

The wealth limit is written as

$$\beta a_i^2 e^{\varepsilon_i} \tag{6}$$

where a_i is the founder's age, ε_i is normally distributed and β is an arbitrary constant to be estimated. Taking logarithms, we have

$$Ln(\beta) + 2Ln(a_i) + \varepsilon_i \tag{7}$$

So we see that the wealth limit is distributed lognormally, given the age of the founder. The standard deviation of ε_i is σ, another arbitrary constant to be estimated. The probability of an asset constraint is modeled as

$$\frac{\alpha}{a_i} \tag{8}$$

where α is a third arbitrary constant. The idea is that as the founder gets older, the probability increases that he can raise enough investment capital for an efficient scale of the business.

We want to choose values of α, β and σ so that the model comes close to the facts. This is called calibration of the model. In econometrics, we use statistical procedures to do that. However, the authors instead use a trial-and-error approach. They simulate the distribution of firm sizes for a large number of values of α, β and σ and compare the results. The computer simulation of the size distribution relies on a kind of program called a pseudorandom number generator. Such a program gives a series of numbers distributed like a particular distribution of random numbers — normal, for example. The computation process is

1. Choose trial values for α, β and σ.
2. Using a pseudorandom number generator with standard deviation σ, choose a trial value of ε_i.
3. Using a pseudorandom number generator and some algebra, choose a trial value of a_i corresponding to the actual distribution of ages.
4. Compute $\beta a_i^2 e^{\varepsilon_i}$
5. Again, using a pseudorandom number generator choose a trial value of s^* that corresponds to the actual distribution in the later year. Yet again, using a pseudorandom number generator, replace $\beta a_i^2 e^{\varepsilon_i}$ with s^* with probability α/a_i. This gives us a starting scale for a hypothetical firm with those constants.

Repeat this process many times: The authors used that loop to generate 515 simulations for each of 2,000 sets of arbitrary constants α, β and σ. They chose constants that gave distributions that best matched the distribution of their 515 observations from 1984 and 1991, statistically speaking. For this "best fit," the constants are $\alpha = 26.15$, $\beta = 0.00460815$, $\sigma = 0.344$. The resulting fit is shown in Figure 11.

To measure the explanatory power of their model, the authors compare it to another model that makes the 1984 and 1991 sizes proportional. They calculate a measure of improved fit somewhat like R^2, which would be the proportion of the observed variation that is explained by the model. On that basis, they say that the model explains between 70% and 75% of the difference between the simple model of proportionate growth and the size distribution observed.

How much confidence can we put in the conclusions of this paper? If it were the only evidence we have, it would be persuasive, but not conclusive. It is one stone in the balance. But, as we have seen,

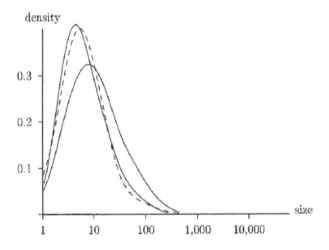

FINANCIAL CONSTRAINTS AND FIRM SIZE
DISTRIBUTION: DENSITIES BASED ON ACTUAL DATA FOR
1984 AND 1991 (SOLID LINES) AND CALIBRATED 1984
DATA (DASHED LINE)

Figure 11. Simulated and Actual Start-up Distributions.

Source: Cabral and Mata (2003, p. 1083, Figure 5).

this study agrees with a large number of studies of other countries based on other datasets. It goes further than many of those studies, with an explanation of the deviations of small-firm growth from Gibrat's law. This explanation relies on the ideas that newly founded small businesses will often be liquidity constrained, and other studies support this assumption. We can be reasonably certain that the tendency of smaller and newer firms to grow more rapidly than other firms is real, and reflects the fact that those firms are founded at an inefficiently small scale, at least in part because of size limits that result from liquidity constraint.

4. Summary and Conclusion

With the evidence available in the first half of the 20th century, Gibrat's law seemed to be true to a good order of approximation. The "law" said that the rate of growth of a firm would be a random variate independent of the size at which the firm began the period and inferred that the distribution of sizes of firms would converge to a lognormal distribution. The lognormal distribution seemed to be a good fit. However, these data were limited, and in particular they were data mostly for large, mature firms. As the second half of the 20th century passed by, economists were able to use more detailed data and more precise methods to revisit Gibrat's idea. It now seems clear that Gibrat's law does not apply to small firms or recently founded firms. For this category, smaller and younger firms tend to grow more rapidly on the average, and their growth is somewhat persistent from one period to the next, though their growth is also more unpredictable and they are less likely to survive. By contrast, Gibrat's law may be true to a good approximation for large, mature firms, though the recent studies are less consistent on that judgment.

Discussion Questions

(1) What is "Gibrat's Law?" Explain in detail. How did Gibrat support his "law" on the basis of evidence? Why is this "law" controversial?

(2) Describe some deviations or exceptions from "Gibrat's law" that are often observed in the evidence.

(3) Explain the meaning of θ in the paper by Cabral and Mata (2003).

(4) How does limited access to capital influence the size distribution of firms, according to the paper by Cabral and Mata (2003)?

(5) Criticize the statistical approach of the paper by Cabral and Mata (2003).

(6) The paper by Cabral and Mata (2003) is based on data from Portugal. Would you expect different results if the study were done on another country? Why or why not?

References

Bentzen, J., Madsen, E. S. and Smith, V. (2012), "Do Firms' Growth Rates Depend on Firm Size?," *Small Business Economics*, v. 39, pp. 937–947.

Cabral, L. M. B. and Mata, J. (2003), "On the Evolution of the Firm Size Distribution: Facts and Theory," *The American Economic Review*, v. 93, no. 4, pp. 1075–1090.

Calvo, J. L. (2006), "Testing Gibrat's Law for Small, Young and Innovating Firms," *Small Business Economics*, v. 26, no. 2, pp. 117–123.

Chesher, A. (1979), "Testing the Law of Proportionate Effect," *The Journal of Industrial Economics*, v. 27, no. 4, pp. 403–411.

Evans, D. S. (1987), "The Relationship Between Firm Growth, Size, and Age: Estimates for 100 Manufacturing Industries," *The Journal of Industrial Economics*, v. 35, no. 4, 567–581.

Fotopoulos, G. and Giotopoulos, I. (2010), "Gibrat's Law and Persistence of Growth in Greek Manufacturing," *Small Business Economics*, v. 35, no. 2, pp. 191–202.

Hart, P. E. and Oulton, N. (1996), "Growth and Size of Firms," *Economic Journal*, v. 106, no. 438, pp. 1242–1252.

Hart, P. E. and Oulton, N. (1999), "Gibrat, Galton and Job Generation", *International Journal of the Economics of Business*, v. 6, no. 2, 149–164.

Hart, P. E. and Oulton, N. (2001), *Variance of Growth and Size of Firm*, Discussion Papers in Economics and Management, The University of Reading Department of Economics, no. 429.

Mansfield, E. (1962), "Entry, Gibrat's Law, Innovation, and the Growth of Firms," *American Economic Review*, v. 52, no. 5, pp. 1023–1051.

Mukhopadhyay, A. and AmirKhalkhali, S. (2010), "Profitability Performance and Firm Size-Growth Relationship," *Journal of Business & Economics Research*, v. 8, no. 9, pp. 121–126.

Nunes, P. M., Goncalves, M. and Serrasqueiro, Z. (2013), "The Influence of Age on SME's Growth Determinants: Empirical Evidence," *Small Business Economics*, v. 40, no. 2, pp. 249–272.

Petrunia, R. (2008), "Does Gibrat's Law Hold? Evidence from Canadian Retail and Manufacturing Firms, *Small Business Economics*, v. 30, no. 2, pp. 201–214.

Santarelli, E., Klomp, L. and Thurik, A. R. (2006), "Gibrat's Law: An Overview of the Empirical Literature," in *Entrepreneurship, Growth, and Innovation: the Dynamics of Firms and Industries: International Studies in Entrepreneurship*, Enrico Santarelli (ed.) (Springer Science, Berlin), pp. 41–73.

Sutton, J. (1997), "Gibrat's Legacy," *Journal of Economic Literature*, v. 35, no. 1, pp. 40–59.

Yang, C.-H. and Huang, C.-H. (2005), "R&D, Size and Firm Growth in Taiwan's Electronics Industry," *Small Business Economics*, v. 25, no. 5, pp. 477–487.

Chapter 12

Small Business and Happiness

In some previous chapters, we have seen evidence that nonpecuniary motives are often important in the formation of small businesses. Some nonpecuniary motives that have been mentioned include a desire to be one's own boss, to make one's own schedule, to do work one enjoys, or to benefit family members. This chapter returns to the topic, with more detailed information from questionnaire studies on the importance and nature of nonpecuniary motives in small business, and a model of small business formation that is focused on nonpecuniary motives.

1. Some Useful Theory: The Economics of Happiness

Economists traditionally assume that people make decisions so as to maximize their utility or the preference ranking they assign to the results of their decisions. To the extent that they do, we may be able to infer their utility or preference ranking from their decisions. If John Doe chooses to vacation in California rather than Florida, we would infer that he prefers California to Florida, that the California vacation increases his utility more than the Florida vacation would. This is called "revealed preference" — the idea being that the person's preferences are revealed by his decisions. However, other social scientists, such as sociologists and psychologists, have often used a more direct approach: ask him. Since the middle of the 20th century, many questionnaire studies have asked the participants to rate their satisfaction with their life, on a scale of worse to better. Satisfaction with jobs, residence and healthcare and other activities have also been studied in this way. One limitation common to all these studies must be mentioned. It is clear that most of the variation in reported satisfaction is an idiosyncratic variation from one person to another. Where happiness is concerned, different people are different, and that is the biggest influence. Nevertheless, we see some differences in the *average* responses that are associated with different economic circumstances.

Richard Easterlin (1974) was the first economist to use data from these quality-of-life studies in economics. In further work, Easterlin (2003, pp. 11176–11177) explained his approach as follows: "I take the terms happiness, utility, well-being, life satisfaction, and welfare to be interchangeable and measured by the answer to a question such as that asked since 1972 in the United States General Social Survey (GSS): 'Taken all together, how would you say things are these days-would you say that you are very happy, pretty happy, or not too happy?' A substantial methodological literature has developed on the reliability, validity, and comparability of the answers to such questions. The consensus is that the responses, although not without their problems, are meaningful and reasonably comparable among groups of individuals.... Needless to say, I am speaking of average effects; there is considerable dispersion about the mean."

Di Tella and MacCulloch (2006, p. 26) write "Most utility functions assume that higher levels of current personal income lead to higher utility. In 1974, Richard Easterlin introduced happiness data into economics and observed that their basic pattern was at odds with this assumption. Specifically, Easterlin (1974) observed that happiness responses are positively correlated with individual income at any point in time: the rich report greater happiness than the poor within the United States in a given year. Yet since World War II in the United States, happiness responses are flat in the face of considerable increases in average income.... A similar pattern has been observed in a large number of countries, including France, the United Kingdom, Germany and Japan, and for different periods of time."

This challenging result reflects the fact that *relative* income has an important impact on self-reported happiness; but when everyone is richer the average person's relative wealth is unchanged. Other studies, correcting for this, find that absolute income also affects happiness. In 2001 (previously cited p. 461) Easterlin writes "As far as I am aware, in every representative national survey ever done a significant positive bivariate relationship between happiness and income has been found." Stevenson and Wolfers (2008, p. 2) write "Across the world's population, variation in income explains a sizable proportion of the variation in subjective well-being. There appears to be a very strong relationship between subjective well-being and income, which holds for both rich and poor countries,..." Not surprisingly, this is subject to the principle of diminishing marginal utility: happiness rises most rapidly with increasing income when income is low. Easterlin observes (2001, p. 468) that the reduced impact of income on happiness at higher income levels "does not occur when happiness is regressed on log income, rather than absolute income. Put differently — if the same proportional rather than absolute increase in income is assumed to yield the same increase in happiness, then income change at upper income levels causes the same increase in happiness as at lower." Stevenson and Wolfers (2008, Figures 7–9, Appendix B) also find that life satisfaction varies linearly with the logarithm of income.

Using data on personal circumstances other than income, this approach allows us to estimate the effect, for example, of age, health and marital status on self-reported happiness. Some of these effects are unsurprising. For example, Easterlin (2003, p. 11177) writes of a study that "examines the life satisfaction (on a 5-point scale) of a national sample of 675 persons reporting disabling conditions and compares them with a national sample of >1,000 nondisabled persons. This study finds that the life satisfaction of those with disabilities is, on average, significantly less than those who report no disabilities." Similarly, married people tend to be happier than unmarried, those who are unemployed are unhappier than those who are employed, even if they have the same income (Clark and Oswald, 1994) and, in the words of Blanchflower and Oswald (2004,

p. 400) "sexual activity enters strongly positively in an equation where reported happiness is the dependent variable. The more sex, the happier the person."

2.   Are Small Businessmen Happier?

A study by Benz and Frey (2008) applied this approach to the motives of self-employed persons and small businesspeople. We have seen some evidence that nonpecuniary motives are important in leading people to start up small businesses. If small business proprietors really benefit from nonpecuniary advantages, we might expect them to report more job satisfaction or more satisfaction with life or both. The study by Benz and Frey (2008) addresses this. They study European data from questionnaire panels carried out in Germany, Switzerland and Britain. They do find that self-employed people report greater job satisfaction than employees. They also find that employees in smaller firms report greater job satisfaction! Benz and Frey (2008, p. 367) write

> In the (German) GSOEP job satisfaction is assessed using the following question: 'How satisfied are you today with the following areas of your life: your job?' Individuals are asked to state their job satisfaction on a scale from 0 (totally unhappy) to 10 (totally happy).
>
> The question asked in the (British) BHPS is similar: 'All things considered, how satisfied or dissatisfied are you with your present job overall?' Answers are coded here on a somewhat narrower scale from 1 (not satisfied at all) to 7 (completely satisfied).
>
> In Switzerland the related question is: 'On a scale from 0 'not at all satisfied' to 10 'completely satisfied', can you indicate your degree of satisfaction with your job in general?' The question was asked only in 1999, which leaves one year of observation available for Switzerland.
>
> In general, individuals in the countries considered seem to be quite satisfied with their jobs. In West Germany, over the period 1984–2000, average job satisfaction of the individuals included in our sample was 7.25 (st. dev. 2.00) on a scale of 0–10.... In Britain, from 1991 to 1999 workers were even somewhat more satisfied with their jobs, indicating an average value of 5.43 (st. dev. 1.36) on a scale of 1–7. Job satisfaction was highest in Switzerland in 1999,

where the average worker stated a job satisfaction score of 8.10 (st. dev 1.72) on a scale of 0–10.

In principle, this difference might be a result of some other differences — for example, self-employed businessmen might be happier because they make more money, or because they work different hours. Benz and Frey (2008) adjust for this, of course, using the economist's usual method: regression, using methods that correct for some known problems. Correlation is not causation! It could be, for example, that the correlation between self-employment and happiness is seen because happier people become self-employed. In the economist's jargon, we would then say that self-employment is an "endogenous" variable. The authors apply some tests for this, and conclude that the results are reliable.

In place of "nonpecuniary benefits," they use the term "procedural utility." Benz and Frey (2008, p. 363) write "Procedural utility refers to the value that individuals place not only on outcomes, as usually assumed in economics, but also on the processes and conditions leading to outcomes. People care not only about the 'what', but also about the 'how'; or they value the 'means' beyond the 'ends'. The concept of procedural utility aims at integrating an aspect of human utility into economics that has largely been neglected in economic theory or empirical research." That is, "Outcome utility" is the utility we get by spending the wages or profits. "Procedural utility" is the utility we get from the way we earn the wages or profits — from the "procedures" we go through to earn the money. Benz and Frey (2008, p. 363) offer another example of procedural utility. "Citizens may reap procedural utility from democracy over and above the outcome generated in the political process, because it provides a feeling of being involved and having political influence, as well as a notion of inclusion, identity and self-determination. Frey and Stutzer (2005) show empirically that Swiss citizens reap such procedural utility from extended democratic participation rights."

The authors argue that self-employment satisfies some "basic psychological needs" for self-determination and/or autonomy. That's not a new idea, but it is difficult to find evidence that bears *directly* on this assumption. The basic assumption is that having one's work directed in a hierarchy is unpleasant, and the bigger the hierarchy the more unpleasant. This leads to two hypotheses:

- "Self-employed people derive higher procedural utility from work than people employed in organizations."
- People working in smaller firms enjoy higher procedural utility than people working in larger firms.

To represent self-employment, Benz and Frey (2008, pp. 367–368) use an approach that by now must be familiar: "The dummy 'self-employed' takes on the value 1 when individuals state that they are self-employed in a given year, and 0 when people in the workforce are employed by an organization.... In West Germany an average 8.3% of the total workforce sampled in the GSOEP was self-employed in the years 1984–2000, and this ratio was relatively constant over the period.... In Britain an average 12.0% of the workforce was self-employed during the years 1991–99.... In Switzerland the ratio amounted to 10.5% in 1999."

Their regression findings are shown in Table 1. We may take these results step by step. The dependent variable is the job satisfaction rating, and a "logit regression" is a method that predicts the average response from a limited, ordered set of responses such as the ones we see here. For each country, the first column gives us the averages for each variable, and the second gives the regression coefficient for the variable. "Employed" is the "reference group," which means that it corresponds to the zero in the dummy variable, and so has no separate coefficient in the regression studies. The first line tells us that self-employment increases average job satisfaction by 0.196 in Germany, 0.258 in Britain and 0.418 in Switzerland, relative to employed workers, the reference group, and the probability that this estimate would be computed if the true value were zero is less than 1 percent; that is, the estimate is statistically significant at the 99 percent level. The third line tells us that an increase of 1 in the log of net income increases job satisfaction rating by an average of 0.374 in Germany, for example. This seems to vary among the three

Table 1. Regression Findings by Benz and Frey (2008).
Self-employment and Job Satisfaction in Germany, Great Britain and Switzerland

Variable	West Germany		Great Britain		Switzerland	
	Mean job satisfaction (scale 0–10)	Ordered logit regression	Mean job satisfaction (scale 1–7)	Ordered logit regression	Mean job satisfaction (scale 0–10)	Ordered logit regression
Self-employed	7.45**	0.196**	5.61**	0.278**	8.47**	0.418**
	(1.92)	(0.064)	(1.31)	(0.056)	(1.77)	(0.112)
Employed	7.24	Ref.group	5.40	Ref.group	8.05	Ref.group
	(2.01)		(1.37)		(1.71)	
Total net income		0.374**		0.081**		0.050
(log)		(0.035)		(0.021)		(0.061)
Working hours		−0.022**		−0.007		−0.036**
per week		(0.004)		(0.004)		(0.012)
(Working hours)^2		0.0001**		0.0001*		0.0004**
		(0.0000)		(0.0000)		(0.0001)
Working		−0.035		0.401**		−0.367**
part-time		(0.032)		(0.064)		(0.123)
Tenure		−0.013**		−0.029**		0.010
		(0.004)		(0.006)		(0.012)
Tenure^2		0.0003*		0.0007**		−0.0003
		(0.0001)		(0.0002)		(0.0003)
Age		−0.035**		−0.066**		−0.036*
		(0.009)		(0.007)		(0.020)

(*Continued*)

Table 1. (*Continued*)

Variable	West Germany		Great Britain		Switzerland	
	Mean job satisfaction (scale 0–10)	Ordered logit regression	Mean job satisfaction (scale 1–7)	Ordered logit regression	Mean job satisfaction (scale 0–10)	Ordered logit regression
Age²		−0.0004**		0.001**		0.0007**
		(0.0001)		(0.0001)		(0.0002)
Sex (female)		0.079*		0.308**		0.287**
		(0.039)*		(0.041)		(0.092)
Education		7 categ.		12 categ.		10 categ.
Job dummies		88 categ.		73 categ.		31 categ.
Industry dummies		45 categ.		10 categ.		14 categ.
Year dummies		17 categ.		9 categ.		—
No. of observations		70,229		52,022		3431
No. of Individuals		11,700		13,380		3431
Time period		1984–2000		1991–99		1999
F		5.85**		13.84**		3.38**

Notes: Dependent variable: Job satisfaction.
Weighted ordered logit regression. Robust standard errors in parentheses (corrected) for repeated observations on individuals). Significance levels:
*0.05 < p < 0.1, *0.01 < P < 0.05, **p < 0.01.
Sources: Benz and Frey (2008, p. 369). GSOEP 1984, 2000, BHPS 1991, 1999 and SHP 1999.

samples. Working hours, tenure on the job and age have important impacts, but these impacts are nonlinear, as shown by the coefficients on the squares of these variables. A number of other, "conditioning," variables are not presented in detail.

The authors do some double-checks with the data sets that allow them to analyze individual movements in and out of self-employment and on those in east Germany who became self-employed only after the political changeover there permitted them to. They offer these as evidence that the causation runs from self-employment to happiness. Another issue is this: The typical self-employed person works in a much smaller firm than the typical employed person. If working in a small firm has nonpecuniary benefits, then it could be that part of this effect comes from the size of the firm and not the fact of ownership. Accordingly, they run a new regression with dummy variables for the size classes of firms. The results are consistent with their hypotheses. Working in a firm bigger than the smallest size class is associated with lower ratings for job satisfaction. (The worst tends to be in the 100–1,000 range.) Proprietors do report higher job satisfaction after allowing for enterprise size, but by a smaller and less significant margin than in the regressions that do not allow for firm size.

This poses an interesting question that they do *not* consider. We know that, on average, small firm employees are paid less than employees of large firms. We also know that they are different in other ways — still: Could it be that large firm employees are paid more to compensate them for their lower job satisfaction?

The British survey asked some specific questions about the sources of the differences in well-being:

- Two were satisfaction with "outcomes": job security and work load.
- Two were "procedural": use of initiative and the actual work itself.

When the latter two were included, there is no separate satisfaction with proprietorship. Satisfaction with small firm employment is reduced, though not eliminated. Inclusion of "job security" and "workload" has no such effect. The coefficients for those variables are large, always "significant," and stable. Thus, they are important variables — but they *do not* explain the satisfaction of proprietors, as the "procedural" variables do. The evidence suggests, and the authors conclude, that (1) the satisfaction derived from small-business proprietorship is *identical with* the (procedural) utility of the use of the proprietor's initiative and the work itself. (2) Some important part of the satisfaction derived from small-business employment is also from those sources. (3) Job security and workload, while important, do not contribute to these other satisfactions.

All in all, the Benz and Frey (2008) study provide a strong case that, on the one hand, nonpecuniary motives are important in the decision to conduct or be employed by a small business, and on the other hand that questionnaire studies of self-reported satisfaction can be used to measure those nonpecuniary motives.

3.   A Model of Nonpecuniary Motives in Small Business Formation

In previous chapters, we have discussed models that attempt to explain the size distribution of business, including those of Lucas (1978), Evans and Jovanovic (1989) and Cabral and Mata (2003). None of these models takes nonpecuniary motives into account. Hurst and Pugsley (2015), however, have recently proposed a model of a similar kind that does take nonpecuniary motives into account. Whereas Lucas assumes that the talent for management or entrepreneurship is distributed idiosyncratically over the population, Hurst and Pugsley (2015) assume that talent is homogenous, but that the nonpecuniary benefit from running a business is distributed idiosyncratically over the population. Their model uses quite advanced methods, but we will discuss some of the ideas behind it.

As in Lucas' model, an individual may choose to found a business or get a job. An individual's utility is an increasing function of consumption, with diminishing marginal utility, plus a fixed increment (zero or positive) if the person founds a business. Individuals differ in the self-employment increment of utility they derive from business ownership and also in their household wealth. Business ownership is a "normal good." To say that business ownership is a normal good is to say that the "demand" to be an owner increases with increasing wealth. This is a result of the diminishing marginal utility of consumption. They write the utility function as

$$U = \log C + \gamma E \tag{1}$$

where C is consumption, E is 1 if the individual is a business owner and zero otherwise, and γ varies from one person to another.[1]

Given the utility function $U = \log C + \gamma E$

> The marginal utility of consumption is $1/C$.
> The marginal utility of owning a business is constant at γ.
> The wealthier the person is, for a given value of γ, the greater the marginal utility of business ownership is, *relative to that of consumption.*
> Thus, the likelier the person is to form a business.
> Given wealth, however, the bigger γ is, also, the likelier the person is to form a business.

Hurst and Pugsley (2015, p. 21) express the point this way: "At low levels of initial income, the marginal utility of consumption is large relative to the marginal utility of the non-pecuniary benefits of business ownership. Likewise the wealthy pay an opportunity cost to run the business in the form of lost wages because they enjoy running a business relative to other forms of consumption."

In the Hurst and Pugsley (2015) model, the rate of return to a small business will be less, in a market equilibrium, than the rate of return to other forms of investment, so that people who establish businesses actually give up some of the wealth they could otherwise spend on consumption, now or in the future. To picture the trade-off

---

[1]This logarithmic utility function was probably chosen for simplicity, but notice that it is consistent with the consensus interpretation of the evidence on the long-run relationship between income and self-reported happiness (compare Stevenson and Wolfers, 2008) In fact the idea that utility varies proportionately with the logarithm of income is quite an old idea, traceable to F. Y. Edgeworth (1881), *Mathematical Psychics* (C. Kegan Paul), though, according to Stigler (1950), he later rejected it.

in their model, we might indicate the loss of consumption spending for a small businessperson as z. That is, if the person does not form a business he can spend all of his wealth on consumption (now or in the future, and including the consumption of his heirs if he leaves a bequest.) If he does form a business, then he can spend only wealth minus z. Thus, in Figure 1, the horizontal axis shows values of consumption spending from 100,000 to 200,000 per year, if no business is formed. For this range, utility varies from 11.5 to 12.2. We suppose that business proprietorship reduces annual consumption spending by $z = 5{,}000$, 7,000 or 9,000. The vertical axis shows the values of gamma that are large enough that the person would get more utility from business proprietorship than from the greater consumption spending. We see that either a greater gamma

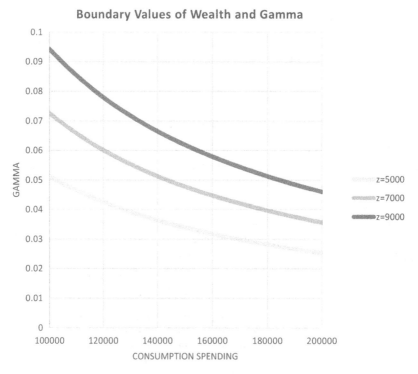

Figure 1. Boundary Values of Wealth and Gamma.

Source: The author's numerical example.

or a greater wealth will shift the person from passive consumption to business proprietorship.

Hurst and Pugsley (2015) also assume that economies of scale differ from one sector of production ("industry") to another. Their approach is typical of 21st century research in economic theory, in that they treat production as the production of *intermediate* goods, which are combined by a black-box market economy to produce a single aggregate consumption good. These assumptions enable them to take a more or less macroeconomic perspective and ignore consumers' choices among different consumer goods (since there is only one). They use integral calculus to capture the assumption that developments in one industry have only negligible influences on developments in other industries.

Capital investment plays no part in their model. Hurst and Pugsley (2015, p. 3) write "...we assume that capital is not needed to start a new business. As a result, there is no role for liquidity constraints in explaining small business entry within our model." The purpose of this is to focus on other things, specifically the nonpecuniary benefit of running a business, as they observe (p. 4) "...our goal is to highlight how a simple model of non-pecuniary benefits of small business ownership has predictions that are similar to many canonical models used in the literature that rely on heterogeneity in ability, luck or liquidity constraints to explain small business entry and dynamics." Production can be carried out by "firms" (corporations) or "small businesses" (family businesses). For a corporation, output is

$$Q = Ah^\theta - b \tag{2}$$

where h is the firm's labor force and the constants differ from industry to industry. This production function gives rise to a long-run average cost function that first declines and then rises, as shown in Figure 2. For this example, the optimum scale is 10 employees. The constants are $A = 100$, $\theta = 0.9$ and $b = 80$.

In Hurst and Pugsley's (2015) stylized model, businesses are of two kinds: corporations and small businesses. A corporation can hire as many employees as it chooses; so, in equilibrium, it will operate

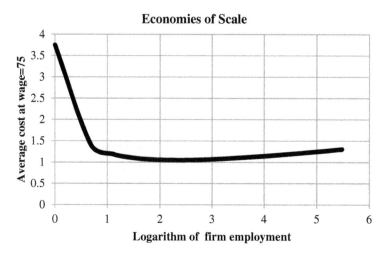

Figure 2. Average Cost with $A = 100$, $\theta = 0.9$ and $b = 80$.

Source: The author's numerical example.

at the optimum scale. However, a "small business" cannot hire labor in this model. The labor force of a small business can be no more than the owner's family can supply. Thus, most "small businesses" will operate at less than the optimal scale. In this model, in equilibrium, individuals sort themselves out so that the wealthier, and those whose taste for business ownership is greater, tend to form "small businesses", and these "small businesses" are more concentrated in industries with a smaller optimal scale. The returns to each industry, "corporation" and "small business" are the same, but for "small businesses" this is the sum of (lesser) profits and a component of utility. In this model, a subsidy to small business is inefficient and favors the rich as against the poor.

There are two obvious weak points in this model: (1) capital investment plays no role; (2) small businesses cannot hire labor. A more "realistic" — and only slightly more complex — model might assume instead that (1) business foundation requires investment proportionate to total employment; (2) hiring and scale for a small business are limited by the founder's initial wealth. Hurst and Pugsley (2015, pp. 29–30) write "One attempt to do this . . . introduces preference heterogeneity to an otherwise standard model of entrepreneurship with credit frictions [that might result in liquidity constraints]. The preference heterogeneity, similar to the form in this paper, generates non-pecuniary compensation from business ownership that effectively shifts the productivity and wealth thresholds for which business ownership is viable. He uses the model to determine to what extent the distribution of firm size is driven by selection on tastes, and finds using the structural model that roughly 40 percent of the distribution of firms (all very small firms) would not be viable without some further non-pecuniary compensation from running the business."

The Hurst and Pugsley (2015) model is an important advance in our understanding of small business, and should be the basis of further work. As they are aware, nonpecuniary benefits are not the only influence on the size distribution of business, but they are an important one. Models that do not allow for nonpecuniary benefits are likely to give biased results. As Hurst and Pugsley (2015, p. 4) write "This complicates the inferences made in many empirical studies that look for exogenous changes in wealth and subsequent business entry as evidence of binding liquidity constraints." Further, their conclusion that subsidies to small businesses are regressive is very likely correct, even if their explanation for the correlation of business proprietorship with wealth is not correct or not complete. If such subsidies do not result in increases in productivity, then the case for them is very weak. Nonpecuniary motivation is no less important for small business than profit motivation is — and probably no more important, but not to be neglected for that.

4. Summary

We have seen evidence in earlier chapters that nonpecuniary motivation is important in small business. This chapter enlarges the point in two ways. First, we see that questionnaire studies that ask people how satisfied they are with their jobs, salaries and with their lives overall can give us insights about the average nonpecuniary benefits obtained by business owners and employees of small business. But those same studies make it clear that much of the difference in "happiness" is simply the result of idiosyncratic differences between individuals. The remarkable diversity of small business has for decades been confronted by models based precisely on the idiosyncratic differences among individuals with respect to talent, human capital or wealth. Recent work takes the same approach in bringing idiosyncratic nonpecuniary motives into the model, and this seems a promising area for future development.

Discussion Questions

(1) How may questionnaire studies be used to study the subjective satisfactions of people with their lives, jobs and/or businesses? Criticize this approach.

(2) Define "procedural utility" as the term is used in the paper by Benz and Frey (2008).

(3) Criticize the use of regression methods in the paper by Benz and Frey (2008).

(4) What evidence does the paper by Benz and Frey (2008) use to argue that "procedural utility" accounts for the greater job satisfaction of proprietors and employees in smaller businesses?

(5) If people differ in the satisfaction they derive from being business proprietors, and also in wealth, what implications will this have for the decisions of people in general to become business proprietors? How is this influenced by economies of scale?

(6) What does it mean to say that business ownership is a normal good? Is there a simple way to express this in an individual's "utility function?"

(7) Assess the overall importance of nonpecuniary benefits in determining the extent and distribution of small business ownership, and give reasons for your assessment.

References

Benz, M. and Frey, B. S. (2008), "Being Independent Is a Great Thing: Subjective Evaluations of Self-Employment and Hierarchy," *Economica*, New Series, v. 75, no. 298, pp. 362–383.

Blanchflower, D. and Oswald, A. J. (2004), "Well-Being Over Time in Britain and the USA," *Journal of Public Economics*, v. 88, no. 7–8, pp. 1359–386.

Cabral, L. M. B. and Mata, J. (2003), "On the Evolution of the Firm Size Distribution: Facts and Theory," *The American Economic Review*, v. 93, no. 4, pp. 1075–1090.

Clark, A. E. and Oswald, A. J. (1994), "Unhappiness and Unemployment," *Economic Journal*, v. 104, no. 424, pp. 648–659.

Easterlin, R. A. (1974), "Does Economic Growth Improve the Human Lot?," in *Nations and Households in Economic Growth: Essays in Honour of Moses Abramovitz*, P. A. David and M. W. Reder (eds.) (New York: Academic Press Inc.).

Easterlin, R. A. (2001), "Income and Happiness: Towards a Unified Theory," *The Economic Journal*, v. 111, no. 473, pp. 465–484.

Easterlin, R. A. (2003), "Explaining Happiness," *Proceedings of the National Academy of Sciences of the United States of America*, v. 100, no. 19, pp. 11176–11183.

Evans, D. S. and Jovanovic, B. (1989), "An Estimated Model of Entrepreneurial Choice under Liquidity Constraints," *Journal of Political Economy*, v. 97, no. 4, pp. 808–827.

Frey, B. S. and Stutzer, A. (2005), "Beyond Outcomes: Measuring Procedural Utility," *Oxford Economic Papers*, v. 57, pp. 90–111.

Hurst, E. G. and Pugsley, B. W. (2015), "Wealth, Tastes, and Entrepreneurial Choice," NBER Working Paper No. 21644, Issued in October 2015.

Lucas, Jr., R. E. (1978), "On the Size Distribution of Business Firms," *The Bell Journal of Economics*, v. 9, no. 2, pp. 508–523.

Stevenson, B. and Wolfers, J. (2008), "Economic Growth and Subjective Well-Being: Reassessing The Easterlin Paradox," National Bureau of Economic Research, Working Paper 14282, http://www.nber.org/papers/w14282.

Stigler, G. J. (1950), "The Development of Utility Theory II," *The Journal of Political Economy*, v. 58, no. 5, pp. 373–396.

Tella, R. D. and MacCulloch, R. (2006), "Some Uses of Happiness Data in Economics," *The Journal of Economic Perspectives*, v. 20, no. 1, pp. 25–46.

Chapter 13

Small Business, Women and
People of Color

We have seen (in Chapter 1) that women, African-Americans and Hispanics in the United States are less likely to be business proprietors than to be employees. In the late 20th and the early 21st centuries, it has been a major policy goal in the United States and some other countries to increase the role of women and people of color in small business. This chapter will explore the status of women and people of color in small business, along with some of the policy responses and some attempt to understand the reasons for the difference in status between people of different kinds in a market economy.

Differences in small business opportunities by gender seem to be worldwide. According to a conference at the Gerald Ford School of Public Policy at the University of Michigan in 2009, "the fact that women everywhere play a less than proportionate entrepreneurial role suggests, on the one hand, the existence of gender-based obstacles and, on the other hand, the potential for major welfare gains if the reasons could be understood and addressed through economic policy" (Acs *et al.*, 2011). "The basic facts about women's rates of participation in entrepreneurship are stark. Regardless of whether 'entrepreneurship' is defined in terms of 'new venture creation', 'business ownership' or 'self-employment' a higher proportion of men than women engage in this activity in industrialized economies."

Klapper and Parker (2011) report that "...various government and institutional policies have been tried in an effort to increase the number of women borrowers. These include financial literacy training programs; public awareness workshops; business development services (Bangladesh and South Africa); promotions of sectors dominated by women entrepreneurs (Bangladesh, India, West Africa, Chile, the Philippines and Canada); marketing support; business training (Peru, India); legal aid; and female business networks." The authors of this literature review (Klapper and Parker, 2011, p. 249), however, attribute these differences largely to differences in the access of women to financial capital.

Issues of this kind do differ from country to country. In the island nation of Fiji, for example, 52 percent of the population are native Fijian, but 42 percent are Indo-Fijians, that is, the descendants of people transported from India to Fiji in colonial times, largely (probably) as indentured laborers. However, "most of the businesses are run by Indo-Fijians." Further, they are "mostly married and males. The gender bias again reflects dominant role of males as heads of businesses in small developing societies" (Reddy, 2007). In a study in India, it was found that female-owned firms face particular barriers to growth (Coad and Tamvada, 2012). These examples could be extended: differences in the status of women are shown for many countries, and differences among ethnic or social groups must be quite common as well. Once again, though, this chapter will focus mainly on the United States, where the issues and policies directed to them have been extensively studied.

1. Differences in Status in Employment and Proprietorship

It is also well known that women earn less as employees than do males. Mary Bowler (1999, p. 16) writes, "Although women earned just 76 percent of what men did in 1998, the gap has closed considerably since 1979, the result of a 14-percent increase in women's real earnings and a 7-percent decline in men's.... Despite the relative improvement for women, earnings disparities with men continued, whether comparisons are made by age, education, or occupation." Further, "As a group, white workers earned more than blacks or Hispanics." These quotations are from a study in 1999. More recently, (Bureau of Labor Statistics, BLS, 2014, p. 6) "Women who were paid hourly rates had median hourly earnings of $12.12, which was 87 percent of the median for men paid by the hour." Women's earnings overall remain less than 90 percent of those of men (p. 35), although there are differences by age and race and national origin (p. 36). Figure 1 below shows the limited progress of women's wages in recent decades.

This raises two related questions. First, could women and members of minorities escape from these low wages by starting small businesses? Loscocco and Robinson (1991, p. 511) write "Small-business ownership has always represented a potential escape route for frustrated employees. It is particularly attractive to members of disadvantaged groups whose opportunities as wage and salary workers are seriously limited." But, second, would they face obstacles to success in small business similar to those they face in the labor markets? Again quoting Loscocco and Robinson (1991, p. 513), "As recently as 1984, woman-owned businesses constituted only about 9.5 percent of all U.S. firms. . . . Perhaps most important, the majority of

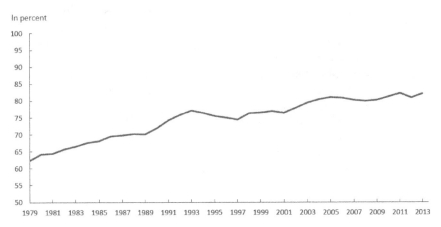

Figure 1. Women's Earnings as a Percentage of Men's.

Source: Bureau of Labor Statistics (2014).

businesses owned by women are low in profitability compared to those owned by men.... In 1980, the average business receipts of women's sole proprietorships was only 27 percent of the average for men's sole proprietorships. Thus, despite the health of the U.S. small-business sector, ownership does not permit women levels of economic success that are comparable to men's." Table 1 shows how the situation has changed in the 21st century.

Taking a sociological perspective, Loscocco and Robinson (1991, pp. 514–515) write

> Drawing from past work on gender stratification as well as small businesses, we propose an explanatory framework that identifies four sets of barriers, some of which exert their influence prior to ownership and some of which are ongoing. Specifically, we identify as key variables gender segregation, skill deficits, lack of access to capital and government contracts, and family responsibilities.
>
> Across a broad spectrum of industries and occupations, women are segregated in the low-paid, low-prestige positions that men do not want.... We expect that a major part of the explanation of U.S. women's lesser success in the small-business arena can be attributed to their concentration in the least profitable fields. A major tenet of sociological research on small business is that opportunities become available to disadvantaged groups when their more privileged counterparts define a particular niche as undesirable.... From this perspective, the tremendous growth of the service sector in the United States... has opened up ownership opportunities for women because men are not as interested in pursuing such opportunities.
>
> Moreover, small-business research emphasizes the strong link between employment field and small-business type.... Women, drawing on their experiences in "female work," paid and unpaid, may choose small businesses that draw on female-typed skills, and the services and products they offer may be as devalued as female-typed occupations....
>
> Business and managerial skills developed in employment contexts are extremely important to small-business success....
>
> As owners, women depend on those who control capital and contracts, who are most likely to be men....

"Patterns of small business economic success, as noted by Loscocco and Robinson (1991) ... are consistent with gender queuing

Table 1. Gender Differences in Business Ownership.
Number and Characteristics

	Women-owned[1]			Equally Men-/Women-owned			Men-owned		
	Number	2007 to 2012 % Change	Share	Number	2007 to 2012 % Change	Share	Number	2007 to 2012 % Change	Share
U.S. Firms	9,932,434	27.5%	36.2%	2,495,756	−45.8%	9.1%	14,999,525	7.9%	54.8%
Receipts of all firms	$1.62 trillion	35.1%	11.2%	$1.36 trillion	6.7%	9.4%	$11.34 trillion	33.8%	78.6%
Employer firms	1,052,876	15.7%	20.1%	779,149	−25.8%	14.9%	3,401,293	5.3%	65.0%
Receipts of employer firms	$1.38 trillion	36.4%	10.3%	$1.24 trillion	13.2%	9.2%	$10.67 trillion	34.9%	79.6%
Employment	8,982,588	19.4%	14.5%	7,093,515	−11.9%	11.4%	45,768,326	11.5%	73.8%
Payroll	$290 billion	35.3%	11.1%	$213 billion	−.9%	11.1%	$1.90 trillion	25.8%	77.8%

Source: National Women's Business Council (2015).

perspectives . . . because women-owned businesses are overrepresented in the least profitable industries and sectors." While Bird and Sapp (2004, pp. 15–23) in this paper document the complexity of the relationship between gender and economic opportunity, they conclude that "These findings are consistent with gender queuing arguments. The smaller gender gap in small business success in rural places appears to reflect declining opportunities for rural owners overall. But rural men-owned businesses also appear to have an advantage over women-owned businesses in drawing customers. In urban areas, men-owned businesses appear to be better positioned than women-owned businesses to take advantage of economic recovery (p. 23).

A British study found that (Rosa *et al.*, 1996, p. 475) ". . . the value of assets in female businesses is significantly lower than in male firms. Access to and control over resources may also play a part in inhibiting women from seeking lateral expansion." A more recent report (Cantwell, 2014, p. 3) to the American Senate also found that "In the area of capital, studies find that women do not get sufficient access to loans and venture capital. Women account for only 16 percent of conventional small business loans and 17 percent of [Government guaranteed] SBA loans even though they represent 30 percent of all small companies." In addition, they found (p. 4) that "women entrepreneurs still do not have equal access to government contracts, . . ." despite longstanding government policies designed to open those opportunities to them. Similar disadvantages can also limit the participation in small business ownership by people of color, Hispanics and other members of less advantaged minority groups in the United States and elsewhere.

These barriers to women's participation in small business proprietorship have justified a number of policies of the United States and other governments to encourage women-owned and minority-owned businesses. In the United States, district offices of the Small Business Administration provide consulting services with particular emphasis on small business startups by women and members of less advantaged minority groups. The Small Business Administration also cooperates with banks and nonprofits to assure that small business startups and expansions can obtain loan capital even if they would not qualify for a conventional loan. These do not, in general, prefer women or minority members, but to the extent that those groups might be less likely to qualify for conventional loans, the loan programs could nevertheless "level the playing field" somewhat. Finally, there has been a good deal of stress on programs to shift more government contracts to firms owned by women, nonwhite and Hispanic people, though there is little evidence of success in this. All in all, the proportion of small businesses owned by women has increased substantially in the last generation, but it would be hasty to attribute this to the favorable government policies, as it has also been a period of profound cultural change, and that must also be a factor in the growth of women-owned businesses.

2. Some Useful Theory: Nash Equilibrium

The gender queuing theory that Loscocco and Robinson (1991) share with Bird and Sapp (2004) will seem to an economist to pose the questions, not to answer them. In fairness, though, those questions challenge the economist's perspective. An economist would like to explain it all by reference to the equilibrium of supply and demand, but supply and demand probably cannot do the job. We might, however, be able to find an explanation in a related concept of equilibrium, one derived from game theory: Nash equilibrium.[1] This idea comes to us from Nobel Laureate (1994) John Nash. Accordingly, we will digress on Nash equilibrium before returning to the economics of women and members of minorities and small business.

The best-known example of Nash equilibrium is an example called "The Prisoner's Dilemma," so the digression will begin with that example to introduce the reader to Nash equilibrium more generally. The following is quoted from my own game theory textbook

---

[1]Subgame perfect equilibrium, considered in an earlier chapter, is one particular kind of Nash equilibrium. In this section, we will consider a different kind, which relies on the expression of the "game" as a table rather than a decision tree.

(McCain, 2014):

> [T]wo burglars, Bob and Al, are captured near the scene of a burglary and are given the "third degree" separately by the police. Each has to choose whether or not to confess and implicate the other. If neither man confesses, then both will serve one year on a charge of carrying a concealed weapon. If each confesses and implicates the other, both will go to prison for 10 years. However, if one burglar confesses and implicates the other, and the other burglar does not confess, the one who has collaborated with the police will go free, while the other burglar will go to prison for 20 years on the maximum charge.
>
> The strategies in this case are: confess or don't confess. The payoffs (penalties, actually) are the sentences served. We can express all this compactly in a "payoff table" of a kind that has become pretty standard in game theory. Here is the payoff table for the Prisoners' Dilemma game:

The table is read like this: Each prisoner chooses one of the two strategies. In effect, Al chooses a column and Bob chooses a row. The two numbers in each cell tell the outcomes for the two prisoners when the corresponding pair of strategies is chosen. The number to the left of the comma tells the payoff to the person who chooses the rows (Bob) while the number to the right of the cell tells the payoff to the person who chooses the columns (Al). Thus (reading down the first column) if they both confess, each gets 10 years, but if Al confesses and Bob does not, Bob gets 20 and Al goes free.

> So: how to solve this game? What strategies are "rational" if both men want to minimize the time they spend in jail? Al might reason as follows: "Two things can happen: Bob can confess or Bob can keep quiet. Suppose Bob confesses. Then I get 20 years if I don't confess, 10 years if I do, so in that case it's best to confess. On the

Table 2. The Prisoner's Dilemma.

		Al	
		Confess	Don't
Bob	Confess	10 years, 10 years	0, 20 years
	Don't	20 years, 0	1 year, 1 year

other hand, if Bob doesn't confess, and I don't either, I get a year; but in that case, if I confess I can go free. Either way, it's best if I confess. Therefore, I'll confess."

But Bob can and presumably will reason in the same way — so that they both confess and go to prison for 10 years each. Yet, if they had acted "irrationally," and kept quiet, they each could have gotten off with one year each.

The Prisoner's Dilemma provides an example of Nash equilibrium. Notice that, when Al chooses "confess," Bob is better off to choose "confess" for 10 years rather than "don't" for 20. Thus "confess" is Bob's *best response* to a strategy of "confess" for Al. But, similarly, Al is better off choosing "confess" when Bob chooses "confess" — that is his best response also. Thus, when each chooses "confess," each is choosing his best response to the other's best response to his strategy. This is what defines a Nash equilibrium. In a Nash equilibrium, each "player" chooses her or his best response to the strategy or strategies chosen by the other player or players.

What is striking about the Prisoner's Dilemma is that although each person is making the decision that is in his self-interest in the circumstances, both are worse off than they would be if they both chose the other strategy. "Best response does *not* mean best result." This is what has made the Prisoner's Dilemma influential and is the reason it is widely studied. But it is a very special case in a number of ways. In particular, it has only one Nash equilibrium. This is not always true — there are some pretty simple games that have more than one Nash equilibrium. Here is an example. We will call it the complementary effort (CE) game.

For this game, two individuals must work together to get a result that benefits them both. Each must make an effort — and the efforts of one increase the productivity of the efforts of the other, that is, the efforts are complementary. If each makes an effort, then together they produce an outcome that is worth a payoff of 10 to each of them. (For this game, the payoffs are rated on a scale of 10, so 10 is just the maximum payoff in the game.) However, effort is costly — it may be unpleasant or require some scarce resources, or both — so if either person makes an effort, that person's payoff is reduced by 3. Thus,

Table 3. A Complementary Effort Game.

		B	
		Make an effort	Don't
A	Make an effort	7, 7	−1, 2
	Don't	2, −1	0, 0

if each makes an effort, the payoff to each is $10 - 3 = 7$, as shown in Table 3.

If only one of them makes an effort, then the value of the product to each of them is less than half. (That is what it means to say their efforts are complementary.) It is just 2 for each of them. Then the one who makes no effort gets a payoff of 2, but the one who makes an effort gets a payoff of $2 - 3 = -1$. This is shown in the upper right and lower left cells of Table 3. Finally, if nobody makes any effort, the payoff to each individual is 0, as shown in the lower left cell of Table 3.

Now we ask, has this game any Nash equilibrium? When each of the two chooses to "make an effort," we have a Nash equilibrium. A's best response to B's strategy of "make an effort" is to do the same, for 7, rather than "Don't" for 2. And conversely, B is also choosing the best response to A's strategy. But the lower right cell also corresponds to a Nash equilibrium. If B chooses "Don't," then A is better off to choose "Don't" for zero rather than minus one, and conversely "Don't" is B's best response when A chooses "Don't." In this game, we have a Nash equilibrium whenever both individuals choose the same strategy, and for that reason it is called a "coordination game." The CE game is one instance of a coordination game — there are others with different properties — but this one has some properties that are of interest to us.

- The Nash equilibrium at the upper left is Pareto-preferred to the one at the lower right. That is, both individuals are better off in the Nash equilibrium at the upper left than they are at the lower right. When a shift from one situation to another makes at least some individuals better off and none worse off, the new situation is said (in economics) to be preferred in the sense due to Vilfredo Pareto. Conversely, the Nash equilibrium at the lower right is Pareto-inferior to the one at the upper left.

- Each individual has a problem of deciding which Nash equilibrium is likely to be realized. This problem does not arise in the Prisoner's Dilemma, since it has only one equilibrium. To be more exact, to decide which strategy is the best response, A must make a judgment as to which equilibrium B thinks will occur, because that will determine what strategy B chooses and so determine A's best response. And B needs to make a judgment as to which Nash equilibrium A thinks B expects, since that will determine what strategy A chooses and so determine B's best response. And that means A needs to make a judgment about what B's judgment as to what A thinks B thinks the Nash equilibrium will be. . . .

The infinite regression in our second bullet point may seem to be a deep problem. From one point of view it is, and a more advanced discussion will be reserved for Appendix A. Students with some background in game theory may want to read Appendix A for a better understanding of the game-theoretic interpretation of economic discrimination. However, Nobel Laureate (2005) Thomas Schelling (1960) pointed out that people solve this deep problem in some pretty simple ways. In deciding the best response, A will be aware of some signals that may suggest an answer. The signals may not have anything to do with the payoffs of the game. To take a somewhat classical example, A may believe that when sunspots are near the top of their cycle, it is a good time to "Make an effort," and when sunspots are in the lower part of their cycle, it is not. If B knows that A believes this, and both know that sunspots are near the top of their cycle, then both have reasons to choose "Make an effort," and that Nash equilibrium is likely to be realized.

The signal might, in principle, be something about the other individual. One of the two might have big ears or blue eyes or some such, and the other might take that as a signal. Suppose, for example, that A believes that "Whenever I get in this kind of a game with a person who has big ears, 'Don't' is the Nash equilibrium that is realized." Suppose also that B has big ears, and (this is crucial!) that B knows that A believes that the "Don't" equilibrium will be played when the person at B's position has big ears. Then B knows that A will choose "don't," and accordingly, B's best response is "Don't." In turn, acting on his (baseless!) belief, A chooses "Don't," and it is his best response. More than that, A's experience — that in fact B chose "Don't" — seems to support his belief, even though the belief has no basis in the "rules of the game" nor in objective fact.

It seems that beliefs of this kind can be very persistent, *because* they correspond to Nash equilibria. Such beliefs can be very persistent *despite* the fact that they make both parties worse off. Of course, if A were to try the experiment of playing "Make an Effort" and B knew that A would do that, then B could prove A's beliefs once and all to be baseless and indeed wrong; but if A's beliefs are widespread, then B may never get the opportunity to prove that the beliefs are wrong — nor the opportunity to gain experience that could influence the payoffs, something this example does not allow for.

In the real world, we have much more than two parties and two strategies. But we shall not attempt to describe the real world in such detail here. Instead — it seems safer — we will close with a story about an imaginary world, to show how the concept of a Pareto-inferior Nash equilibrium might be applied to a much more complex world.

Let us imagine a universe in which "everybody knows" (that is, most people believe) that people with big ears are ineffective at business management and better adapted to other occupations, such as goatherding. Thus, they believe, businesses headed by people with big ears are significantly more likely to fail than other businesses.

Suppose, nevertheless, that a person with big ears proposes to start a business with a business plan that would, in itself, be promising. The aspiring businessperson goes to a bank to ask for a loan. Believing that businesses headed by people with big ears are more likely to fail, so that the bank would lose money, the banker (even if she herself has big ears) rationally refuses to make the loan. Established business people who might form business-to-business (B2B) relationships with the new business rationally choose not to, since they may face losses if the new business fails — which, they believe, it is likely to do. As a result of this inability to obtain finance and business partners, the new business fails — providing more evidence in support of "what everyone knows."

Most people with big ears, anticipating all this, rationally choose to become goatherds. The few exceptions who do establish successful businesses are in goat-connected fields, like shearing or spinning goat wool, where their experience gives them some advantage. These fields, being crowded with competitors who have few options, are not very profitable. That is, we observe ear-size segregation. Notice that everybody (except the one big-eared person who applied for the business loan) is rationally choosing the "best response" to the rational decisions of others. This is a Nash equilibrium. But there may be other Nash equilibria.

Now, think of a less imaginary universe in which "Everybody knows" (that is, most people believe) that people with big and small ears are, on the average, equally effective business managers. Thus, they believe, businesses headed by big-eared people are no more likely to fail than other businesses. Then the banker has no reason to refuse a loan for a good business plan. B2B links can be formed just as usefully for a big-eared person as for a person without big ears. Big-eared businesses fail at about the same rate as other businesses, which provides evidence that the belief in equal business aptitude regardless of ear size is correct. There is no ear-size segregation and rational big-eared people choose to start businesses about as often as anybody else. Since the resource of the talent of big-eared people does not go to waste (as in the imaginary universe), everybody is better off than they would be in the imaginary universe. Since, again, everybody has chosen the "best response" to the rational decisions of others, this is another Nash equilibrium. It is a better, "Pareto preferable," Nash equilibrium.

I have chosen the example of big-eared goatherds precisely because, to the best of my knowledge, there is no discrimination against people with big ears (and the goat-farmers I know seem to do OK for profits. Yes, I have met one or two.) This is not just to avoid offense, although I certainly hope I have not offended. It is also to point out that the Pareto-preferable Nash equilibrium is not just utopian — some of us are living in it! It may be overoptimistic in one way. The real-world game is not symmetrical as the one in Table 3 is. If everyone had equal opportunities, white male businessmen would face more competition, and that increase in competition could force them to work a little harder to keep the business going. They might find themselves with a smaller slice of the pie. But it is true too that a better use of resources will increase the size of the pie. That, after all, is the argument of free-market economics in general: since a more efficient use of resources will increase total production, even those who lose *relatively* need not lose absolutely. And that argument applies no less to equal opportunities for women, people of color and Hispanics than it does to other policy changes that increase the efficiency of resource use.

3. What Does This Mean for Policy?

The game-theory model of "ear-size segregation" may or may not supply a plausible explanation for what Loscocco and Robinson (1991) call gender segregation. Because it draws on a kind of equilibrium theory, it is an explanation that economists will probably find workable. But — what does it tell us about policy? We can observe that the elimination of the less-efficient Nash equilibrium would improve both overall productivity and the distribution of the product, and that is reason enough[2] to seek policies that would realize the better equilibrium. But how to do it?

It is easy enough to say that public policies for this purpose must "change the rules of the game," but we need to be more specific. Since the less-efficient equilibrium depends on particular "signals," such as big ears, policies might attempt to make business decisions "blind" to the relevant signals. This could be quite difficult for visible

---

[2]This applies the "Little criterion." See Little (2002, pp. viii–x). As Little observes, this presupposes a value judgment on distribution — in this case a judgment that distribution ought to be neutral to such things as skin color, gender and dialect — in addition to the rather complex value judgments expressed words like "efficient" and "productivity."

characteristics such as skin color and gender, and, conversely, that suggests a reason why "visible" groups have often been discriminated against. And even to the extent that such a policy might be effective, it would not necessarily succeed — the inefficient Nash equilibrium remains a Nash equilibrium and if some signals are suppressed, the decision-makers will find other signals to inform their decisions. These signals may very well lead to an equally bad or even worse equilibrium. (In a complex game like the one we play in the real world, there may be many more than two equilibria.) Now, at the very least, the government might make its own decisions "blind" to discriminatory signals and, at the same time, direct those decisions toward the more productive outcomes. We have seen that this sort of idea has played some role in policies of the United States government, although with limited success.

In a more positive sense, government policy might target the "segregated" population with programs that would serve to assure an equal chance at success for their businesses, such as targeted loan programs, subsidized educational activities to assure that the "segregated" population can obtain skills that others might derive from other sources, and that would encourage and reward B2B contacts and services among and with businesses owned or directed by members of the segregated community. Policies of this kind, too, have played a role in the activities of the U.S. government. To the extent that they succeed, so that the number of business successes by people of the "segregated" community increases, evidence would be supplied that "what everybody knows" ain't so — that in fact there are no differences in the business ability between the differentiated groups — and so realize the better Nash equilibrium in more and more cases. Perhaps the gradual progress we have seen is evidence that is happening.

4. Concluding Summary

The smaller number of enterprises headed by women, nonwhites and Hispanics seems to reflect special difficulties that they face, and that should be removed. This has been a target of public policy in the United States and some other countries for decades. The number of women-headed small businesses has increased relatively rapidly, though there is still a "gap." It is not clear whether this is a result of public policy or of cultural change, or both.

Appendix A. Games of Incomplete Information and Discriminatory Equilibria

In the example in Section 2 of this chapter, agent A believes that the less preferred Nash equilibrium is to be expected if A's counterpart, B, is a big-eared person, even though there is nothing about B *directly relevant to the game* that is different from A. That seems an odd and arbitrary belief. That it is odd and arbitrary doesn't mean that people would not believe it — people believe many odd and arbitrary things, especially on the basis of experience and "common sense." But people also often believe that others are different than they are, and justify their beliefs about *what the other person will do* with other beliefs about *what kind of person the other person is*. Game theory teaches us that this can be fallacious — that people may do different things although they are just alike, because otherwise they could not arrive at a Nash equilibrium (McCain, 2014, pp. 144–147, 207–211, 213–216). But game theory also offers some tools to deal with a case when there can be differences in the games the agents believe they are playing.

Suppose, once again, that A believes that, because of something about B, a "Don't" Nash equilibrium is most likely. In particular, suppose that A believes B is "lazy." What could that mean? If B finds effort more unpleasant or costly than A does, then B might supply less effort in the same circumstances. Suppose in particular the cost of effort to B is not 3 but 9. Then, the payoffs are as shown in Table A.1. If so, then, even when A makes an effort, B is better off to choose "Don't" for 2 rather than 1, and there is only one Nash equilibrium, the one at the lower right.

In a game like those in Tables 3 and A.1, people can observe their own payoffs, but may not be able to observe the payoffs of others. Thus, A can only rely on judgment to estimate the payoffs to B for any choices of strategies, and conversely. If some players do

Table A.1. A Complementary Effort Game with a "Lazy" Player B.

		B	
		Make an effort	Don't
A	Make an effort	7, 1	−1, 2
	Don't	2, −7	0, 0

not know what the payoffs (or strategies) are, then we have a game of incomplete information — and that is a deep problem indeed. But Nobel Laureate (1994) John Harsanyi (1967) has shown us how, with a little simplification, we can deal with games of incomplete information. The simplification has already been sneaked into the example: the idea that players may be of more than one type. Then, in order to make a rational decision between the strategies, each person must make some judgment as to what type the other player or players are. A player in a game such as this might base her judgments on an estimate of probabilities, and since the best mathematical rule for estimating probabilities is called "Bayes' Rule"; this will lead to a "Bayesian Nash Equilibrium."

Specifically, we suppose

(1) It is possible that players in this game are of more than one "type," and specifically just two types: lazy and nonlazy players. (It is also possible that there is only one type — possibility is not fact.)
(2) This possibility is known to both players.
(3) A believes that if B has big ears, then it is very probable that B is a lazy player, so that his expected value for playing "Don't" is greater than his expected value for playing "Make an effort."
(4) B is in fact a nonlazy player, and there is no correlation between ear size and laziness. Indeed, so far as B knows there are no lazy players.
(5) B knows that A believes that it is very probable that a big-eared person is lazy and that this will lead him to choose "Don't" as his best response.

Knowing that A mistakenly believes B to be lazy, B's rational strategy choice is "Don't," and that leaves us with the Pareto-inferior Nash equilibrium in the game that is actually being played. But it also reinforces A's mistaken belief! A, who is a "Positive Economist," reasons "My hypothesis that B is of a different type is consistent with what I observe, so I will treat it as a proven hypothesis until I observe contrary evidence." Such hypotheses can be very persistent indeed.

It was Nobel Laureate John Harsanyi (1967) who pioneered this approach, in which "games" of imperfect information are games in which there may be players of more than one type, and in which each player must make a judgment as to what type his counterpart is. The example here can be an illustration of what Robert Aumann (1999) called "interactive epistemology." As Chant and Ernst (2008, p. 559) note, Aumann's interactive epistemology leads to some propositions about knowledge that are "highly dubious," but Aumann's theory can be applied, with caution, without making use of those dubious propositions. For this example, it is sufficient to distinguish between knowledge and belief. Everyone believes what he knows to be true, but may believe some other things as well, and some of those things might prove to be false. The example of black swans is often used to illustrate this. In the wild, black swans exist only in Australia, so before Australia was explored, Europeans (and Africans and Asians) might well have believed the proposition "All swans are white," and they had good evidence to base the belief on. But it is beliefs that enter into business decisions, especially when the questions have no certain answers.[3] In Aumann (1999) part 2, belief is relative and is measured by subjective probabilities. In particular, a person may assign probability 1, the highest degree of belief, to a proposition that is not known and may not be so. If experience gives the person no evidence that would require revision of that probability or of his strategy, then the result is a Bayesian Nash equilibrium. Of course,

---

[3]This concept of probability has been prominent, but also controversial, in the 20th century. Aumann's objective in his paper was to reconcile that concept with another concept of probability that was also prominent, and less controversial, in the 20th century. It is here that Aumann's "highly dubious" propositions come in.

people are often less rational than Bayes' rule prescribes, and cling to their beliefs even in the presence of negative evidence, but the point of this discussion is that *even if they are perfectly rational*, the Pareto-inferior Nash equilibrium may persist.

Discussion Questions

(1) Discuss the role of young and old people, women and members of historically disadvantaged minorities in small business and in government policy toward small business.

(2) Economic theory suggests that if some people are paid less than others as employees, those who are paid less will have more incentive to choose self-employment, and so we would expect to see a higher proportion of those people as business proprietors. Evaluate this hypothesis.

(3) Contrast the Nash equilibrium and the market equilibrium of supply and demand as alternative explanations of the different economic status of people of different kinds.

References

Acs, Z. J., Bardasi, E., Estrin, S. and Svejnar, J. (2011), "Introduction to Special Issue of '*Small Business Economics*' on Female Entrepreneurship in Developed and Developing Economies," *Small Business Economics*, v. 37, no. 4, pp. 393–396. See p. 234, 248.

Aumann, R. J. (1999), "Interactive Epistemology I and II," *International Journal of Game Theory*, v. 28, pp. 263–314.

Bird, S. R. and Sapp, S. G. (2004), "Understanding the Gender Gap in Small Business Success: Urban and Rural Comparisons," *Gender and Society*, v. 18, no. 1, pp. 5–28.

Bowler, M. (1999), "Women's Earnings: An Overview," *Monthly Labor Review*, v. 122, no. 12, pp. 13–21.

Bureau of Labor Statistics. (2014), Report 1051: *Highlights of Women's Earnings in 2013*, December.

Cantwell, M. (2014), Chairman, U. S. Senate Committee on Small Business and Entrepreneurship, *21st Century Barriers to Women's Entrepreneurship*, U.S. Senate.

Chant, S. R. and Ernst, Z. (2008), "Epistemic Conditions for Collective Action," *Mind*, v. 117, no. 476, pp. 549–573.

Coad, A. and Tamvada, J. P. (2012), "Firm Growth and Barriers to Growth Among Small Firms in India," *Small Business Economics*, v. 39, no. 2, pp. 383–400. See pp. 383–384.

Harsanyi, J. C. (1967), "Games with Incomplete Information Played by 'Bayesian' Players," *Management Science*, v. 14. See Part I, pp. 159–183; Part II, pp. 320–334; Part III, pp 486–502.

Klapper, L. F. and Parker, S. C. (2011), "Gender and the Business Environment for New Firm Creation," *The World Bank Research Observer*, v. 26, no. 2, pp. 237–257. See p. 239, 249.

Little, I. M. D. (2002), *A Critique of Welfare Economics*, reissued (Oxford University Press).

Loscocco, K. A. and Robinson, J. (1991), "Barriers to Women's Small-Business Success in the United States," *Gender and Society*, v. 5, n. 4 (December), pp. 511–532.

McCain, R. A. (2014), *Game Theory: A Nontechnical Introduction to the Analysis of Strategy* (World Scientific).

McCain, R. A. (2014), *Game Theory: A Nontechnical Introduction to the Analysis of Strategy*, 3rd Edition (Singapore: World Scientific), pp. 144–147, 207–211, 213–216.

National Women's Business Council. (2015), *Fact Sheet: Gender Differences in U.S. Business*, available at https://www.nwbc.gov/facts/new-fact-sheet-gender-differences-us-businesses (accessed on 20/12/2015).

Reddy, M. (2007), "Small Business in Small Economies: Constraints and Opportunities for Growth," *Social and Economic Studies*, v. 56, no. 1/2, pp. 304–321. See p. 309.

Rosa, P., Carter, S. and Hamilton, D. (1996), "Gender as a Determinant of Small Business Performance: Insights from a British Study," *Small Business Economics*, v. 8, no. 6, pp. 463–478.

Schelling, T. (1960), *The Strategy of Conflict* (Cambridge: Harvard University Press).

Chapter 14

Economic Policy for Small Business

Economics is a policy science. One of the best reasons to explore the economics of small business is to form a basis for the evaluation of policy. This chapter will focus mainly on the United States, and specifically on activities of and coordinated through the Small Business Administration (SBA), since most federal public policy for small business is administered through that agency, and many state, local, and nonprofit and voluntary activities in favor of small business are coordinated with the SBA. Some comparisons with other countries will be given.

1. Public Policy and the SBA

How do we approach the study of public policy? To quote — once again! — Roger A. McCain (2015, p. 4)

> Public policy is a pragmatic field. The pragmatic perspective leads to a view of public policy as an outcome of a *process*, and public policy *analysis* is often carried on in terms of the *public policy process*. We might sketch the public policy process roughly as follows: (1) A *problem* is identified which seems to call for public initiative as a solution. (2) Alternative solutions are proposed. (3) Solutions are evaluated, and to the extent possible, the most promising solution specified. At this point the process may be abandoned, if it is found that the best solution does not require public initiatives. We should note, too, that different individuals with different values

or interests may regard different proposals as best, and this is the stuff of which politics is made. From this point we suppose that one particular political perspective has been adopted, and the proposal is considered best from that particular perspective. (4) The proposal is advocated and public support for it sought, in the course of which new interest groups and organizations may come into being. (5) The proposal is brought before the legislative or executive branch of government at an appropriate level. (6) The proposal is enacted with or without modification. (7) The proposal is implemented. (8) Experience with the program as implemented leads to feedback from those affected. (9) The cycle begins again with proposals for improvement, replacement or abandonment of the policy.

It is natural then to begin by asking: what problems are there that might be addressed by a public policy in support of (or, for that matter, aimed at limiting or suppressing) small business? One such "problem" will have to be dismissed. This is the "problem" of insufficient growth of employment or production. This may be a real problem, but as we have seen, policies in support of small business do not seem to be the way to deal with it, since most small businesses are not high-impact firms or "Gazelles." (For this refer back to Chapter 5, and note also topics in Chapters 11 and 12.) To quote Veronique de Rugy (2005, pp. 15–16)

> Economic policy is appropriately directed towards economic growth whether it takes the form of additional jobs or increase of productivity in existing jobs is all that matters. And unlike the common belief there is no reason to base our policies on the idea that new jobs are creating more economic value than existing jobs or that small businesses are more deserving of government favor than big companies ... most small-firm job creation occurs within a relatively few firms, firms [called] "Gazelles." Gazelles are high-growth entrepreneurial companies that started small and quickly grew larger. This subset of small firms, not small firms in general, is the powerful job creator and innovation producer that should be targeted by government policies. But no one can identify a Gazelle before it takes off. The label can be applied only by looking at past growth, long after the firm has created new jobs. Because no one knows where new jobs or the innovation will

come from, it is impossible to accurately target the job-creating or entrepreneurial firms.

So it does not make sense to support small businesses in order to solve the problem of slow employment growth. There may however be two public policy problems that policies in support of small businesses can address. These two problems are associated with capital of two different kinds, human capital and financial capital.

We have seen that human capital plays a great role in the success of small businesses. While some human capital is idiosyncratic, there are also skills of management that can be useful in many if not all business situations. (Refer back especially to Chapter 7.) Since proprietors of small businesses are often only part-time managers, they may benefit from assistance and training in these skills, and subsidies for such assistance and training could have the potential to increase the productivity of their businesses, with benefits not only to the proprietors but also to their employees and customers.

Second, we have seen that many small businesses are "liquidity constrained" and thus have inadequate access to capital markets. (Refer back to Chapter 8 and some topics in Chapters 9 and 11.) Here, again, public policy might be aimed at improving the access of small businesses to capital, and thus improving the allocation of capital and increasing the productivity of the small business sector. In any case, these two objectives — increasing small business access to human and financial capital — seem to be central to many of the activities of the SBA.

Accordingly, it will be convenient to address the policies of the SBA under two headings: lending and loan-guarantee programs (on the one hand) and non-lending programs (on the other hand.) In the following two sections, these will be taken in the opposite order. One further "problem" is the limited opportunities available to women, nonwhite, indigenous and Hispanic people. So far as small business opportunities and opportunities for government contracts are concerned, the SBA has been charged with some responsibilities to relax these limits, and also for measures to encourage opportunities for military veterans in small business and government contracting.

These activities may be grouped along with non-lending or lending programs depending on the form they take.

The SBA (2016) was established in 1953. Quoting from the official history, "its philosophy and mission began to take shape years earlier in a number of predecessor agencies, largely as a response to the pressures of the Great Depression and World War II.... The Reconstruction Finance Corporation (RFC), created by President Herbert Hoover in 1932 to alleviate the financial crisis of the Great Depression, was SBA's 'grandparent'; The RFC was basically a federal lending program for all businesses hurt by the Depression, large and small. It was adopted as the personal project of Hoover's successor, President Franklin D. Roosevelt, and was staffed by some of Roosevelt's most capable and dedicated workers." Wartime agencies to encourage war production by small businesses were also established. This was the origin of public assistance to small businesses to obtain government contracts, which is continued by the SBA. After World War II "... the Office of Small Business (OSB) in the Department of Commerce also assumed some responsibilities that would later become characteristic duties of SBA. Its services were primarily educational. Believing that a lack of information and expertise was the main cause of small business failure, the OSB produced brochures and conducted management counseling for individual entrepreneurs.... By 1952, a move was on to abolish the RFC. To continue the important functions of the earlier agencies, President Dwight Eisenhower proposed creation of a new small business agency — Small Business Administration (SBA)." A critic of the SBA, however, writes (DeHaven, 2011) "Dwight Eisenhower was against creating the SBA in principle, but he signed the legislation as a politically expedient move that would counter criticisms that Republicans were beholden to big business."'

As that quotation indicates, the SBA has remained controversial. Advocates for free markets regard it as unnecessary and see it as creating market distortions, not correcting them. However, it has remained politically popular enough to continue, and has continued the functions that were entrusted to it in 1953. In addition, the SBA was later charged to promote equal opportunity for women and members of disadvantaged minorities, and to encourage opportunities for military veterans in small business. This continues today.

2.   Non-Lending Programs

Non-lending programs of the SBA include the Office of Advocacy, the District Offices, and a wide range of activities in cooperation with state, local, private sector, and nonprofit organizations and volunteers.

The Office of Advocacy is tasked to advocate for small businesses. It (U.S. Small Business Administration, 2015, p. 36) "examines the role and status of small business in the economy and independently represents the views of small business to federal agencies, Congress, the president and federal appellate courts as friends of the court." It seems fair to say that in this it acts as a lobbyist for small business in general. In addition, it (SBA, 2015, p. 36) "...compiles and interprets statistics on small business and is the primary entity within the federal government to disseminate small business data ... the office also funds outside research of small business issues and produces numerous publications to inform policy makers about the important role of small businesses in the economy and the impact of government policies on small businesses" (SBA, 2015, p. 36). Much of the data and some discussions used in this book have come from Office of Advocacy publications or from research they have sponsored.

As part of the SBA, the National Ombudsman (SBA, 2015, p. 36) "...has helped thousands of small businesses save time and money by resolving difficult regulatory compliance and enforcement issues." This office is relatively new, having been established by Congress in 1996. Its primary role is to mediate between small businesses and government agencies where there are difficulties of compliance with regulation. Indeed, small businesses are exempt from many regulations, though the upper limit for such exemption varies from 15 to 50 employees. In some cases, penalties for violations are reduced for small businesses.

A large part of the non-lending activity of the SBA is educational. The SBA has 68 district offices. Each state has at least one, and California, Texas and some other states have more than one. These district offices provide counseling and coordinate with other programs of the SBA and with other, more specialized and non-federal bodies to enable small businesses to have access to resources. According to their Resource Guide, (SBA, 2015, p. 6) "In addition to our district offices, which serve every state and territory, the SBA works with a variety of local resource partners to meet your small business needs: SCORE chapters, Small Business Development Centers (SBDCs), and Women's Business Centers (WBCs). This partner network reaches into communities across America: More than 13,000 business counselors, mentors and trainers available through over 900 SBDCs, 110 WBCs and 350 SCORE chapters. These professionals can help with writing a formal business plan, locating sources of financial assistance, managing and expanding your business...." (SBA, 2015, p. 7). "SCORE is a national network of more than 11,000 entrepreneurs, business leaders and executives who volunteer as mentors to America's small businesses." The SBDCs collaborate with local and state government agencies and are focused largely on counseling small business proprietors and potential small businesspeople.

Public policy also requires federal agencies to award some proportion of their contracts for supply of goods and services, building, etc. to small businesses. The target is 23 percent. Businesses headed by women, historically disadvantaged minorities, disabled veterans or in designated distressed neighborhoods (HUBZones) have their own targets. Generally, 51 percent ownership by an American citizen or resident alien of the appropriate category will be required. These preferred contracting programs are vulnerable to abuse.

A common pattern is that large firms headed by businessmen who would not qualify use more or less fictitious "front" firms to channel the contracts to themselves. Since 2010, there has been something of a crackdown. In Pennsylvania and in Philadelphia, Southeast Pennsylvania Transit Authority (SEPTA) and the Pennsylvania Department of Transportation (PennDOT) were prominently scammed; the fraudulent contractors were convicted in 2012. Quoting a criticism of the SBA (McElhatton, 2013), "...the American Small Business

League, a nonprofit group … estimates large companies received more than $16 billion from the federal government's top 100 small-business contracts in fiscal 2001." In a case under investigation, International Business Machines (IBM) may have received 98 percent of the revenues from contracts awarded to a firm headed by a "disabled veteran" whose disability stemmed from an injury received in military prep school. (It should be stressed that these are allegations, not proven facts!)

These are complex programs, and any complex program under political pressures will be subject to some abuse. However, these may be good reasons to find other, less complex means to promote good ends, if possible. Contracting usually begins by inviting bids or negotiations. Policies that assure that some proportion of the invitations are sent to small and policy-supported businesses probably do no harm, may promote competition and cost little. Beyond that, the case is much less clear.

A critic of the SBA, Veronique de Rugy (2005, p. 6, paper previously cited) "The efficiency of these programs has often been challenged, yet no politicians seem to have the will to abolish them. In fiscal year 2006, the total budget of the SBA will be roughly $600 million." She notes "To be sure large firms also receive abundant preferential treatments and subsidies." A later section will return to the question whether the programs may be justified on economic grounds or not.

3. Lending and Loan Guarantee Programs

Since the Herbert Hoover administration, the SBA and its predecessors have supported lending to businesses deemed to be unable to obtain credit otherwise. According to a Treasury briefing document (Community Affairs Department, 2008, p. 1) "… one of the largest federal loan guarantee programs [is] the Small Business Administration's (SBA's) 7(a) Loan Program. In fiscal year (FY) 2007, this program provided federal loan guarantees on approximately $14.3 billion privately originated small business loans…. The SBA 7(a) Loan Program was established by Congress in 1953. The program's mission is to help small businesses receive credit. The program provides loan originators a guaranty that if a loan defaults, the SBA will pay off a portion of the remaining balance. Lenders and the SBA share the risk at different levels. There are more than 5,000 lenders with outstanding 7(a) loans. Between 1997 and 2005, the program's guarantees have supported nearly $87 billion in loans to small businesses. In terms of market share, 7(a) loans in 2005 amounted to 4 percent of all U.S. small business loans under $1 million."

There are several other lending programs, some in cooperation with local nonprofit organizations. In general (SBA, 2015, p. 13), "The three principal players in most of these programs are the applicant small business, the lender and the SBA. The Agency does not actually provide the loan, but rather they guaranty a portion of the loan provided by a lender (except for microloans). The lender can be a regulated bank or credit union, or a community based lending organization.... The business applies directly to a lender by providing them the documents they require.... The lender will analyze the application to see if it meets their criteria and make a determination if they will need an SBA guaranty in order to provide the loan.... SBA only guarantees a portion or percentage of every loan not the whole debt, so in the event of default the lender will only get partially repaid by SBA. This means that if the borrower can't make the payments and defaults, the lender can recover the guaranteed portion of the defaulted debt from the SBA. The borrower is still obligated for the full amount." The proportion of the loan guaranteed has varied from time to time. There was (Dilger, 2013, p. 2) "...congressional action taken during the 111th Congress (2009–2011) ... to temporarily increase the 7(a) program's maximum loan guaranty percentage to 90%."

Canada, too, has a small business loan guarantee program. This program is somewhat more targeted on businesses that intend to invest in growth (Chandler, 2012, p. 254). Chandler estimates (2012, p. 260) that the loan guarantees "created" about 5,000 jobs, about 3.8 percent of new positions in small businesses in Canada in 2004–2006. These are new hires attributable (as a statistical estimate) to businesses that expanded thanks to government-guaranteed finance, but does not estimate whether or to what extent these employees would have found jobs in other firms had the loans not been guaranteed. In the Russian Republic, the Bank Kreditovaniya Malogo Biznesa, KMB, was founded by the European Bank for Reconstruction and Development, and focuses largely on small businesses, but is now in majority private ownership (Buyske, p. 160). In the Republic of Korea, companies with public credit guarantees were judged to perform well, but perhaps because the guarantees were given to companies that were better established to begin with (Kang *et al.*, 2008). In general, microfinance (lending to very small businesses, especially in less-developed countries) has been an important strategy of economic development in the 21st century (Buyske, 2007, pp. 11–48), but it has been argued that loan guarantees are less appropriate for the less-developed members of the European union than would be programs more focused on human capital (Liargovas, 1998). Worldwide, support for small business loans is a fairly widespread policy for support of small businesses. Indeed, "well over 2000 such schemes exist in almost 100 countries. Thus more than half of all countries – and all but a handful of the OECD countries — have some form of credit guarantee scheme..." (Honohan, 2008).

However, again quoting Veronique de Rugy (2005, p. 6) "the SBA hosts many special lending programs for small businesses that might not be able to get loans from regular banks. These credit programs are authorized to guarantee \$42 billion in loans in FY2006. In theory, most of these loans are zero-subsidy loans (see for instance the 7A loan program) and should not cost taxpayers anything. However, their design bears the risk that if the economy takes a downturn, the fee charged by SBA to guaranty these loans are unlikely to be sufficient to cope with the number of small businesses defaulting on their loans."

Following the recession of 2008–2009, this did occur. According to Dilger, (2013, p. 14) "One of the SBA's goals is to achieve a zero subsidy rate for its loan guaranty programs. A zero subsidy rate occurs when the SBA's loan guaranty programs generate sufficient revenue through fee collections and recoveries of collateral on purchased (defaulted) loans to not require appropriations to issue new loan guarantees. From 2005 to 2009, the SBA did not request appropriations to subsidize the cost of any of its loan guaranty programs, including the 7(a) program. However, in recent years, loan guaranty fees and loan liquidation recoveries have not generated enough revenue to cover loan losses, resulting in the need for additional appropriations to account for the shortfall. In FY2010, and again in FY2011, the SBA was provided $80.0 million to cover loan subsidy costs for the 7(a) program.... The Obama Administration reported that the 7(a) loan guaranty program will not require funding for loan credit subsidies in FY2014."

There have also been scandals. In 2007, the *New York Times* reported (Girard, 2007) "When federal agents swept into the offices of [name removed] last January, they were on their way to cracking the largest loan fraud scandal in the history of the Small Business Administration. [name removed], 44, then an executive vice president in the Detroit office of [a loan company], had bilked the SBA's flagship 7(a) loan program out of at least $76 million, and perhaps as much as $96 million. One business magazine dubbed the caper 'Cookie Jar Capitalism.'" The position of the SBA was that budget cuts had made it impossible for them to enforce their regulations. According to the New York Times report, "in the face of withering Bush administration budget cuts (reducing SBA staff by 25 percent), the agency delegated almost all oversight to the major lenders themselves, or third parties." It also appears, in retrospect, that questionable lending processes had become pretty common in all sectors of the American economy in 2007.

The example from Chapter 8 illustrating liquidity constraint indicates that liquidity constraint may arise because the risk of a very bad outcome cannot be shared symmetrically between the lender and the borrower. If the outcome is bad enough that the borrower goes bankrupt, then the risk falls disproportionately on the lender. The lender will limit the amount lent in order to limit that risk. By assuming part of the risk, a public lending program such as those operated by the SBA could relax that constraint and increase the access of businessmen to capital, perhaps increasing the efficiency in the allocation of resources as a result. At the same time, because the public lending program assumes only part of the risk, the lender has an incentive to carefully monitor the loan. To the extent that these benefits occur, they have to be balanced against the public assumption of the risk of large losses and of fraud. These risks exist in any lending, of course, but in the case of a public lending program, they are risks assumed by the public purse, and as such cannot be neglected.

4. Evaluation

As we have seen, both public lending programs and non-lending programs have the *potential* to increase the efficiency or productivity of the small business sector. This, however, poses two questions. First, are these potentialities realized — do they exist in the actual world? And second, supposing they do, are the benefits sufficient to justify the costs?

On the first question, advocates of free markets would argue that the potential is not realized. We know also that a market system has the potential, in ideal circumstances, to bring about an efficient allocation of resources. There would then be no potentiality that public policy could improve on efficiency that is already perfect. Now, probably nobody believes that we live in an ideal world, so the free market position is a little more pragmatic: it is that *given* the imperfections of both governments and markets, market allocations are *systematically* more efficient than governmental interventions. This would lead to the conclusion that public initiatives would *systematically* worsen the allocation of resources, so that they should be avoided unless they are justified by other values unrelated to efficiency. This idea that markets are systematically more efficient than government initiatives will depend on one's opinions both on economic theory and political science. In any case, there is no consensus among economists that markets systematically yield better allocations of resources in this sense.

The second question is, of course, a question of cost–benefit analysis. It seems certain that some benefits are gained by some people. Some resources are transferred to small business proprietors that they would not obtain otherwise. Unless they are obtained fraudulently, these resources will increase the productivity of the small business sector. The increase in productivity would then give rise to three kinds of individual benefits: first, higher profits; second, possibly, higher wages; third, cheaper prices or better service for customers, resulting in increases of consumers' surplus. Studies of government programs in support of *agriculture* have focused on the increase in consumers' surplus and have found that it, alone, has provided sufficient benefits in some cases to more than offset the government expenditures. However, the impacts of the programs on productivity of the nonagricultural small business sector, and thus indirectly on the three categories of individual benefits, does not seem to have been studied. Perhaps it could not be, since it would be a very large and complex cost benefit study, and much of the data would be hard to get.

There is another kind of benefit that should not be ignored. We have seen that nonpecuniary motives play an important part in the formation of small businesses (refer especially to Chapter 12 as well as Chapter 5). That is to say, some people prefer to be self-employed in small businesses rather than the alternatives they may have in other activities. We also have some evidence that some people prefer to be employed in small businesses rather than other businesses. Now, economists take preferences as the final basis for evaluating economic activity. Some people prefer coffee to tea; some the reverse. A market system is well adapted to accommodate those different preferences for coffee and tea, and all economists would agree that this is an important benefit of a market system. Preferences for small business activity deserve no less respect. Thus, we might find that the profits from small businesses are often less than the income the proprietor could earn in the alternative opportunities she has. If she operates a small business, she does so because she is better off, taking the utility of being an independent businessperson into account — as Hurst and Pugsley (2015) observe (refer to Chapter 12). Thus, the benefits to the proprietor should be valued at no less than the alternative income available outside the small business sector. This is a minimum — the benefit to the proprietor can be no less than the alternative income that she gives up to be a proprietor.

This, of course, is a further complication. If this comprehensive cost–benefit analysis has not been done, and probably cannot, what is the point? The point is that it provides a baseline to think carefully about arguments for and against public policy in support of small business. Arguments that neglect one side or another of this hypothetical cost–benefit analysis are incomplete to some extent. It seems fair to say that none of the arguments for or against these policies is conclusive. At this stage, all one can do is use one's best judgment to balance the arguments on both sides and arrive at a "reflective equilibrium" (Rawls, 1971) on the evaluation of programs in support of small business. For what it is worth, the author's judgment is that they probably do make a positive contribution, on net, but could almost certainly be refined and improved in detail.

5. Conclusion

In this chapter, we have seen that a number of public programs in the United States support small businesses, and there are such policies in other countries as well. In this discussion, we have drawn on the previous chapters to better understand the role of small businesses.

In earlier chapters, we have learned to be cautious in applying the idea of a representative or average agent in the study of small business, since small businesses are not distributed along a bell curve and are very diverse in other ways, and because some sections of our population have fewer opportunities for small business entrepreneurship. We have seen that they differ from other businesses in other ways, including the characteristics of the employees. We have seen that economies of scale have different implications for small businesses. We have seen that nonpecuniary motives and family ownership and management may play key roles in small businesses. The role of family ownership and management may be ambiguous. We have reason to believe that family management may increase the productivity of labor, but reduce that of capital, relative to non-family firms.

Small business and entrepreneurship are distinct, but interrelated topics. Just how they are interrelated depends on the definition we adopt for the word "entrepreneurship." If we adopt the Schumpeterian definition popular in the 21st century, there is little relation. If we adopt a definition closer to the consensus of economists in the 19th and 20th centuries, we find that most small businesspeople are entrepreneurs, if in many cases only part-time.

We have seen that human capital is important, and an important component of the human capital is idiosyncratic. This idiosyncratic human capital, a product of experience, seems to reinforce the importance of family management and other means to limit opportunism. However, another important component of human capital useful to a business comprises common skills of business management that can be acquired through experience as an employee in a successful business or through formal training. Opportunities to acquire this sort of human capital may vary, however, depending both on personal identity and on other, more idiosyncratic differences.

Financial capital is no less important, and all businesses can face constraints in their ability to raise the capital needed for efficient operation. However, there is reason to believe that many small businesses are limited in their ability to operate at an efficient scale because of limited access to financial capital.

All in all, the study of small business is now a mature subfield of economics, one that shares many ideas with other subspecializations but combines them in a distinctive way to better understand the economics of the small business sector.

Discussion Questions

(1) Assess the relative importance of loan guarantees and other programs in the activities of the SBA and in U.S. government policy in general.

(2) Are the policies of the SBA likely to be cost-effective in promoting rapid economic growth? Why or why not? In your answer, enumerate various policies and answer the questions separately for each.

(3) Supposing policies in support of small business are not cost-effective in promoting rapid economic growth, does that mean that they should be eliminated? Why or why not? In your answer, enumerate various policies and answer the questions separately for each.

References

Buyske, G. (2007), *Banking on Small Business* (Cornell University Press).

Chandler, V. (2012), "The Economic Impact of the Canada Small Business Financing Program," *Small Business Economics*, v. 39, no. 1, pp. 253–264.

Community Affairs Department. (2008), "Insights: The SBA's 7(a) Loan Program, A Flexible Tool for Commercial Lenders," Comptroller of the Currency, Administrator of National Banks, US Department of the Treasury.

DeHaven, T. (2011), "Waste, Fraud, and Abuse in Small Business Administration Programs," Testimony Before the Committee on Small Business and Entrepreneurship, United States Senate, Published by the Cato Institute, available at http://www.cato.org/publications/congressional-test imony/waste-fraud-abuse-small-business-administration-programs (accessed on 5/1/2016). It should be noted that the Cato Institute is consistently committed to supporting free market economics.

de Rugy, V. (2005), "Are Small Businesses The Engine of Growth?" *American Enterprise Institute*, AEI Working Paper #123, December 8, 2005. It should be noted that the American Enterprise Institute is consistently committed to supporting free market economics.

Dilger, R. J. (2013), "Small Business Administration 7(a) Loan Guaranty Program," Congressional Research Service.

Girard, K. (2007), "Business Intelligence: S.B.A. Tries to Conceal Its Role in Massive Loan Fraud," *New York Times*, available at http://www.nytimes.com/allbusiness/07girard.html(accessedon5/1/2016).

Honohan, P. (2008), "Partial Credit Guarantees: Principles and Practice, Trinity College Dublin," in Presented at the *Conference on Partial Credit Guarantees*, Washington, DC, March 13–14.

Hurst, E. G. and Pugsley, B. W. (2015), "Wealth, Tastes, and Entrepreneurial Choice," NBER Working Paper No. 21644, Issued in October 2015.

Kang, J. W., Heshmati, A. and Choi, G.-G. (2008), "Effect of Credit Guarantee Policy on Survival and Performance of SMEs in Republic of Korea," *Small Business Economics*, v. 31, no. 4, pp. 445–462.

Liargovas, P. (1998) "'The White Paper on Growth, Competitiveness and Employment' and Greek Small and Medium Sized Enterprises," *Small Business Economics*, v. 11, no. 3, pp. 201–214.

McCain, R. A. (2015), *Game Theory and Public Policy*, 2nd Edition (Elgar), p. 4.

McElhatton, J. (2013), "IRS Scandal Exposes Small-Biz Pass-Throughs," *Federal Times,* available via the American Small Business League at http://www.asbl.com/showmedia.php?id=2079 (accessed on 7/1/2016).

Rawls, J. (1971), *A Theory of Justice* (Belknap Press), p. 20.

Small Business Administration (SBA). (2016), "History," available at https://www.sba.gov/about-sba/what-we-do/history (accessed on 5/1/2016).

U.S. Small Business Administration. (2015), *Resource Guide for Small Business,* National Edition, available at https://www.sba.gov/sites/default/files/files/resourceguide_national.pdf(accessedon5/1/2016).

Index

CPSIA information can be obtained
at www.ICGtesting.com
Printed in the USA
LVHW011914130720
660546LV00016B/532

9 789813 231245